Could I Hear That Again, Please?

Other Bramber Press books by Peter Thorogood

Thomas Hood: Poems Comic and Serious
Selected with an introduction and notes
Illustrated with Hood's own comic woodcuts 119pp
ISBN 0 9526786 - 0 - 8

In These Places...At These Times
Selected poems by Peter Thorogood. Beautifully illustrated
with the author's watercolours 84pp
ISBN 0 9526786 - 1 - 6

St. Mary's Bramber: A Sussex House and its Gardens
Five hundred years of history. Illustrated with old photographs 40pp
ISBN 0 9526786 - 4 - 0

St. Mary's Bramber: A Pictorial Souvenir
A delightful portrait of a much-loved house and its gardens
Fine colour photographs by Henry Wilson
Additional photographs by Roger Linton and Peter Smith
Nostalgic memories in prose and verse 32pp
ISBN 0 9526786 - 6 - 7

*The Complete Comic and Curious Verse
of Peter Thorogood*
With over eighty humorous pen-and-ink sketches by the author 162pp
ISBN 0 9538281 - 2 - 3

South of the River
A Novel of the Fifties
in Eighteen Episodes and over Eighty Scenes 442pp
ISBN 0 9538281 - 8 - 2

Could I Hear That Again, Please?

*Views and Reviews
of a Well-Tuned Listener*

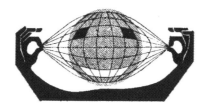

Peter Thorogood

Published in Great Britain by

St. Mary's House, Bramber, West Sussex BN44 3WE
Tel/Fax: (44) 01903 816205
www.bramberpress.co.uk

ISBN 1 - 905206 - 02 - X

Copyright © Peter Thorogood 2006

The right of Peter Thorogood to be identified as the author of this work has been asserted by him in accordance with the Copyright, Designs and Patents Act 1988.

All rights reserved. No part of this publication may be reproduced, stored in or introduced into a retrieval system, or transmitted, in any form, or by any means (electronic, mechanical, photocopying, recording or otherwise) without the prior written permission of the publisher. Any person who does any unauthorised act in relation to this publication may be liable to criminal prosecution and civil claims for damages.

The articles and shorter pieces in *Could I Hear that Again Please?* were written between May 1966 and July 1967, a time when 'political correctness' was a concept neither widely understood nor practised. Certain passages may, for a variety of reasons, appear not acceptable to some readers. In the interests of historical accuracy, these passages have been retained.

Some of the pen-and-ink sketches from the *Radio Times* (May 1966 to July 1967) are by anonymous artists. We have been unable to trace their copyright holders and would be grateful to receive any information as to their identity. Every effort has been made to trace other copyright holders, and the publishers will be happy to correct mistakes or omissions in future editions. The same also applies to a small number of the thumb-nail portraits, though the majority are included by kind permission of the National Portrait Gallery, London.

Cover design by Alan Durden and Tony Ketteman from an idea by the author.

Printed and bound by CPI Antony Rowe
Eastbourne

In memory

of

Oleg Kerensky

Literary Editor of *The Listener* 1963-67

and

David Bowes

Poet, painter, friend
and enthusiastic reader of these reviews

*With thanks to all those BBC broadcasters,
presenters, producers, technicians, researchers
and freelance contributors who provided me with so many hours
of pleasant listening*

Author's Note

Could I Hear That Again, Please? is a kind of 'Radio Diary' which records the spoken words, thoughts and theories of a large number of broadcasters. Its intention is to present, promote and perpetuate the wealth of knowledge contained in a wide variety of radio talks. However, the dates of the pieces refer to their publication in *The Listener*, and though the book may have the appearance of a diary, I have not kept to a chronological sequence, preferring to arrange the material thematically.

In addition to my newly edited material previously printed in its original form in *The Listener*, I have gathered together a number of fugitive pieces which escaped the Literary Editor's critical eye because, although I hoped to review the broadcasts, the pieces could not be included for lack of space or because they did not fit into a theme. Some developed into miniature essays and might have found a home in another kind of periodical, or book such as this. Whatever the reason for the original exclusion of these errant pieces, they can now be remembered in these pages. Together with their published counterparts, they are testimony to the remarkable range of subject-matter that could be found in any week's listening on any of the four radio channels. Published and unpublished pieces are designated (P) and (U) respectively.

I willingly acknowledge my incalculable debt to all those people whose research and writings were a vital contribution to the many programmes reviewed and revived in this volume. Without these contributors, this book could never have been written. Wherever possible the names of authors have been mentioned and attributions noted. The extensive index of names gives the reader some idea of the infinite variety and content of contributions.

Many of the broadcast talks reviewed in these pages can be found in past issues of *The Listener*, which, from 1929 to 1991, remained the perfect mirror of the changing times. Copies may be found in most of the major public libraries.

P. T.

✶

In the Beginning

Writing for *The Listener* 20

Art and Architecture

Portrait of the Artist as a Young Amateur 24
Thoughts on a Raphael Madonna 26
Gombrich and the Historical Imagination 27
Artists and Environment 29
The Sense of Pure Vision 31
The Poetry of Pictures 33
In Search of the Unexpected 34
City of Flowers 35

Birds and Beasts

It Takes All Sorts 38
Snakes Alive! 38
'And Don't Spare the Horses!' 39
Man Eats Dog 39
'El Ingles' 40
The Countryside in February 40
Animal Etiquette 40
Pets Corner 41
From my notebook: A False Start — The Habits of the Cuckoo .. 42
In Cloud-Cuckoo-Land! 42
From my notebook: Notes for 'In Praise of the Hare' 43
The Lore of Nature! 44
Great Scott! 46

Books and Authors

What the Dickens? 50
'The Bubble Reputation' 51
The Pessimistic Optimist 52
Looking Forward to Looking Back 54
H. G. Again! 56
From my notebook: Literary Neighbours 57
Grrrrgh! Wow! Yaroo! 58
The Myth of Greyfriars 58
B. O. P. — R. I. P. 60
Big Pot of the Potteries 62
The Arnold Bennett Centenary 63
Arnold Bennett: A Literary Portrait 64
The Arnold Bennett Memorial Lecture 65
A Man of Contrasts 65
Letter from Somerset! 66
Delderfield in Devon 67
A Raffish Raconteur 68
Beyond 'The Outsider' 70
Samuel Beckett's Dream 71
The New Science Fiction 71
Prospective Narrative 73

Christmas and New Year

Nine Lessons and Carols 76
'Ten to Eight' and 'Five to Ten' 77
A Christmas Meditation 77
Ghosts of Christmas Past 78

Peace and Goodwill 80
Announcing the Winners! 81
Letter from America 82

Conformists and Radicals

Portrait of a Radical 84
Diplomacy at the Vatican 86
The Life of a Saint — without a Shadow of Doubt 86
Holy Smoke! 89
A New Dawn? 90
From my notebook: A Voice for Peace 93

Crime and Punishment

Essay in Malice 96
The Smiler with the Knife 97
Habitual Criminals 97
The Hi-Jackers 98
No Offence, Mate! 99
The Tottenham Outrage 100

England and the English

From my notebook: Scripts for Review 104
As Others See Us: The Popular View 105
As Others See Us: The Classic View 106
Studying Contemporary English 107
Focus on Visitors to Britain 108
Corner of a Foreign Land 108

Anything to Declare? 109
Waving or Wavering? 110
Achievements of a Lifetime 112
Collectomania! 113

Entertainers and Performers

'G. B. S.' 116
'Corno di Basso' — Behind the Mask 116
Nijinsky's Diary 118
From my notebook: Mme Nijinsky 119
A Tortured Soul 119
Diva Divina! 120
Gay Paree! 121
Round the Horne! 123
Rule Britannia! 124
Frankie Howerd: A Man of Parts 125
The Spice of Life! 127
From my notebook: The Fabulous Freddy Frinton 128
From my notebook: Herr Frinton of Hamburg 129

Gardens and Countryside:

'Down the Garden Path' 132
Hedging Our Bets! 133
The Raggle-Taggle Gypsies O! 133
Rustic Idyll 134
Fairies at the Bottom of the Garden? 136
The Countryside in May 137

History and Ideas

The Nature of Contemporary History 140
The Mass Portrait Gallery 141
The Biography and Inner Life of Ideas 141
Planning for What? 143
Divided Opinion 144
A Savage Judgement 145
'English People Are Sweet!' 146

Kings and Queens

Pomp and Circumstance 148
Queen of Hearts 149
'My End is My Beginning' 153
The Merry Merry Monarch! 153
America's Last King 155
A Spontaneous Reply from Queen Victoria ... 156
Letter from America 157

Life and Beyond

Measuring Time 160
Happiness is Egg-Shaped! 160
From my notebook: Too Much Choice 161
Death and the Philosophers 162
Time Considered 163
Living Longer 163
What is Life? 164
Science and Mysticism 165

No Ease in Zion 166
'Love Bade Me Welcome' 168
The Meaning of Life 168
Further Deliberations on 'The Meaning of Life'. 170
Rosh Hashanah 172

Mind and Body

Health and Science 176
What is a Freudian in 1967? 176
'Jung and Easily Freudened!' 177
The New Doctor's Dilemma 179
Crisis in the Ward 180
Biological Backlash 181
'Things Fall Apart' 182
Confused Thoughts 183

Music and Myth

A Silence Filled with Greek 186
Labyrinthine Lucubrations 186
From my notebook: Homeric Analogues 189
The Voice of the Gods 190
Aa-aa-um-mm-mm! 191
The Xylophone 193
A Re-sounding Tinkle! 193
Psychedelic Sound 194
The Anxiety of Art 195
The Greek Sound 196

Poets and Poetry

Publish and Be Damned? 198
Golden Corn! 199
Speed, Sound and Sentiment 201
Choices 202
The Originality of Arthur Waley 202
Willow, Willow, Waley O! 203
From my notebook: Tea in Bayswater 204
Betjeman High, Betjeman Low 205
Between Heaven and Hell 207
'In Country Heaven' 209
Logue's ABC 210
L for Logue 211
Anti-Poetry 213
From my notebook: Further Notes on Anti-Poetry 214
Master of Nothing 215
Read on from Here 216
'The Poet Speaks' 216
The Reading of Poetry 218
Sense, Sound and Sensibility 219
Sound Poetry 220

Pop Songs and Pop Stars

Scrambled Egg-Head 224
Pop Goes a Person 225
How It All Popped Up! 226
Permanent Group Mum 227
Pop goes a Hymn Tune 228

'Pop Inn' and 'Pop North' 228
'Where's it at, Man?' 230
The Fan Cult 230
Square on Pop! 231
The Wind of Change 233

Poverty and Population

Born Free! 236
Population Explosion 237
Champion of the Poor 239
Over-Crowded Britain? 241
Underfed and Overcrowded 242
Hit the Road, Jack! 243
Cap in Hand and a Begging Bowl 244
House-Hunting Safari 245
Storming the Barricades! 246
On the Bread Line 248
Trouble in Hong Kong 249
A Cheap Home for Life 249
Wherever Next? 250

Revolution and Revolt

Russia in 1916 252
The BBC Sound Archives 252
More About Rasputin 253
China in Turmoil 254
Culture and Revolution 254

All Greece and No Fat Living! 257
The Great Dictator! 259
What's in a Name? 260
Myth and Nationalism 261

Scandal and Intrigue

A Secret Shared by All Europe 264
Sex and Mr. Gladstone 265
Pros and Cons! 267

Shirkers and Workers

Focus on the Lazy British 270
Pride, Prejudice and the British Working Man 271
When is a Worker not a Worker? 272
What a Waste! 274

Sportsmen and Gamblers

Moral Ethos and Social Evil 276
The Lone Navigator 277
Honi Soit Qui Mal y Pense! 278
The Stanley Matthews Story 279
It's Just Not Cricket, Old Chap! 280

Technology and Pussy Galore

The World of Marshall McLuhan 284
Brave New World! 284

The Old Woman of Redditch 286
Is Technology Unnatural? 286
A Bond Dishonoured 287
Paradise Lost? 288
A Universal Cure-All 289

Travel and Foreign Places

Misconceptions 292
The Eskimo Solution 292
There is a 'Greenland' Far Away! 292
Paradise Islands 293
Utopia Down Under 295
Health and Efficiency 295
Balancing Act 296
Journey to Jerusalem 296
Down, Out and Broke in Syria 297
Living on the Edge 298
Travelling Light 299
On the Track of Lawrence! 299
In the Public Eye 300
Two-and-a-half Square Miles 300
Social Conflict and National Myth 301
A Seasoned Traveller 302
East is East and West is West 304
Understanding Other Societies 305

War and Peace

The Custer Legend 308

The Decline of the Western 308
Bader's Battle of Britain 309
War in the Countryside 310
Vietnam Horror 310
Into the Firing Line 311
No Winners, Only Losers 312
Bluff and Counter-Bluff................................ 312
The Peacemaker 314
From my notebook: War and Peace 315
The Rise and Fall of CND 316
A Certain Anachronistic Inconsistency 317
An Old Soldier's New Year Thoughts 318
Spring in Washington 319
Last Words 320
My Very Last Words! 321

The End of the Line

On the Grapevine 324
Coup de Grâce 324
Looking Back: Decline and Fall 325

Diary of Events for the 1960s 330
Acknowledgements 338
Note on the Vignettes 339
Index of Persons 342

'We hope that in these pages, with their catholicity of interests — studies, hobbies, recreations — everyone will find at least some congenial feature, and also some new means of extending and deepening the enjoyment of broadcast programmes.'

From the Editorial of the first issue of *The Listener*, 16 January, 1929.

In the Beginning

Writing for *The Listener*

In 1966, Oleg Kerensky, Literary Editor of the BBC weekly *The Listener*, invited me to take over as independent freelance critic of 'The Spoken Word', initially to stand in for the current incumbent, Kevin Crossley-Holland, who was on holiday. At the time David Wade reviewed the previous week's radio drama and Alan Blyth covered music programmes. In view of the temporary nature of my literary contributions, I had no contract of any kind. As it turned out, I remained as an independent critic for fifteen months.

The Listener began its life under the aegis of Lord Reith in 1929 as a vehicle for printing broadcast talks. It became a popular weekly which, with its unique purpose of making the spoken word available in printed form, provided readers with the opportunity to enjoy the wealth of talented writing and broadcasting put out over the air during the previous week.

From the very beginning, *The Listener* could claim as its own such distinguished writers as George Bernard Shaw, Bertrand Russell, Virginia Woolf, George Orwell and E. M. Forster. In a later age, it included the poetry of W. H. Auden, Stephen Spender, Christopher Isherwood, Elizabeth Jennings, Stevie Smith and Philip Larkin.

For all of ninepence, readers could be kept up-to-date on a variety of subjects they were not necessarily specialists in but wished to know more about. There were entertaining insights into the lives and pursuits of a wide range of interesting human beings — always with the knowledge that we were listening to the very best authorities on the subject.

Meeting a remorseless weekly deadline meant sacrificing my social life — parties, dining in favourite restaurants, cosy chats over morning coffee, evenings at the opera, and foregoing all the other pleasurable pursuits currently being enjoyed by the rest of my friends (and readers!) during their leisure hours.

I was, forthwith, locked into a self-imposed *régime* of listening — for twelve months a year, seven days a week, and in sporadic bursts spread over a fifteen-hour day. I was up early in the mornings, listened late into the evenings and invariably wrote up my notes in the small hours, particularly on Sunday nights, since I had to get my copy to the Editor's office by ten o'clock every Monday morning. A journalist friend who had a regular column in one of the national newspapers gave me the best piece of advice: 'Take the telephone off the hook and deactivate the door-bell!'

A selection from literally hundreds of programmes every week meant the choice was bound to be haphazard and invite confusion, as the material was so disparate. To select a few of the most important talks simply doubled up on what was being reported in other newspapers and journals. I settled on making a personal choice. In due course, a theme would emerge, a title would present itself and I would start writing my final draft.

Reading through these brief pieces again I have been surprised at the wide range of subject-matter that had to be covered over the fifteen-month period. I had to be prepared to write on any subject, as any journalist might be called upon to do.

Along the way, I am pleased to have had the chance of making the acquaintance over the air-waves of a variety of remarkable people: poets Robert Browning, Alfred Lord Tennyson, W. B. Yeats, Dame Edith Sitwell, Sir John Betjeman, Dylan Thomas and Christopher Logue; influential thinkers Marshall MacLuhan, Teilhard de Chardin, Simone Weil and Professor Galbraith; psychologists Jung and Freud; brilliant *raconteurs* Sir Compton Mackenzie and Peter Ustinov; modernist poet Nicanor Parra and science fiction author J. G. Ballard. There were plenty of villains too: Rasputin and Jack the Ripper come immediately to mind!

I covered a surprising amount of ground in a comparatively short time, including Professor J. M. Cohen on the eccentricities of 'anti-poetry', Sir Paul Dukes on Russia during the Revolution, Bertrand Russell and the Campaign for Nuclear Disarmament, Frank Richards and his 'Billy Bunter' books, H. G. Wells and his view of history, Arnold Bennett and 'The Five Towns', Turgenev's love affair with opera *diva*, Pauline Viardot-Garcia, an English bullfighter called 'El Ingles', footballer Sir Stanley Matthews, playwrights George Bernard Shaw and Samuel Beckett, not to mention passing glances at Queen Victoria, Emperor Haile Selassie, Maria Callas, and some Eskimos.

These reviews show the changing values and direction of the social, political and cultural life in Britain and around the world at a particular time in our history. We are reminded of the many people, both famous and infamous, who, though they may now have passed into oblivion, nevertheless made their mark through the medium of broadcasting. There are the 'ordinary' people too, who went about their 'daily round and common task', people who provided us with a fascinating picture of the way the world was in the 1960s.

My brief as critic for 'The Spoken Word' was to convey to readers the essence of the broadcast, the viewpoint of the speaker, and my personal response to it. I had to be careful not to exceed the prescribed 600-word limit. If I missed a broadcast I could, in exceptional circumstances, arrange with the producer to go into a studio and listen to a re-run, hence my title for this book. In practice, with the *Radio Times* as my guide, I listened to, at the very least, twice the number of programmes I ever came round to reviewing. I made sure I wrote notes on all of those I listened to. I sometimes wrote up complete first drafts about broadcasts of marginal importance in case they might turn out to be of use in the finished article. Inevitably, some of these *essais* had to be rejected for lack of space and have now been included in this volume.

Looking at my notes now, I see that I scribbled at speed, even developing my own primitive shorthand. Sometimes copious notes were jumbled together, sometimes only three or four key words spread over a page with a great deal of space between.

Being new to journalism, I was, in retrospect, too cautious as a critic, too willing to praise rather than criticise, too keen to put myself into the shoes of the contributors in an effort to be fair in my judgements, though I do admit to being unnecessarily cavalier and waspish in reviewing John Betjeman's volume of poems, *High and Low*. In petulant mood, I once made unkind and personal remarks about the voice of the venerable Sir Paul Dukes. These solecisms aside, I see no reason to provide an *apologia* for my literary misdemeanours. Ultimately, my role was to record something of the wealth and breadth of broadcasting in the brief period at my disposal, recognising that the comparatively little I was able to review was only a ripple in the vast expanse of BBC programmes.

Art and Architecture

19 January 1967 (U)

Portrait of the Artist as a Young Amateur

Water-colour painting coincided with my 'first love'. I heard that an attractive new art teacher had arrived in my school. Her name was Phyllis Hall, and the news very soon spread round the Upper Fourth that she had beautiful blonde hair and a peaches-and-cream complexion. I plucked up enough courage to leave a note for her and before long I was enjoying a weekly painting lesson instead of having to play silly-mid-on in the inter-house cricket match. Of course, there were lots of jokes and gibes, especially from the maths master, who showed me no mercy.

It was in the delicious company of the adorable Miss Hall that I learnt how to manage a paint-brush and mix my colours. Although I am proud of those first attempts (they still hang on my sitting-room wall), I have to admit that she helped me in the finer points. I achieved with difficulty (and not entirely without her practised hand) a modest self-portrait by sitting in front of a pair of mirrors. Next came quite an acceptable *gouache* painting of the garden and house of the prep school. As with most of the activities I enthused over in those days, I gave up just as I was beginning to make progress.

This overly indulgent introduction is by way of saying how much, as an untried amateur artist, I enjoyed Robert Brazil's talks in the 'Schools' programme with the slightly forbidding title (for young people at least): 'The Artist and the Shape of Natural Structure'.

Mr Brazil begins by drawing our attention to the importance of landscapes. After all, he says, 'artists have been painting them for three hundred years.'

Trees are things of beauty in themselves. We should mark the form and nature of the tree — viz. Smollett's observation about 'the treeness of a tree.' Warning: if you paint trees, it helps to put in a few people to emphasise the scale of things.

Mountains and clouds are things of beauty too. If you are attempting to paint them, you must remember that they have a 'relationship with each other' in your painting. Gently dragging the brush lightly across the moistened paper, we can create the illusion of dampness, of cold, as it often is before rain comes. Black clouds may well serve as a warning to sailors; they are 'a revelation to the artist.'

Sometimes we can discern 'a spiral movement' in nature, as with a snow-storm or a windswept landscape; wild waves breaking on the seashore, branches of trees blowing in the storm, so the twisting lines begin to appear in the painting. There is a 'romantic' energy there.

Well! Not until you have painted the scene ten times over! In any case, you have lost the moment. The storm has blown over. Your paints and brushes have fallen into the mud. It's time to go home. Try again another day. Or is it time to bite the dust and take up metal-work?

Ideally, says Mr. Brazil, 'the artist seeks to discover the forces and tensions' in the natural forms. He attempts to create nature from nature rather than merely making a copy of it. The artist can visualise the finished work, its scale, its form, even its range of colours, before he puts brush to paper. The degree of inspiration is the measure of his emotional and intellectual response to his subject. The rest is pure technique. We have, at this point, the impression that we are being asked not to be impatient. Let us, then, stop and observe closely.

There may be trees surrounding a pond. They stand firmly rooted in the soil and rocks. They thrust against the sky pressing against the descending clouds. Wild shapes begin to form in blocks of colour. We may begin to see the 'tensions' emerge as the painting proceeds. The trees begin to 'embrace' the pond, to overshadow it. The surface of the water does not appear at first to be troubled by any breeze— quiescent. But wait!

A figure appears, at the touch of the brush. We see him leaning forward, his hair, his clothes, swept backwards as if by a strong wind. Some layers of paint are added to the pale wash of the pond surface and suddenly we see an element of struggle entering the picture. Another part-figure appears, head and arms raised up above the water. The branches of the trees begin, by a few strokes of the brush, to look 'troubled'. There is clearly a story developing. 'Figures in a landscape' is all the title will tell us. We have to interpret what is happening before we can appreciate the artist's intention. So there is an inescapable bond between the viewer and the painting which has to be recognised and fully understood. Robert Brazil admirably defines the subtleties of that relationship.

The much-lamented Phyllis Hall, sitting in the peaceful garden of my school, viewing my clumsy efforts at verisimilitude, would, I am sure have continued to teach me along these lines, though in my case, the end result would have been greatly tempered by my lack of practice. I believe I could be easily encouraged to take up my brush again when I think of those tranquil moments in her company, exchanging confidences in a secluded garden on those warmest of summer afternoons.

8 and 15 January 1967 (P)

Thoughts on a Raphael Madonna

The distinguished art historian, E. H. Gombrich, in his new set of eleven essays on the Italian Renaissance, *Norm and Form*, has invented an entirely original and refreshing perspective on art criticism. The book was, this week, the subject of a radio review by Professor Leopold Ettlinger.

Imagine you are in Florence. You are wandering through the galleries of the Pitti Palace. You find yourself in the Hall of Saturn and your eye is irresistibly drawn to Raphael's portrait of the 'Madonna della Sedia'. Your attention is momentarily distracted by a gentleman who is absorbed in the painting before him. He screws up his eyes and holds up his hands like blinkers to shut out the ornate gilt frame that encloses the picture. Many people believe the model for this Madonna to have been a Roman peasant woman but this gentleman does not. You and I may think she is oriental, for she is wearing an eastern head-dress and

Raphael: Madonna della Sedia (c.1556)

embroidered scarf, but this gentleman does not. Indeed, he may even scoff at the tale told in Florence about the work being painted on the end of a wine-barrel but, because it is set in a circular frame, we rather like the story. When he gets home, he scrutinises his face in the round shaving mirror to observe the subtle distortions of the facial features, as in a *tondo*. He knows what Raphael is trying to do.

Only a remarkable luminary like Gombrich would do such a thing. He has just the right degree of humour (and humanity) for it. The result is a fine chapter on tradition and creativity in the painting of the 'Madonna della Sedia'.

On the other hand I cannot see, as the Professor does, that Raphael's idea of portraying an Italian peasant woman in middle-eastern costume in any way 'threatens the integrity of the work.' Neither do I understand, in the title chapter, how Leonardo da Vinci's painting of 'The Last Supper' should be less symmetrical than the Monterchi 'Madonna', for surely all the lines of perspective converge on the head of Christ. And is not the whole work based on an ancient ratio? It naturally depends on what the Professor means by 'symmetry' in this context. Reading Gombrich on Leonardo and Raphael is like reading Ruskin on Giotto: both illuminate and enhance the work of the artist because they go to the very roots of creativity.

9 January 1967 (P)

Gombrich and the Historical Imagination

To hear one distinguished art historian talking about the work of another should be a worth-while experience and it is difficult to say why Professor Leopold Ettlinger's review of Gombrich's *Norm and Form*, 'Classification and Its Discontents', was not completely satisfying. Beyond a lengthy summary of the book, little came through of the scholarship, the breadth of vision, the intense humanism of the Gombrich canon. It seems to me, after all, that Gombrich has carried on where Ruskin left off, drawing inspiration on the way from Wölfflin[1] and Burckhardt[2] As always with Gombrich, there are fine oracular moments and a number of favourite art historian's idols are smashed in the process. Professor Ettlinger chooses to ignore these points.

Prof. Ernst Gombrich

It would seem to me a commonplace to suggest that the historical context of art is of prime importance. I fail to see why it should be unfashionable today. If it is, then it might appear to be a terrible indictment of all pre-Gombrichian art criticism that it should have encouraged students of art to tread upon such stony ground.

Norbert Lynton[3], in his review in *The Guardian*, quoted Gombrich as saying that there was no such thing as art, only artists — an idea that might well give future art historians food for thought!

Quentin Bell, writing in *The Listener* last week, whilst not considering Gombrich a stylish writer — an unfair criticism since Gombrich was not writing in his native language — does admire his 'enormous erudition with fine gifts of historical imagination'. While he considers Gombrich defective in his style, he does praise him as 'a great teacher' with 'a passionate interest in what he is saying.'

Norm and Form, in Bell's view, and I am inclined to agree, is 'not the happiest of titles.' That ambiguity aside, Gombrich's achievement in *Norm and Form* is astonishing. Where there is complexity he brings simplicity. In the end, in every work of art he explores, he creates the illusion for us that we have always understood it from the very beginning. Through his logic and his sensitivity we can come to know the secrets of the marvels he puts before us. Above all else, he is endearing in his compulsive affection for his readers.

[1] *Heinrich Wölflin, Der klassische kunst.1898. Introduced the idea of comparative studies in art criticism. Used two lanterns in his lectures to show differences between two paintings of the same subject by different painters. Gombrich warned of the dangers of this method.*

[2]*Jacob Burckhardt*, The Civilisation of the Renaissance in Italy (1860). *Seminal work on life and manners in the age of Dante and Michelangelo.*

[3]*Norbert Lynton, Professor of the History of Art, Head of Department of Art History at the Chelsea School of Art, and Art Critic for 'The Guardian', describes Gombrich's method as taking inherited concepts of style and function and rediscovering their meaning by uncovering roots. 'The roots are the stuff of history, fascinating in themselves....but I should guess that his impulse is the modern impatient one of wanting to blow the dust off the past achievements, even when it is gold dust.'*

18 January 1967 (U)

Artists and Environment

Can it be as long ago as 1954 that the Peterlee project courageously brought in Victor Pasmore* to add an aesthetic element to the architectural heritage of County Durham? It was a bold move, though for those who now live under its shadow, it may seem rather dated. The suggestion that painting and sculpture enter into the mind of the architect may seem, on balance, a good idea, considering the horrendously ugly buildings that shoot up from the streets of our towns and cities. The whole question was discussed by a panel of artists and architects under the able direction of Andrew Forge.

One can understand that sculpture has an ancient and distinguished link with architecture. One can also see that, given the eccentricity of modern buildings these days, we can envisage a time when painting would be the only means of bringing beauty to the beast. Unhappily, given the state of contemporary painting, there is no guarantee that the enhancement achieved by the marriage of architecture with the plastic arts would in any way allow us to make any seriously objective judgements. There will no doubt, with the modern trend for experimentalism, be some hot discussion as to the relative merits.

Art is by its nature a synthesis. Its relationship with its

surroundings is therefore of vital importance. The paintings on the walls of the houses in Pompei are as empathetic as the frescos of Giotto at Assisi and Leonardo's 'Last Supper' at San Lorenzo in Milan. More recent alliances of art and architecture, such as Mondrian with Le Corbusier, have succeeded. But we do have to ask 'what part artists can play in the development of our surroundings.' Generally speaking, architects regard artists as 'naïve'. Furthermore, the artist expects to see the completion of his work comparatively quickly, where as the architect may have to wait years to see the finished product of his endeavours. Whatever the degree of co-operation, there will, by necessity, have to be a consideration of space, dimension and perspective. These problems were ably dealt with and brought together by Andrew Forge, himself a distinguished artist and sculptor.

There was the constructivist, Anthony Gilbert, who surprised everyone by asking the question: 'Is the architect a necessary ingredient?', and saw television sets as 'unconscious sculpture'! After all, 'the artist is always showing the way for the architect.'

Whereas, in former times, art was 'embedded in religion', nowadays, we tend to believe in more 'totemistic objects'. This in some ways shows the irrelevance of architecture in real terms. We rarely notice the buildings we work in or even inhabit. The trouble is that we do not see art in our surroundings until it is taken away. Another contributor, Matthew Carder, remarked that, without Eros, Piccadilly would be just another roundabout. 'Eros controls the element of space around it.' I would have preferred to call it 'quality of space'.

Architect Theo Crosby, emphasised the importance of the sociological factor in art. Like da Vinci, he believed 'the most relevant function is the human function.' In the 1930s there was emphasis on the structural and organisational functions. In the 1960s, 'architecture is an architecture of totality or it is nothing.' In Mondrian's view, the artist was a new kind of specialist, at a time when there was 'a free and open association of artist and architecture.'

In the view of artists, Ken Turner and Maurice Agis, there should always be 'mobility and change'. A building can be transformed by light and sound. A sense of space can be achieved by new techniques, through colour experimentation and the highlighting of textures. Spots of light can revolve around a room and sunlight reflect on brass discs.

The discussion looked into the future. Squads of artists would be recruited to work for municipal authorities. They would provide public art, sculptures for the community. There would be 'throw-away houses'. Brick and concrete would be replaced by steel and plastic. Houses could be made so that they could be 'melted down' when no longer needed.

Well! At the end of that, narrator and interviewer, Andrew Forge, could see no alternative but to close the programme in case of melt-down. Clearly the Big Bad Wolf had puffed once too often and there was nowhere for anyone to live, not even a house of straw.

Victor Pasmore, artist. Associated with the formation of the Euston Road School (1937-39) and the first post-war exhibition of abstract art. Consultant urban and architectural designer, Peterlee New Town (1955-77). Exhibited widely: Venice Biennale 1960, Musée des Arts Decoratifs, Paris 1961, Palais des Beaux Arts, Brussels 1961, Tate Gallery 1965, etc.

16,21,30 May, 8 June 1967 (U)

The Sense of Pure Vision

What makes painting different from the other arts? Is there some special attitude of mind, some special functioning of perception that separates it in our minds when we attempt to make an assessment of its merits? These are questions which Michael Podro sought to answer in his four talks.

After dismissing the eighteenth-century aesthetic canon — 'a very barren subject' — he pursued a convincing line of argument, stemming largely from the notion that, by the eighteenth century, art had become separated from knowledge and morality, though Schiller and Diderot considered that a truly beautiful work of art should be improving, 'a crucial and central function of the human mind'.

An analogy to sentence patterns as being 'graspable patterns', intelligible structures leading to a fluency of understanding, was a suitable opening to the thorny subject of the relationship between art and poetry.

Schiller pointed to the dual nature of man as being vital in the understanding of a work of art: man as part of Nature and feeling, man morally and intellectually free.

In the second talk, Mr. Podro examined two theories leading from this view of duality. First, art as pure undistorted vision, and second, as sensuous perception, in both cases drawing widely from Schopenhauer[1] and Schiller[2], Roger Fry[3] and Baudelaire[4]. Particularly in the case of Roger Fry, the argument gained weight through the additional concept of the painting as 'form set out in space', and then, 'as a real life scene around which he produces an accidental fantasy'. In other words, Rembrandt could be seen in terms of both spatial vision and psychological narrative. He could be seen not only as a great painter but also a great poet. As Mr. Podro affirmed in Goethe's words: 'The arts have a tendency to merge.'

I might, as a layman, have been terribly lost in the associationist psychology of Johann Friedrich Herbart had not some allusion been made to musical analogy: 'Play me a part of a familiar tune and I will anticipate the rest....Play me a familiar tune and I will hear it more clearly than something strange for which I have no ready expectations. Or play me a tune which is not familiar and I will hear that aspect of it which is like other tunes I have known. I will hear more clearly the familiar aspect of it than others I have not heard before.'

Wait a minute! Could I hear that again, please?

[1]*Arthur Schopenhauer (!788-1860) philosopher of pessimism. Believed the world to be basically malignant. The Human Will perpetuated its survival through the will to reproduce and perpetuate life. Therefore Asceticism and Chastity are the duty of man if evil is to be extinguished.*

[2]*Friedrich Wilhelm Joseph von Schiller (1759-1805), lyrical and reflective poet as well as one of Germany's greatest dramatists. He believed in the humanising influence of art.*

[3]*Roger Fry (1856-1934) English artist and critic. Art critic* The Athenaeum *1901, Director Metropolitan Museum of Art, New York*

1905-10, in 1906, Discovered' Cézanne and introduced Post-Impressionists at the Grafton Galleries, London 1910.
⁴Charles Baudelaire (1821-67), French poet of 'Les Fleurs du Mal', a work reflecting a morbid (some thought unhealthy and decadent) sense of beauty which lead to six of the poems being banned.

*

25 May 1967 (U)

The Poetry of Pictures

I derived particular pleasure from the talks on the impact of painting on English poetry in the mid-nineteenth century. Ian Fletcher opened the series with a penetrating analysis of types and emblems in poetry, beginning with the basic principle that Victorian poetry was over-painterly and Victorian painting over-literary.

Dante Gabriel Rossetti

Word-painting was a form which led to feeble excesses if unchecked, though Rossetti (following the example of Keats's *Ode to a Grecian Urn*) admittedly turned out some tolerable sonnets on pictures and sculptures. One can, however, understand Whistler's remark: 'But Gabriel, why not simply frame the sonnet?'

The comparison of the painting of 'Mariana' by Millais and Tennyson's 'Mariana in the Moated Grange' was illuminating. Yet the unwholesome morbidity of Rossetti's poetry, especially the poem written while on a journey through Belgium and France in 1849, in which the corpse of a man stabbed and tumbled into the Seine is described in all its clinical detail, is as perverse an exercise in grotesquerie as ever I have heard.

Edward Lucie-Smith's talk on Rossetti was notable for its clarity of style and in many ways was the most 'likeable' of all, since the play on gruesome or morbid detail was gratifyingly resisted. The analysis of Rossetti's turgid sensitivity, his shrinking from reality, was very clearly defined.

Amidst all this aesthetic allure of medievalism, it was almost a relief to move into the more strident atmosphere of Tennyson's 'Idylls of the King', with D. J. Palmer's interpretation of 'Old, unhappy, far-off things/ And battles long ago.' Compared with the occasionally effete and wan Pre-Raphaelites, the pictorial vividness of Tennyson's King Arthur, marching against the godless kingdom of the Red Knight, was a triumphant appeasement of the Muse.

*

20 June 1967 (P)

In Search of the Unexpected

Florence has an ageless dignity which Seán O'Fáolain[1] has called 'everness', in contrast to the light arabesques and broken Gothic that constitute the 'neverness' of Venice. Like Maurice Barrès[2], most travellers come to Florence with the thought that they are about to experience 'le plus grand plaisir de ma vie,' as he wrote of his first view of the Parthenon in *Le Voyage de Sparte,*

The weary tourist, guide-book in hand, wandering aimlessly along one of the narrow, labyrinthine streets of Florence, darkened by the shadows of solid Romanesque architecture, may be faced by that 'serene height of alabaster, 'coloured like a morning cloud and chased like a seashell' — John Ruskin's memorable description of Giotto's Florentine *campanile.* It is then that we realise that this city is truly one of the most important aesthetic experiences, indeed, even, as with Barrès, 'one of the greatest pleasures of my whole life.'

[1]*Prolific Irish writer, who became Director of the Arts Council of Ireland 1957. Popular works included 'An Irish Journey', 'Summer in Italy' and his short stories.*
[2]*Maurice Barrès (1862-1923). Intensely lyrical French writer.*

Author of the popular novel, 'Colette Baudoche' and important works such as 'Du Sang, de la Volupté et de la Mort'.,and 'Les Déracinés',

20 June 1967 (U)

City of Flowers

At the very moment when the great deluge of the River Arno was sweeping through Florence, the BBC was issuing a beautiful booklet to accompany George Walton Scott's enthralling series of programmes for 'Study Session', entitled 'City of Florence', designed primarily to present the greatness of the art of the City from the eleventh to the sixteenth centuries — to present, that is, not merely the treasure house of painting and sculpture, but also to reveal the artists and their patrons as a vital force.

Brian Robb, Senior Tutor at the Royal College of Art, concerned himself with the visual impact of the city, beginning with an account of the magnificence of San Miniato, with its rich inlays of green and white marble, set in roundel, diamond and all manner of geometrical shapes, enhancing the 'delicate justice of their relationships'. The raised steps and the ornate choir-screen served 'to isolate and emphasize the sanctity of the altar and the mystery of the Eucharist', an observation which led Mr. Robb to delineate the changes which came to Florence at this time through the schism between the Catholic and Orthodox churches, the decline of the Byzantine Empire after the Crusades, and the rise of the merchant classes, bringing a vital reassessment of art and philosophy which ultimately flowered into the

San Miniato, Florence

Renaissance.

Few tourists would fail to appreciate the remark that the buildings of Dante's Florence 'were designed to intimidate rather than to please.' There followed other illuminating moments on Donatello, Uccello and Masaccio, and, with a felicitous clarity, Mr. Robb described the fascinating façade of Santa Maria Novella.

The next four talks were given by Francis Hoyland, who, like Barrès, experienced a moment of utter revelation when, arriving in the scruffy piazza, he came face-to-face with the bare façade of Santo Spirito, amid the gloom of the oppressive Florentine rain. Once inside, however, he discovered marvel which he described with almost Ruskinesque appraisal. An impressive section on Botticelli led him into a very logical account of the neo-Platonism of the High Renaissance. Here was the artist speaking, in contrast to the art historian: 'The design of any work of art can affect us through some answering impulse in our bodies', a physical empathy which goes beyond the heart of humanism and the Socratic code, with man at the centre of the universe.

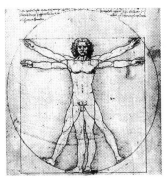

'Human Figure in a Circle'
(Leonardo)

The Leonardo drawing of a male figure, limbs outstretched to fill a circle, becomes a central symbol of the Renaissance view of man. In Alexander Pope's famous lines from his *Essay on Man*:

> Know then thyself, presume not God to scan;
> The proper study of mankind is man.

Birds and Beasts

20 February 1967 (P)

It Takes All Sorts

Gerald Durrell

When Tom Salmon asked Gerald Durrell* if he didn't find the fearsome noises of the jungle frightening, the reply came swiftly back: 'The only fearsome noise I ever hear is my bank manager clearing his throat!'

From then on, the tone was set for Mr. Durrell to talk about his life as a zoologist and traveller. While he was out on safari, Mrs. Durrell would be back at base-camp, chewing platefuls of spinach to feed to a young fledgling that could only digest regurgitated leaves, or coaxing a baby crocodile with peppermints because it refused the more succulent pieces of mouse-meat.

*Born in India in 1925 and a regular contributor to BBC programmes. As a zoologist, he travelled widely, particularly to the Cameroons, Mexico and Mauritius. He was author of many best-selling books, including 'My Family and Other Animals'.

21 September 1966 (U)

Snakes Alive!

Gerald Durrell chatted about his ordeal of descending into a snake-pit. First, he lost one of his shoes. In spite of this undeniable misfortune, he had to touch down in the semi-darkness barefoot — straight into a nest of vipers!

(Pick of the Week Notes)

20 February 1967 (P)

'And Don't Spare the Horses!'

I wonder how Mr. Durrell would have fared in the discussion between Jeremy Sandford (author of *Cathy Come Home*) and Miss M. Raymonde-Hawkins in 'Home This Afternoon', when Gordon Snell asked them: 'Do we care more about our animals than our children?'

Miss Raymonde-Hawkins was a tough nut to crack. She rose defiantly to defend the cause of animal-welfare.

'Children are far more fond of themselves on a horse than the horse they are on.'

Mr. Sandford's quiet but persuasive tone did not quite match the sweeping dedication of his formidable opponent.

18 February 1967 (P)

Man Eats Dog

Messrs Durrell and Raymonde-Hawkins would certainly have had a thing or two to say to popular biologist and broadcaster, Dr. Magnus Pyke, whose talk for 'Science Survey' dealt plainly with the problems of nutrition in an over-populated world and the necessity for the breaking down of taboos and prejudices. Captain Cook, for example, had eaten dog flesh in Tahiti in 1769, and what is more, he liked it. The chow, Dr. Pyke informed us with a clinical detachment, was specially bred for culinary delight. What could be more nutritious than a succulent puppy ham?

Can you feel Miss Raymonde-Hawkins' hackles rising? Frankly, I'd rather keep to the pork-lamb-beef permutation and steer clear of frogs, snails, bird's nests, and especially anything remotely canine or even reptilian, come to that!

24 February 1967 (P)

'El Ingles'

When Charles Vincent Hitchcock went into the ring to fight his first bull, a black cat ran out in front of him. That cat was to be the mark of success for the most celebrated of English bull-fighters, 'El Ingles', as his Spanish fans called him. Now he has retired at the age of thirty-nine to keep a bar in Palma, after a career which, from the first 'baptism of blood', was destined for brilliance. 'Is bull-fighting cruel?' Roy Cross asked him in 'Home This Afternoon' from the north of England. 'Well,' he said, 'the English always associate blood with pain. The bull does not suffer as much as we think.' Where is Miss Raymonde-Hawkins?

24 February 1967 (P)

The Countryside in February

I was glad to escape to 'The Countryside in February', which took us once more through that beguiling world of the poetical C. Gordon Glover, who, in soothing tones, led us over 'the grim unlovely pebbled snout of Dungeness' and across Romney Marsh to view the 'swans on a slate-grey mere.' It may not be to everybody's taste, but to a country-born lad like me, the evocative freshness of this staunch old BBC series is always a welcome escape from what most town-dwellers think of as the real world.

22 February 1967 (P)

Animal Etiquette

All animals possess elaborate codes of communication which, says Dr. J. M. Cullen, can be confidently interpreted according to a complex system of signals and responses. In a discussion with Professor Robbins (educationist), J. M. Argyle commented on the relationship between human language and animal display, and drew attention to the language of the eyes, comparing the emotive expression of the human eye with the glacial stare of the cockerel, and all the psychological ramifications which that involves. I shall never feel quite at ease now at a cocktail party!

*

28 May 1966 (P)

Pets Corner

A programme about pets informed us that a kestrel was nesting on top of the BBC building. And did you know that nightingales were no longer singing in Berkeley Square but now entertained twice nightly in the gardens of Buckingham Palace?

We were told the momentous news that Diana Dors* had sold her cockatoo, that lizards could be bought for 3s. 6d., alligators for 7s. 6d., mice for 1s. 3d. each and miniature Japanese squirrels had sold out at £3. They apparently make very good pets. I wonder if Dr. Pyke might like one for dinner!

Diana Dors

Diana Dors, an icon of British films from the 1950s to the 1970s, was born Mary Fluck in 1931 and quickly rose to stardom as a sex symbol with her portrayal of glamorous and provocative roles earning her the soubriquet of 'The English Marilyn Monroe'. Diana starred in many popular films, including 'The Sandwich Man', 'Berserk', 'Passport to Shame', and 'There's a Girl in My Soup'. Her last film, 'Steaming', came out in 1984, but in May of that year she died, following a long battle with cancer. A programme, about her sensational life on and off the film set, entitled 'The Blonde Bombshell' was subsequently shown on television.

*

From my notebook: 28 May 1966 (U)

A False Start: The Habits of the Cuckoo

I have to admit that, nature-lover as I am, the curious habits of the voracious cuckoo seem to me to be highly reprehensible and, if I think about them too much, I could really begin to dislike the wretched creature. As I listen now, a revolting kind of bubbly noise assails my ears. We are told it is its mating call. 'Bubble, bubble, bubble!' it goes. 'Bubble, bubble, bubble!' just like a thirsty child sucking lemonade through a straw. So that's what goes on in 'Nature's Parliament'!

28 May 1966 (U)
In Cloud-Cuckoo-Land!

What is it that makes us wax romantic over the ceaseless, repetitive call of the cuckoo? Delius rhapsodized over it to very good effect. Wordsworth rejoiced in its song. The sly creature inveigled Robert Browning into calling it 'Sweet Bird', if you please!

But what of the facts? First of all, it is nothing but a selfish squatter. It settles down in the nice warm nest of a poor little unsuspecting dunnock who had just popped out for a bit of foraging in the fields. It proceeds in a thoroughly heartless manner to turf out the sweet little dunnock eggs and lays its own look-alike replacement. Then she flies off to pastures new, leaving the poor little foster mother to feed the newly-hatched cuckoo chick, which rapidly grows to three times its size. This monstrous babe throws out the remaining little dunnocks, leaving the foster parent to fly to and fro with sustenance to satisfy this squatter's increasingly voracious appetite. No wonder I cannot bring myself to write about such a voracious ogre as the cuckoo! It is nothing but a parasite! Can Nature have devised a more gross and beguiling deception than this?

From my notebook: *25 December 1966* (U)

Notes for 'In Praise of the Hare'

A range of Irish, Scots and English accents gave an air of authenticity to an account of the extraordinary life-cycle of the hare, in a programme especially compiled by George Ewart Evans and David Thomson. Ancient mythology joined with present-day oral tradition to provide a fascinating glimpse into the secret world of this mysterious creature.

We were told a number of basic facts to begin with.

1. The doe never puts all her young leverets in one nest and, unlike rabbits, they are born with their pelts.

2. Hares never leave the field they are born in. They sit in a wide circle, sometimes as many as thirty or forty at a time, as if in a coven, while one or two gambol and frolic in the centre. Perhaps, we are told,

this is a mating ritual. We don't really know. There is always the mystery, you see.

3. The jack-hares box and 'spur' their enemies (i.e. kick them!). In March, a great deal of hare-boxing on hind legs takes place. Perhaps they are selecting a mate. Some appear to thump the ground with their feet. (Just like my bank manager!)

4. With very poor sight and being extremely nervous animals, hares have a highly-developed sense of smell and hearing. They appear to have an uncanny sixth sense too. An old Irishman put it like this:

"To be sure, they have hindsight — or whatever you call it — well, it's a kind of foresight, only backwards, don't you see!"

5. Like human beings hares go grey with age. Now, that I find hair-raising! There's something scary about a ghostly old grey hare staring you in the face! It could be just like suddenly catching sight of oneself in a mirror! Strange tales are told of hares turning into witches and

witches turning into hares.

Well! Interesting as these facts are, we are not any nearer to understanding the creature. There is no end to the stories about it, many of them conflicting and perplexing, tales lost to us now, as rural communities disappear, and the ancient beliefs and superstitions with them. As the Irishman said:

"We've grown more Christian-like 'n what we was years ago.'

24 February 1967 (U)

The Lore of Nature!

This week I have learnt a great deal about the habits of animals. I don't mean all that schoolboy stuff about the birds and the bees. I mean really interesting things that might well change my view of all that highly contentious propaganda about humans being the highest form of living creature.

When I was a little six year-old I would sometimes watch our old farm foreman, Pomfret, pluck our chicken for Sunday lunch. I used to hear him say that the bird didn't feel a thing as he wrung its neck. So why did I see it twitching for minutes afterwards?

Which reminds me of what I heard Charles Vincent Hitchcock ('El Ingles'), the English bull-fighter, say the other day on the radio. You

might not believe it, but it's straight from the horse's mouth. He claims that, when the bull has been prodded and poked with metal spikes and finally brought to its knees to receive the final thrust of the sword, the enraged and humbled animal 'doesn't feel it as much as we think'! That means that it feels it a deal more than the matadors let on. With those words, he might be said to have scored a *bull's-eye* in the 'cruelty-to-animals' stakes. After all, 'matador' is the Spanish for 'killer', and a killer isn't going to plunge a sword between the shoulder blades of a bull without causing pain and drawing a considerable amount of blood. But the English, he says, always associate blood with pain. Now, what a strange idea!

Let us think of something less gory! Let us turn to birds of the feathery kind. Now, we hear, the ears of birds are sensitive to pitch, as Dr. S.M. Cullen, Lecturer in Zoology at the University of Oxford, told us on the Third. That I can believe when I am woken up by the joyous chorus of trillings, pipings and squawkings outside my bedroom window when Spring comes. It would be more than likely that a sweet little trilling robin would respond to the ugly squawking of a magpie with nothing short of revulsion.

There followed some observations on animal behaviour in comparison with human behaviour. For example, when a dog looks at you as you approach him along a path, it almost instantaneously decides whether it likes you or not and either it will attack you with a vengeance or it will run off like greased lightning.

On the other hand, you can tell immediately what plans you have to adopt over the next few seconds by observing how the dog is holding its tail and whether its ears are drawn back ready for attack. In which case, run for your life!

According to Dr. Cullen, animal display and language contain 'dangers of ambiguity'. Do we run for it if we see a lion yawning? We certainly would if it was roaring. But watch out! You really must be sure to read the signs in double quick time. The animal is thinking to itself, not in as many words, mind, one of three things as it stares you out:

1. I am hungry. I want you for my dinner!
2. I am about to attack you. I just don't like the cut of your gib!
3. I am desperate for a mate. How about coming round to my place?

In all of these cases there is only one thing to do — leap onto your bike and make for the hills — PDQ!

In this discussion Dr. Cullen was ably assisted by Professor R.H. Robbins, the well-known authority of phonetics and linguistics at the School of African and Oriental Studies, who pointed out how important the 'language of the eyes' is in human communication. It is all done through 'expression'. Unlike the cockerel, it is virtually impossible for us humans to look a person straight in the eye for more than a few minutes unless there is some other element present such as curiosity or aggression. Usually, we are embarrassed if someone stares at us for no apparent reason.

*

25 March 1967 (U)

Great Scott!

Happy the man, and happy he alone,
He who can call today his own;
He who, secure within, can say:
Tomorrow do thy worst, for I have lived today.

With Dryden's famous words, BBC Radio has aptly chosen, this week, to celebrate the work of Peter Scott by bringing together two friends, Gillie Potter and S. J. Lotbiniere, in Suzanne Gibbs' production, 'The Happy Man'. They were joined by a variety of musicians including Gipsy Zsiga Burai and his Band, and chorister Christopher John Elliott, and there were readings by John Welsh, Hedley Goodall, Clive Ray and Brian Roberts.

Peter Scott

Scott, son of Scott of the Antarctic, was born in 1909, the year in which Bleriot made the first cross-channel flight. Scott's mother had studied under Auguste Rodin in Paris. His godfather was Sir James Barrie. George Bernard Shaw was a friend of the family.

Scott claims that he was 'a perfectly poisonous small boy with an angelic voice' and sang 'Polly-wolly-doodle-all-the-day' very prettily.

His mother took a coastguard cottage at Sandwich so that her young son could be encouraged to take an interest in natural history. There he became more aware of the habits of sea-birds, learnt to identify birdsong and watched the wild geese come and go.

To train his memory, he learnt the whole of *The Hunting of the Snark*, all thirty-five minutes of it. He irritated his art master by persistently sketching flowers and stuffed birds and was told to 'Go and draw a pudding!'

Up at Cambridge, he read zoology, botany and geology. He had some photographs published in *Country Life* and began to take an interest in maps and seafaring. He went racing in dinghies designed by Uffa Fox, who 'had a splendid repertoire of songs.' He developed a love of music, including among favourite works the Brahms Violin Concerto and the *Sinfonia Antarctica* by Vaughan Williams.

He saw Richard Strauss conduct *Der Rosenkavalier* in Munich and, through a mutual friend, had an *entrée* to Franz Knapperbusch's apartment to play cards.

It is clear from all this that Peter Scott is an all-round man. He painted bird scenes, took a lighthouse on The Wash, went in search of red-breasted geese in Hungary and later brought back snow geese from Canada.

His world was darkened by the Nazi threat, Hitler's rantings and Chamberlain's announcement of war in Europe. 'In the war, as ever, my luck held' — enough to hear Churchill's announcement at the end of hostilities.

Scott's aim crystallised into a wish 'to save birds and teach people to enjoy them. Aren't the great skeins of wild geese part of the glory of God?'

I think the most moving part of the programme was his visit to his father's hut in the Antarctic snows — a deep personal experience that stayed with him for the rest of his life.

Above all, Suzanne Gibbs and John Sparks brought out the humane qualities of a man devoted to bird-life. One gets from all this the abiding impression of a deep reverence for nature and his earnest wish for the conservation of wildlife 'for the benefit of mankind.' He believes that wild swans symbolise the ideal relationship between man and nature.' 'They and their kind,' he said, 'have contributed to my happiness.'

Books and Authors

3 January 1967 (U)

What the Dickens?

Whenever Professor K. J. Fielding's name appears in the *Radio Times* we can be sure of some very sound criticism. His talk on 'The Popularity of Dickens' was, as expected, stimulating.

Charles Dickens

In the twelve years after Dickens died, his books, in the first three months alone, sold over four million copies. The key to his posthumous success is, as Thackeray pointed out, that he 'remains modern.' Perhaps this is due, says Professor Fielding, to the fact that Dickens speaks to his readers directly. Of course there is the humour, the poetic sense, the irrepressible high spirits and the ability to create an imaginary world which reflects the dilemmas of the human condition. But in his extraordinariness he is the best exponent of the ordinary.

Amidst the comicality and the caricature there are to be discovered 'disturbing truths', as in *Great Expectations*, for example. Pip's long process of self-discovery begins with 'a fearful man, in coarse grey, with a great iron on his leg....who limped, and shivered, and glared and growled.' To this gruesome figure Dickens seeks to reconcile us in the course of time, as he does with Jaggers, Pip's legal guardian, a lawyer who keeps two death masks of hanged men staring down at him from the wall of his office. The detail is so naturally told that we believe every word of it. 'Dickens establishes the story's credibility and a natural standard by which to judge it.'

The Professor dwells interestingly on the imaginative way in which Dickens conceived the character of Miss Havisham, deserted by her husband on her wedding morning, grown self-indulgent in her hopelessness, still clad in her wedding-dress with its faded trimmings, now like 'earthy paper'.

Pip is struck by the fact that one of her shoes is missing. What is it that is so striking about the underlying symbolism? The literary parallel here is as uncanny as the missing shoe of Jacob the assassin of 'The Tottenham Outrage (see p.100). We can almost hear the crowds gasp when the constable says: 'His shoe is missing.' The very realisation sends a shiver down Pip's spine too. The experience is as unfathomable as the lost parentage theme in another Dickensian mystery, *Oliver Twist*.

Professor Fielding is quite clear in his assessment: 'Much of Dickens is missed if we lay all the emphasis on the intensity of his insight into alienation, violence and abnormality, and not enough on the counterparts of normality, security and happiness.'

There are, in the Professor's view, three further reasons for the popularity of Dickens: his belief in men's equality, the responsibility they owe one another, and their need for justice. On one occasion, whilst walking home from a dinner, Dickens was stopped many times by working people in the street 'all eager to thank him for the pleasure his books afforded them.' That surely shows the measure of the man and his message.

Professor Fielding's talk (the first of six) brought together many threads and carried us through to a neat conclusion in a very informative twenty-five minutes.

6 February 1967 (U)

'The Bubble Reputation'

Polly Elwes included an intriguing story in her excellent magazine programme for older listeners, 'This Afternoon', in which Naomi Lewis talked about a long-forgotten writer I knew little or nothing about, and perhaps the same goes for many of Naomi's listeners.

A novelist who invents such exotic titles as *The Soul of Lilith* and *The Sorrows of Satan* surely deserves to be re-invented. Her name was Mary MacKay and nobody, I am sure, has ever heard of her, unless of course they are addicts, as her tens of thousands of readers apparently are in the United States. Her father was Charles MacKay, editor of *The Illustrated London News* and she lived in Earls Court, a place hardly to be associated with high romance. She began her career as a concert pianist and once gave a recital which included fifteen ingenious improvisations. However, piano-playing did not, in a manner of speaking, turn out to be her principal *forte*!

As a novelist, writing under the pen-name of Marie Corelli, Mary MacKay began to have some success with *The Romance of Two Worlds* in 1886 and the more sensational, *Vendetta, or The Story of One Forgotten,* a three-volume novel of the same year. Then, among others, her high society novel, *Thelma,* came along, followed with amazing regularity by a series of novels including *My Wonderful Wife: A Story in Smoke* (1889), *The Silver Domino* (1892), *The Soul of Lilith* (1892), *The Mighty Atom* (1896), and many others.

Marie Corelli

Marie Corelli was a remarkably prolific writer, freely expressing her opinions about modern life and conduct, and mixing her professional work with feminist activities by supporting the suffragette movement. Thus the girl from Earls Court became one of England's most popular novelists, but such is the nature of fame that within a few years of her death in 1924, her books were hardly read in her native land. In other places in the world, her name became synonymous with the passion and romance of her plots, and her work found a new and vital readership across the Atlantic.

20 September 1966 (P)

The Pessimistic Optimist

The producer, Derek Parker introduced a radio-portrait to mark the centenary of the birth on 21st September 1866, of H. G. Wells. The production was compiled from the BBC Sound Archives. We heard H.G.'s shrill, squeaky voice telling us he was 'opposed to people who say Britain for the British', and Sir Julian Huxley, who clearly admired this incredibly active brain 'metabolizing ideas and knowledge'. There was Frank Horrabin's account of how Wells would shut himself up in his library to work on the *Outline of History* so that 'it was almost more than your life was worth to pass the windows'.

An endearing piece of reminiscing concerned Sir Compton Mackenzie's visit to H.G. at Hanover Terrace when Wells remarked on how much he liked Lawrence's *Sons and Lovers* and asked why he had ever gone to Arabia! Yet there was humour even in his last months. Sir Julian Huxley recounted how Wells had been exasperated by a guest who wouldn't leave and finally Wells was forced to say, by way of protest: 'Please, can't you see I'm busy dying?'

Wells was treated at greater length in Robert Pocock's documentary on the Third Programme. Here was Wells the novelist, the sociologist, the popular historian. Among the undeniable attractions were the voices of Professor G. P. Wells and Frank Wells, H.G.'s sons. They told of Wells's abhorrence of sloth, his love of mankind in the abstract and his dislike of it in the flesh; his final despair when his hopes of Utopia were blown up at Hiroshima. There were reminiscences of a touchingly personal kind by Winifred Simmons

H G Wells

and the Dowager Lady Aberconway. Television viewers might have seen Madame Odette Keun, more than a friend to the great little man, talking about Wells splendidly in the BBC1 production, 'Whoosh'.

Here was a man who extended the scope of the novel, who looked into the future, as George Orwell put it, and 'knew that it was not going to be what respectable people imagined', a man who created horrors and marvels out of his imagination and made them plausible. Wells could, at the end of the *Outline of History*, see 'life forever dying to be born afresh', and 'man leaving his ancestral shelters and going out upon the greatest adventure that ever was in time or space'. Is this ' the little man with big ideas' that Malcolm Muggeridge has been talking about lately? No, it seems that the sum total of these impressions is rather less than the whole man. I would have liked more of Wells and less of what his friends and enemies had to say about him.

Somewhere in the back of my mind there lurks an equation told me by my tutor, Harold Laski, when I was reading *The History of Mr. Polly*. It goes: 'Cold pork and pickles + nagging wife = indigestion.' But Mr. Polly's relationship with his remarkable creator is more complex than that.

1 October 1966 (U)

Looking Forward to Looking Back

The H. G. Wells Centenary Celebration

It is always a pleasure to me to listen in to people talking about people. Not that I'm any sort of gossip, mind! No, I'm just fascinated by the infinite variety of the human race. Of course there are limits to the practice, especially in a small 'Clochemerle' type of society, where discretion should be, but rarely is, the better part of valour. But if people will insist on recording their thoughts and memories, however personal, it does seem to be fair play to allow the rest of us to listen in.

The family and friends of H. G. Wells were, by courtesy of BBC Radio, brought together in my sitting-room this week for a discussion organised by Robert Pocock, in the form of a 'radio portrait'. We met composer Sir Arthur Bliss, Lord Ritchie Calder, Lancelot Hogben, Kingsley Martin, Sir Francis Meynell, V. S. Pritchett, Sir Compton Mackenzie (see pp 68-9), Sir Ralph Richardson, and Wells' two sons, G. P. and Frank, all at one fell swoop. What a gathering!

Wells was an inspiration to many young people who wanted to escape from the humdrum pursuits their elders expected them to follow. Here was a man who could show them how to break free of the old social bonds, show them the marvels of the universe, extend the boundaries of experience and render the impossible possible.

Henry James once said of Trollope: 'His great, his inestimable merit was a complete appreciation of the usual.' Wells, in his social novels like *The History of Mr. Polly, Kipps,* and *Love and Mr. Lewisham,* succeeded admirably to convey that quality of 'the usual' which, in his case, stands for the daily trials and tribulations, joys and passions, frustrations and disappointments of every human being who ever lived on this planet. Where Wells shows himself to be a genius is when he carries us into outer space, away from the humdrum pettinesses of life, into the realms of science that had hitherto been the province of boffins.

Mr. Polly could only escape from the boredom of his life by indulging himself with his favourite cold pork and pickles. He was in the habit of getting out of any of life's little difficulties by shouting: "Lil' dog! Lil' dog!" and rushing off out of sight, supposedly in search of the non-existent animal, before the crisis came to a head.

Clearly that was no way to go on. So he does the unforgivable thing and walks out on his job and his dull little wife with her precious cat and canary, and, in his quest for the simple life, finds solace with the comfortable fat lady in the pub on the river, but not before he has to fight off the bully of a bouncer.

You see, in the Wellsian canon, you have to *earn* your happiness. It isn't there just for the asking. It is all to do with the growing pains of the 20th century. Seen from the current Victorian viewpoint, it was unheard of that a nice young lady like Ann Veronica, the eponymous heroine of one of Wells' most daring novels, should want a particular man who excited her, pursue him and, what is more, get him with such gusto!

What comes through in all the programmes about Wells this week is the image of Wells, the great populariser of ideas, a 'non-stop genius' who challenged the heights of Academe with works of literature which, however much they were criticised for their style and content, broke new ground, sweeping away the old conventions. Mr. Polly achieved his breakaway by setting fire to his shop. Small wonder that his creator, this little man with a great vision, was such an inspiration to the young.

21 September 1966 (U)

H. G. Again!

Frank Wells assembled a number of his father's friends to reminisce about the great little man. Frank Swinnerton reminded us that Wells was always kind to young writers, had an ability to put people at their ease, had boundless energy, often writing two novels at the same time, was very sensitive to adverse opinion and would close up like a clam when under threat. As a diabetic, he could be quarrelsome at times. His political views led him to quarrel with the Russians after the revolution and quarrel with the League of Nations, which he despised. In spite of all this, Wells always remained an optimist, as Kingsley Martin explained, though he discovered that in reality men were more gullible and cruel than he could ever have imagined. The atomic bomb left him in a state of despair for the future of mankind; 'it blew up his hopes for good' and, towards the end of his life, he became more somnolent and morose. As Malcolm Muggeridge pointed out, Wells, in his last book, *Mind at the End of Its Tether,* foresaw the universe was going to end, dragging down with it life itself.

V.S. Pritchett, in his critical role, thought Wells was basically second-rate. His prose was 'loose and journalistic', he was 'incapable of describing love', though good at writing about 'naggers and hen-peckers' and vulgar characters.

With his thin, squeaky voice, Wells, as a public speaker, had little effect on his audiences. George Bernard Shaw said he sounded more like the music-hall entertainer, Wee Georgie Wood. He read with the paper close to his face and had no talent whatsoever for speaking extemporaneously. Yet, as J. B. Priestley remarked, he was a good conversationalist at anyone's dinner-party. Whilst Shaw was a natural performer, Wells had to invent his *persona*. He was always honest and frank to a fault, even about any scandal that surrounded him. Sir Julian Huxley maintained that Wells was wrong in some of the detail in his history of the world, but as a pioneer of science fiction he was more imaginative than even Jules Verne.

St. John Irvine told a story of Wells in his last illness.

Doctor: Look here, Wells, I'm just as ill as you are, but I don't moan about it.
Wells: No, but you don't pity yourself as much as I do.

In the end, he wasted away, so thin and frail, with his brain still teeming with ideas. 'I shall die quietly,' he said.

*

From my notebook: *21 September 1966* (U)

Literary Neighbours

A snippet I heard on the Home Service this week:

When Wells was interviewing his new secretary he failed to ask her about her shorthand and type-writing skills and couldn't stop telling her about his extraordinary new neighbour, George Bernard Shaw. As she had never heard of the great playwright, the story passed right over her head.

Here follows a story that was going the rounds of the Chelsea Poetry Circle this week:

Ivy Compton Burnett

After a literary gathering in the West End, T. S. Eliot invited the novelist, Ivy Compton Burnett, to share his taxi home to Cornwall Gardens. What one would have given to be a fly on the windscreen!

Afterwards, the waspish Miss Burnett was asked what illuminating subjects they talked about on the way. Did the very deep Mr. Eliot make a world-shaking remark? Did he utter a few memorable thoughts of the greatest profundity?

"My dear," cried the spiky spinster, "he talked of nothing but his grocery list and the best places to buy lamb chops!'

*

6 October 1966 (U)

Grrrrgh! Wow! Yarroo!

The greedy, cadging, deceitful, incorrigible William George Bunter is the central character in a juvenile mythology that captivated and still captivates the imaginations of countless children. He and his prankish companions, Harry Wharton, Skinner and Coker appeared in the pages of *The Magnet* from its inception in 1908 to its demise brought about by the paper shortage in 1940, after 25,000 words of Greyfriars mythology. The fellows are 'chums' and 'chaps' and 'cads' and 'rats'. The stories are full of sayings and sentences like 'I say, you fellows!' and 'It's a perfect dog's life at this school'. Bunter speaks a language of his own: sounds of woe, of anguish and complaint. He hoots and yarroo's and chortles amidst all the horseplay. He is a slug, a shirker, a complainer, a malingerer. Yet he is a lovable rogue all the same. Fair-play in the school is as rampant as skulduggery.

Gerald Campion as Billy Bunter

'I'm sorry I hurt you the other day.'
'You didn't hurt me enough!'
'Well, if Bunter doesn't take the whole biscuit factory!'
I say, you fellows!

*

6 October 1966 (P)

The Myth of Greyfriars

When I was at school in the 1940s, we had a matron who looked for all the world like Smollett's Mrs Jewkes — bushy eyebrows and a face that looked as if it had been 'pickled for a month in saltpetre.' She scared us almost as much as the dreaded bullies from the 'Long Dorm', who stealthily crept up at night and beat the hell out of us juniors, with wet knotted towels. One night we were frightened by creaking boards outside the door. We attacked, blow upon blow with all our might. When the lights were switched on, we found we had felled matron in a shower of goose feathers. One mother, in defence of her little darling, dismissed these days of violence and terror with the predictable words: "Ah well! Boys will be boys."

Despite the haze of sentiment that surrounds those distant memories, 'The Myth of Greyfriars', written and introduced by John Chandos with readings by Hugh Burden, was a most satisfying and nostalgic excursion into the past as read in the well-thumbed pages of *The Magnet* and *The Gem*.

As a rule, writers of children's books are supremely partisan. *Robinson Crusoe*, *Treasure Island* and *Swallows and Amazons* are all variations on the 'noble savage' theme. Jack and Ralph in *The Coral Island* are splendidly British chaps engaged in their own little piece of empire-building. When they reappear in *Lord of the Flies* they are faced with the more disturbing questions of survival and original sin.

Frank Richard's 'Billy Bunter' stories are all the more remarkable for their realism. Bunter's world is inhabited not only by splendid chaps who idolise clean-living and fair play; it is also filled with rotters, cads, bounders and bullies.

Bunter, like Golding's Piggy, is the perfect modern anti-hero — fat, lazy, dissatisfied with his hard lot. It is difficult not to sympathise with his absurd self-indulgence and pathetic yaroo-ings which punctuate his protestations at the injustice of the world.

If there is truth in Orwell's accusations of snobbishness and cheap patriotism, sexually Greyfriars was beyond reproach. No suspicion of scandal ever darkened dormitory or masters' common-room. True, there were plenty of canings, birchings, form-lickings and bumpings, and a fair amount of spite and selfishness in amongst the horse-play. Ah well! Boys will be boys!

While the myth continued, with its careful admixture of sentiment and violence, the creator of the myth remained, apart from one outburst against Orwell, quietly cultivating his garden.

With remarkable foresight, Denzil Batchelor and John Chandos visited Frank Richards just three months before he died. They found 'a gnome of great age with a wizened parchment face'. The interview turned out to be an unforgettable journey into a world which no longer exists.

Did he like *Tom Brown's Schooldays*? Yes, two or three chapters are well worth reading. Shakespeare? Too long-winded, too involved and 'a beastly snob'. 'Bunter', he said with affection, 'is simple, a little shy. He doesn't realise he is a liar or a young rascal. He thinks he is the only decent fellow at Greyfriars.'

And what about corporal punishment? 'I don't quite see how boys, real boys, could ever be kept in order without it.'

This was a marvellous exchange: the gentle homely voice, the benevolence, the total (to coin a word) immersement in his creation, the sense of humour, the philosophic calm: 'Let youth be happy, or as happy as possible, for the world is, after all, a decent sort of place.'

*

13 February 1967 (U)

B. O. P. — R. I. P.

Boy's Own Paper 1888

"The B. O. P. is dead!" exclaimed contributor Brian Doyle, sadly concluding his interview with its last editor. Countless octogenarians — and many of us younger whippersnappers too — will mourn the demise of *The Boy's Own Paper* which has stopped publication after eighty-eight years. I for one was an avid reader and looked forward to each number as it came out, never giving a thought to who wrote its articles and stories, or how it appeared as regularly as clockwork on the counter of our village paper-shop. All I knew was that I had to get in quick after school on a Friday, before the copies were all sold out. Do you know? I think, if I rooted around on the bottom shelf of my old toy cupboard, I might just find a dog-eared copy or two gathering the dust.

In this week's edition of producer Rosemary Hart's popular magazine programme, 'It Takes All Sorts', Jack Cox, who for twenty years was Editor of *The Boy's Own Paper*, talked to Brian Doyle about his experiences. On hearing Cox's quiet voice, reminiscing with such good sense and in calm, measured tones, I was immediately carried back to another age, a time which belonged to a known and cherished past when reading formed the principal part of a child's leisure hours.

In 1879, a time when there was a demand for reading of all kinds, the Committee of the Religious Tracts Society set up the B. O. P. to combat the 'Penny Dreadfuls' that were flooding the market. The intention was to promote the Christian way of life in an attractive form that would catch the imagination of the undiscerning child. The Society persuaded Jules Verne, the author of *Round the World in Eighty Days*, to contribute a story, together with one by Conan Doyle (before the days of Sherlock Holmes) and one by H. de Vere Stacpoole, author of *The Blue Lagoon*.

News of the success of the magazine spread far and wide throughout the Empire. Presents began to arrive on the Editor's desk — monkey nuts from West Africa — even monkey skins! And would you believe it? Someone on safari in East Africa, 300 miles from the nearest settlement, found a copy of the magazine sticking to a thorn bush.

At first, the paper's image had a strong public school, stiff upper lip look about it — all of it based on the daily routine of a cold bath, a plateful of porridge, regular 'Radio Malt' or 'Virol', and a good dose of healthy exercise — the ideal recipe for moulding character.

Boys in school caps and grey flannel shorts were involved in countless adventures of bravery and bravado. Improving poems with marching rhythms spread the gospel of good living:

> Whatever you are, be frank, boys,
> 'Tis better than money or rank, boys.

In 1904, the editor, Hutchinson, appointed Lord Baden Powell President of the Anti-Smoking Society of the BOP, but they didn't take into account the many pipe-smoking fathers who wrote in to complain!

By the early 1920s the image had changed. Adventure and drama lending an edge to stories like 'The Lost City' by Charles Godson. It was in 1946 that Jack Cox took over the editorship. He had been evacuated to Surrey during the Blitz, later training as a schoolmaster. He eventually joined 'the Fleet Street gang' and became an editor, with offices in Bouverie Street. Now, as the 'Big Chief' of the B. O. P., he has changed the contents of the paper to suit the tastes of the times, especially the craze for hobbies of all kinds. Among his writers nowadays we find Brian Glanville, Henry Blythe and Hammond Innes.

As we have seen, Brian Doyle sadly concluded his interview with the words: 'The B. O. P. is dead!'. For thirty-four years *The Boys Own Paper* had appeared every week of the year. From 1912 to 1967 it came out regularly as a monthly. Now Mr. Doyle could triumphantly proclaim to the fans: 'Long live the B. O. P.' and confirm that there will assuredly be a *Boy's Own Companion* series, and, it seems, a *Boy's Own Annual*.

27 May 1967 (P)

Big Pot of the Potteries

Enoch Arnold Bennett was born on 27th May 1867. Both the 'Home' and the 'Third' programmes celebrated his centenary in style. The renewal of interest in Bennett's work and the extraordinary paradoxes in the man and his philosophy were the starting-points for author John Wain's evocative analysis, 'A Place of the Mind'. The  vignette of the pianist, Harriet Cohen, playing duets with George Bernard Shaw, and Bennett being too shy to join in, was charming. Frank Swinnerton's story of a trip on A. B.'s yacht — 'a sort of barge with a motor'— was a joy. And what one would have given to see that incredible tennis match in which Basil Dean partnered Galsworthy against Arnold

Bennett and H. G. Wells? 'Whenever the ball came Arnold's way he put it in his pocket,' saying that bending was bad for him.

Even though Bennett's marriage to Marguerite Soulie was a disaster, contemporary accounts appear to convey something of its comic side, with Frank Swinnerton once having to appease Marguerite's anger at discovering Arnold's secret apartment. George Beardmore's account of her was a memorable essay in character-study, with her household animals, her imagination, her peacocks, her kitchen full of relations, and her incessant talk of Arnold and his books. Always behind lay the microcosm of Bennett's world — the 'Five Towns'* with their shop-keeping society, thrifty, conservative, clannish. Now the great kilns are replaced by electric ovens. Yet not so long ago, John Wain's father was working among the mechanical sieves and the flint-dust, and dying of 'potter's rot'. As for those who inhabit the 'lost' town of Fenton (the sixth to Bennett's 'Five'!), there is resentment in their hearts for being neglected by the great novelist.

'So I never liked him since,' said a woman of Fenton. 'I never read his books, neither'.

Burslem, Hanley, Stoke, Longton and Tunstall

27 May 1967 (P)

The Arnold Bennett Centenary

The greatest discovery in Edwin Clayhanger's life is that injustice is a tremendous actuality that has to be faced and accepted, and it is therefore in character that he should eventually decide to stay and submit to his environment. In a sense, though critics acknowledge the importance of Arnold Bennett's removal to France as a vital step on his path towards maturity, it was in itself a mere transmigration. The truth is, he never really left the 'Five Towns'. His spirit, whether he liked or not, remained firmly rooted in the grime and smoke and flint-dust of that wen of humanity that comprised the Potteries. The Parisian episodes in *The Old Wives' Tale*, often bizarre and unreal, represent a kind of dream-like back-ground to the real business of the novel, which is the decay of youth and beauty amidst the ravages of time. As E. M. Forster has so aptly expressed it — time is the hero.

Another great quality of Bennett's philosophy of life is his compassion. Everyone who knew him affirms his kindliness, his understanding, his sympathy with those who are forced to submit to the indignities of a life they never chose to live. We must 'brace ourselves to the exquisite burden of life,' says Clayhanger in one of those marvellous moments of the sublime in the midst of chaos that only Bennett  can describe. This stoical acceptance of things as they exist is his great contribution to our literature of this century. As he jotted down in his Journal, the essential characteristic of the really great novelist is 'a Christ-like, all-embracing compassion.'

*

26 May 1967 (P)

Arnold Bennett: A Literary Portrait

In a warm Irish lilt, St. John Irvine presented a splendidly sly assessment of Bennett's place in the long line of great literary men, deploring the fact that Bennett had acquired the wrong way of writing in France (no doubt a reference to his admiration for the works of Émile Zola). But he was, nevertheless, a very likeable man, 'the most generous-minded, human-hearted author I have ever known'. For Bennett, who was voted the best-dressed man of 1928, that is indeed a happy tribute.

*

26 May 1967 (P)

The Arnold Bennett Memorial Lecture

The Arnold Bennett Memorial Lecture on the 'Third' was delivered by J. B. Priestley, who added some lively contributions to the image. The delicate stomach, the neuralgia, the perky rather absurd nose, the strangulated voice, the pronounced stammer — all helped to delineate the 'audio-visual' Arnold.

As for the 'inner man', he went 'hurtling through space like a rocket out of control'. He loved *de luxe* hotels and frilled evening shirts, and the 'smart set'.

The account of Bennett's lingering death was as moving and deeply-felt as anything I have heard on radio. Mr. Priestley's final reading was magnificent, in broad, earthy tones that afterwards drew me irresistibly to my bookshelves in search of my dog-eared copy of *Clayhanger*.

Arnold Bennett

26 May 1967 (U)

A Man of Contrasts

What a week this has been for 'the best dressed man in town'. For an author whose star has been supposedly in decline in recent years, there has been a remarkable willingness on the part of his friends and admirers to rush forward with a host of memories of Arnold Bennett, the man, and praise for Arnold Bennett, the writer. His style of dress was foppish and decidedly expensive. 'He looked,' said St. John Irvine, 'like a masher, but he had no idea how to mash!'

In contrast to the severity of his authorial discipline, which entailed early rising and, as with Trollope*, a daily allotment of words, he was, withal, 'a likeable man', even at times lovable. Sometimes he was endearingly comical, with his tuft of hair, which would neither stay up nor down. The great C. E. Montague of *The Manchester Guardian* exclaimed: 'What a bounder the man is. What a bounder I am, ever to have thought that he was one.'

But he was impatient with people who fancied themselves as authors. 'Half the population of these islands think they are authors,' he once exclaimed. Yet he was, said Irvine, 'unbounded in his zeal for the young with talent'.

*Novelist Anthony Trollope aimed to write two thousand words every morning before he set off for his official work at the Post Office.

21 September 1966 (U)

A Letter from Somerset!

Somerset Maugham

In the series 'Voices', drawn from the BBC Archives, Leslie Perowne introduced us to the real Somerset Maugham. The incomparable, urbane voice, the suave tones, the wit and wisdom of one of the great literary figures of our time were vividly brought to life in this excellent assembly of recordings.

I liked the brief exchange of letters between Maugham and an American lady who wrote to him for advice about how to deal with her wayward son. Maugham replied:

'Dear Mrs. Hale, Give your son a thousand dollars a year and tell him to go to the devil.'

She wrote sometime later:

'Dear Mr. Maugham — My son, after mature consideration, has decided to go into the bond business!'

5 January 1967 (U)
Delderfield in Devon

R. F. Delderfield

The novelist and playwright, R. F. Delderfield, who lives in the seaside town of Sidmouth, talked about his work to Tom Salmon on the 'Home Service' this week. Delderfield left London when he was eleven years old and has lived among Devon folk for over forty years. For eleven years, he spent his apprenticeship by working as a reporter and sub-editor on a local newspaper. Provincial journalism was his 'university of writing', providing him with the raw material for his characters and locations.

Delderfield's years in the Royal Air Force gave him a rich fund of ideas. Life in the ranks was tough and *Worm's Eye View* might just as well have turned into a bitter play. It was, he says, 'conceived on a bus'! Taking twenty-one 'originals' of his acquaintance, he condensed them into five characters that became more real to him than the real-life prototypes.

Admittedly, he writes, in the main, of the fairly recent past, some twenty years ago. Although life is much changed in the intervening years, he is able to say with conviction: 'I might have lost patience but I haven't lost faith. Experience is like wine — it has to be bottled for twenty years.'

He turned his back on literary coteries, 'steadfastly setting his face against the herding instinct'. Quite suddenly, the established playwright turned into the apprentice novelist. Most people who enjoy a good farce can remember the hilarious antics of the characters in *Worm's Eye View*, and now we can look forward to a 'bird's eye' view of Delderfield's life in his latest novel, *A Horseman Riding By*, one of the longest novels written in English in recent times. He claimed that with this novel his identification with the sufferings of his characters made him suffer with them.

Surprisingly, his long-term hero is Napoleon, and his latest book, *The Retreat from Moscow*, is currently with the publishers. Like Byron,

Delderfield admired the courage and determination, the sense of destiny, in fact the whole romantic charisma of the Emperor, whose retreat was 'a feat of endurance, living on horseflesh and eating snow....'

Delderfield admits that some of the most miserable times in his own life have been 'between books'. His happiness comes from making life live through his books, by drawing on his native locale. It could be said that his hero is the Devon countryside. Just as Hardy used the lowering Dorset landscape and the Brontës the bleak Yorkshire moors, Delderfield evoked the Devon scenes out of its distinctive red soil, its smells, its dust, its wild flowers and its beautiful hanging woods. He derived a deeply personal satisfaction from writing and took little notice of his critics. 'A writer knows best about his own work.'

*

14 & 18 July 1967 (U)

A Raffish Raconteur

Sir Compton Mackenzie

Sir Compton Mackenzie is writing the eighth volume of his autobiography, which deals with his move to Edinburgh, though since the age of eight, he has had a passion for the Western Isles. He says he had 'a *penchant* for islands' and read R. M. Ballantyne's *Coral Island* and Arthur Ransome's *The Swiss Family Robinson*.

Success came to him early with his hilarious novel of Scottish high jinks, *Whisky Galore!* In fact, it was his 'highland' books that brought him fame. Few of us can claim, like Sir Compton, that life was 'one long laugh the whole time'. The secret of his happiness, he said, was that he never learnt to drive a car. Indeed, if he had, he would have been without doubt a slow coach!

How slowly he speaks, taking everything word by word, syllable by syllable, so that the pace frequently came almost to a halt. Invariably the interviewer, Archie P. Lee, brought him to life again to tell yet another anecdote.

Mackenzie had a real talent for describing court scenes too. At the time when he was Rector of Edinburgh University, he became unexpectedly involved in an infringement of the Official Secrets Act. Through an indiscretion, the name of a secret service agent was mentioned in one of his stories and 'he was called to book'. The situation was not helped by government officials behaving, as he said, 'like characters out of *Alice in Wonderland*'. The case cost him something in the region of £5,000 in the end. His skit on the Secret Service, *Water on the Brain*, portrayed a wry picture of characters involved in intelligence work, who, he said, 'should do it only for a couple of years. After that, they go dotty!'

He professed to having a 'Protean' approach to travel, identifying with each country, absorbing its culture, not just getting to know the people, but becoming one of them. 'If I am in Greece, I become a Greek,' he claimed. 'If I am in Ireland I become an Irishman. If I am in France I become a Frenchman.' His trouble was, he could never be anything else but a proud Scotsman. Controversially, he believed in a 'common citizenship' between Scotland and France and ever regretted that Mary Queen of Scots did not flee to France.

He adored Virginia Woolf's novel, *The Waves*, the ghost stories of Oliver Onions, and still reads 'Westerns' with pleasure. Like William Cobbett, he hated tea addicts and wrote a diatribe against tea-drinking.

Around and about during the twilight years of Wells, Bennett and Galsworthy, Mackenzie wrote to Wells about the impossibility of dramatising *Kipps*. He succeeded in the end with Wells' approval, who subsequently denied it and called Compton Mackenzie to see him on a rather chilly evening in May.

As for Conrad, he was put out to have to talk French to him, Conrad's English being limited. 'That's why he cut the dialogue out of his novels.' 'What about his own career in the theatre?' he was asked. 'Ah well! I was too good an actor to make a good dramatist!'

3, 10, 17, & 24 April 1967 (P)

Beyond 'The Outsider'*

Trollope once wrote that success is the necessary misfortune of humanity and that it is only to the very unfortunate that it comes early. In four excellent interviews Wilfred De'Ath, who has a real knack of bringing out the most in his subjects, spoke to Colin Wilson and three novelists, Maureen Duffy, Julian Mitchell and Margaret Drabble.

Colin Wilson

Colin Wilson revealed no radical change in his outlook except that success had made him an 'outsider.' Sadly for us, he still dislikes the English and responds more to his American, Arab and Japanese admirers.

Maureen Duffy looked back on her success with anguish and regret, and with wistful reflections on the financial burdens of the novelist, while Julian Mitchell's self-appraisal was delightfully ironic in the true stiff-upper-lip manner.

The most successful interview was with Margaret Drabble. who, in spite of the conflicts of family life, was the most promising of the four.

Colin Wilson, in his essay, 'Beyond the Outsider' (*Declaration* 1957), described the outsider as a man who is made wretched by a yearning for freedom from internal and external problems, but then, which of us does not yearn for such a Utopia? It is in the nature of art that that conflict should never be completely resolved.

**'The Outsider' by Colin Wilson, was a seminal work of the 1950s which high-lighted the situation of the creative artist in an increasingly bourgeois and philistine society. His examples include Albert Camus, H. G. Wells, Nijinsky, Van Gogh, Rimbaud, and T. E. Lawrence.*

18 March 1967 (P)

Samuel Beckett's Dream

Samuel Beckett

'No trace anywhere of life, you say, pah, no difficulty there, imagination not dead yet.' So began Samuel Beckett's abstruse piece of surrealism, *Imagination Dead Imagine*, a personal vision of life, reflecting the symbolism of Coleridge and the metaphysics of Donne. Mr. Beckett finds himself standing outside himself, gazing down, not at a stately pleasure dome nor caves of ice but on a plain rotunda. 'No way in, go in, measure,' is an instruction that indicates the compulsive search for the infinite. Somehow, a life-giving force, 'the light that makes all so white', leads him through a succession of exits and entrances, each adding a new dimension to his understanding. Mr. Beckett's vision is that of a dreamer suspended, neither willingly nor unwillingly, in a limbo akin to one of those floating visions before waking, when life falls neatly into place.

The script was beautifully and solemnly spoken by Jack MacGowran, whose voice blended well with the soft but intense flow of the language. The success of the programme as a whole owed much to Martin Esslin's controlled production and his perceptive embracing of the basic symbolism.

28 & 29 March 1967 (P)

The New Science Fiction

The fascination of science fiction is that it may one day become part of a greater reality. Most of Orwell's *Nineteen-Eighty Four* happened by 1944, and a few of the darker prophecies of H. G. Wells have yet to materialize. Let us hope they never will. Though Tennyson's grim vision of war in the air, in that remarkable poem, *Locksley Hall* (see pp 315-316), took only seventy years to happen, at least his prophecy of a 'Parliament of Nations' has born fruit of a kind. George Macbeth drew on J. G. Ballard's short story, 'You, Me and the Continuum' as a starting-point for a series of discussions with J. G. Ballard, Michael Morrock and Judith Merrill.

'You, Me and the Continuum' is a very original piece of writing. It concerns the Second Coming as it might take place in the twentieth century. When the story begins, there has been an attempt to break into the Tomb of the Unknown Warrior on Good Friday. How is this incident related to 'the strange and confusing figure of an unidentified Air Force pilot' whose body is washed ashore on a beach near Dieppe?

J G Ballard

Ballard's technique of writing is one of extreme concision, coupled with a wide range of reference: surrealist painting, anatomy, politics and radio astronomy, to name only a few. In twenty-six short paragraphs, one for each letter of the alphabet, the central theme is gradually unfolded. The imagery is simple enough in itself but, in its relationship to the theme, it adds an altogether new dimension. Under paragraph D (Delivery System), the lecturer points out that the original story of the Messiah riding into Jerusalem on an ass was 'an unintelligently literal reading of a tautological Hebrew idiom'. Amidst Ballard's brand of futurism there lies a clinical detachment, a sense of non-involvement, for the characters are not deeply drawn but mere shadows of themselves.

*

2 April 1967 (P)

Prospective Narrative

In conversation with George Macbeth, J. G. Ballard expressed his dissatisfaction with linear narrative and sought to explore the depths of narrative rather than the history of it. But the tone of 'You and Me and the Continuum' seemed to me to be derivative, reminiscent of that fear of unavoidable chaos that pervades the pages of Aldous Huxley's *Ape and Essence*, and perhaps a recollection of the symbolism of the dead pilot whose parachute flaps ominously on the mountainside in Golding's *Lord of the Flies*.

Ballard's highly controversial concept that the Messiah will appear, not as a single identity of Jesus, but in an enormous multiplex of contacts is substantiated in the final passage Z (Zodiac): 'as his own identity faded, its last fragments glimmered across the darkening landscape, lost integers in a hundred computer codes, sand-grains on a thousand beaches, fillings in a million mouths'.

On the whole, there is greater listening-value in hearing Ballard* talk about his work and less in hearing others talk about it in 'The Future of Speculation'. The three programmes made a perceptive comment on the development of the English school of Science Fiction writing.

*James Graham Ballard was born in 1930. Author of a number of apocalyptic novels and short stories in surrealistic style including, 'The Terminal Beach' (1964) and 'The Crystal World' (1966). A truly original, philosophically complex writer, he went on to publish 'The Atrocity Exhibition' (1970), 'Crash' (1973), 'Concrete Island' (1974), and 'The Unlimited Dream Company' (1979). He made his name with 'Empire of the Sun' (1984), which was turned into a much-praised film in 1988.

Christmas and New Year

24 December 1966 (U)

Nine Lessons and Carols

Christmas Eve would not be the same for most people who value our English traditions if we did not have the opportunity to enjoy that perfect marriage of words and music exemplified in the Service of Nine Lesson and Carols at King's College, Cambridge, all under the impeccable directing of David Willcocks.

It may be true for some that a kind of mystique has grown up over the years that sets this event in a certain mould uncomfortably close to cliché. Whilst some listeners might feel inclined to say: 'I've heard it all before,' no-one surely would deny that the solo treble voice that echoes through this inspiring place at the beginning of 'Once in royal David's City' would not ever produce the same sensation twice over. After all, we ourselves are inescapably one year older!

The bidding prayer, which carries our thoughts to 'the helpless, the cold, the hungry, and the oppressed, the lonely, the unloved, the aged, and all who know not the Lord Jesus' leads into the murmuring, measured recitation of the Lord's Prayer.

Even the chorister chosen to read the story of Adam and Eve, who pronounces every plosive — 'the Gar-<u>d</u>en of E-<u>d</u>en' — adds to the charmingly natural simplicity of the moment. Up comes 'The Holly and the Ivy', and 'Ding Dong Merrily on High', and 'God Rest You Merry, Gentlemen' (note the position of the comma!), and the haunting melody and simple words of Christina Rossetti's 'In the Bleak Midwinter':

> What can I give him,
> Poor as I am?
> If I were a shepherd
> I would give a lamb.
> If I were a wise man
> I would do my part;
> Yet what I can I give him —
> Give my heart.

19 December 1966 (P)

'Ten to Eight' and 'Five to Ten'

Christmas is a time of birth and rebirth. For some it will have been a time of prayer and meditation. Few of us, however, will have heeded Wordsworth's reprimand about laying waste our powers in too much 'getting and spending'. After carols, we perhaps came home to pagan rituals of Christmas Tree, coloured paper decorations, turkey and ham with all the trimmings, and Christmas Puddings aflame with brandy. Then, for the children at least, the long-awaited exchange of gifts — 'Hideous tie so kindly meant', as Betjeman's poem goes, beautifully read, by the way, by Sir Alec Guinness on the 'Ten to Eight' programme.

Later in the day, Hughie Green, speaking on the 'Five to Ten' programme, put the situation in a nutshell when he described Christmas as a time in which to 'rest, relax and reflect', but for many of us it could be also 'a big bore', the searching for appropriate presents we could ill afford, and the prodigious exchange of Christmas cards.

I can endorse Mr. Green's view of present-day Nazareth and its importunate Arabs with their audacious fleecing of unwary 'pilgrims' seeking the place where Jesus was reputedly born. Mr. Green preferred to remember Christmas in the simple surroundings of an English country church.

These five-minute talks each morning and evening before the daily 'News' have been described by one critic as 'religious commercials', but Hughie Green's was a gem in a series of infinite variety.

25 December 1966 (P)

A Christmas Meditation

Taking Browning's poem 'Christmas Eve' as his text, Professor Owen Chadwick, Master of Selwyn College, Oxford, posed the question:

'Can a man have faith and yet be racked with doubt?'

In Robert Browning's case, with his sense of past corruption in the long history of Christianity, 'his mind still doubted but his faith knelt down.' How could he 'strip the learning of all affection and still have understanding?' Professor Chadwick* spoke in measured language often akin to poetry but with a warm humanity and an immediacy that enchanted the ear as well as captivating the mind.

'No theology is any good,' said the Professor, 'unless it is tested by 'Thy will be done'.' What better message than that for a Christian optimist like Browning, who could see the sickness and transitoriness of the world and yet have hope?

Master of Fellow of Selwyn College, Cambridge, from 1956. Author of perceptive philosophical works including 'From Bossuet to Newman' (1957) and later 'The Secularisation of the European Mind in the Nineteenth Century' (1976). His broadcasts made compulsive listening.

25 December 1966 (U)

Ghosts of Christmas Past

Christmas was a time for ghost stories and 'things that go bump in the night'. After our last day at school, we would hurry home down the lane, past the old gnarled oak, whose dead branches stretched out towards us like the scrawny arms of a witch. We would run helter-skelter down the cinder-path, to find lashings of hot buttered toast waiting for us on the well-scrubbed table in our cosy farmhouse kitchen. Ghosts were not so frightening in the safety of home.

Gale Pedrick brought us some choice items of 'Christmas Past' in his popular 'Pick of the Week' programme. Owen Brannigan sang a very jolly version of 'Little Jack Horner, sat in a corner, eating his Christmas pie' in the style of Handel.

In 'South-East' we were able to enjoy a reminiscence of wartime Christmases twenty years ago when people still spoke of the British Empire, when three inches of snow covered the London streets and food rationing meant a lean time for most of us. At least we had the wireless. A host of fans listened in to ITMA with Tommy Handley ('It's That Man Again') and his cleaning lady, Mona Lott ('Can I do you now, sir?'), Colonel Chinstrap saying: 'I don't mind if I do!' to a gin-and-tonic, and my boyhood favourite at the time, the furtive secret agent with the cavernous voice, Funf ('Deess eess Fu-unf!') ever ready to plant his bomb.

Christmases on our farm remain in the memory as if they were only yesterday. On Christmas Eve, after mother had prepared the turkey for the oven, with a liberal amount of thyme and parsley stuffing and sausage-meat, we all had a 'lucky' stir of the pudding mixture, hoping to find the sixpences before it was tied up tight in its basin to simmer away on the top of the great black kitchen range. After we had all had a go at peeling the Brussels sprouts, we, one by one, crept secretly up the stairs to wrap the presents we had been hiding for weeks from prying parental eyes.

Christmas Eve was also the time when the favourite uncles and aunts arrived and the music began. Auntie Ciss, who gave lunch-hour concerts in the City of London churches and sang in the famous full costume performance of Coleridge-Taylor's *Hiawatha* at the Albert Hall, would give her annual performance of *Bless This House*, while Uncle Joe was a dab hand at *A Pair of Sparkling Eyes* and his brother, John, portly in a suit far too tight for him, regularly burst his buttons with a sturdy rendering of 'A Policeman's lot is not a happy one', which always brought the house down. Then we would all join in with 'Chestnuts roasting on an open fire' and 'I'm dreaming of a white Christmas'. Mind you, in recent years there has been very little snow around to dream about.

Johnny Morris delved into the BBC Archives to bring us some of the happy times spent by a variety of revellers at Christmas parties. It

Johnny Morris

seems to have been a time for charades, comic songs and monologues. There was old Mr. Lovelock, sitting under the gas-light, drinking a glass of stout, doing his imitation of a brass band and 'blowing brown stout spray and fumes all over the front room.' Hetty Fetlock gave her traditional rendering of 'The Robin's Return' and one of the 'nippers' had memorised all three verses of 'God Save the Queen', which was wildly applauded. The monologue by Mr. Hammond was not awaited with the same enthusiasm, but it brought a few smiles when his face suddenly changed from his usual jovial self to a 'very frightening face indeed.' The dog howled his part and even the cat joined in the general caterwauling! As for Mrs. Belcher, who once had a beautiful soprano voice — well! — she certainly lived up to her name when she came out from a large port-and-lemon and gave a sort of Florence Foster Jenkins rendering of 'The Laughing Song' from *Die Fledermaus* that reduced everybody to tears of merriment. Thank you, BBC Archives.

25 December 1966 (P)

Peace and Goodwill

Christmastime was not quite as meaningful to us as children without a carpet of snow covering the fields and rooftops. The traditional card of the three Wise Men riding over a snow-laden landscape towards Bethlehem under a sky of celestial blue, with a brilliant star guiding them to the manger, is a far cry from the reality of getting and spending in shops overladen with Christmas fare. There is too much rush and tear, too much razzmatazz, to be able to stop and ponder the true message of Christmas until it is all over. Only then can we heave a sigh of relief and wait for Lent to purge us of our prodigal indulgence and encourage us to turn over a new leaf.

Should we have had a lie-in on a murky Christmas morning, we could have lightened our darkness with the magnificent sound of English church bells ringing out their message loud and clear, from St. Paul's in the heart of London and Wells in the west, from St. Donard's in Belfast, from Felkirk's St. Peter's in Yorkshire, All Saint's at Allesley in Warwickshire, St. Michael's in Cornhill, and back again to the Church of the Nativity at Bethlehem. There surely can be nothing so exhilarating as the ringing of bells, sending out their message of joy on Christmas morning. What more appropriate sound than that to prelude the theme of the Queen's speech to the peoples of the Commonwealth this year — the bringing of gifts.

The three Wise Men brought gold, frankincense and myrrh. 'The custom of gifts will never die out', but those gifts 'can never overshadow the presents we can give to the future of the world.' 'It is,' said the Queen, 'never more appropriate than now to call upon the gift of goodwill.'

'Mankind has many blemishes but, deep down, in every soul, there is a store of goodwill that can be called upon.' The Queen's heartfelt Christmas wish for 'Peace and goodwill' and her special message of encouragement to the women of the Commonwealth served as a timely reminder of the values we should set for the coming year whatever problems it may have in store for us.

30 December 1966 (P)

Announcing the Winners!

'Any Questions?' this week gave some light relief to the Christmas deliberations. Question-master, Freddy Grisewood, cleverly managed to keep under control an ebullient team of contributors: Baroness Stocks, Lord Mancroft, Bamber Gascoigne and Professor Alan Gemell, as well as a lively and responsive audience from the Oldbury Community Centre.

Harold Wilson

Jackie Kennedy

Up for discussion were 'The Woman of the Year' (Jackie Kennedy) and 'The Man of the Year' (Harold Wilson).

Alan Gemell was suspicious of Wilson, whilst at the same time admiring him for standing up to the Unions and tackling head-on the Rhodesian question. Nevertheless, he was of the opinion that 'you can never trust a man who can run with the hare and hunt with the hounds'!

25 December 1966 (P)

Letter from America

We were all set for Christmas cake and mince pies when on came that excellent man-of-good-sense, Alistair Cooke, reminding us of the Puritan view of Christmas, 'a time of stern prohibition'. Away with the dancing and the merry-making! Away with the eating and the drinking! Away with yule-log and mistletoe! Remember, said Mr. Cooke, Mencken's* definition of a puritan as 'a man who fears that somewhere someone is having a good time!' I took another slice of Christmas cake and a sip of warm mulled wine and hoped that everybody was doing something of the same.

* Henry Louis Mencken (1880-1956), American satirist. Author of 'The American Language', a scholarly work of considerable influence that helped to establish American English in its own right. He held strong views about the European 'patronage' of America and was a powerful influence on the contemporary thinking of his day.

Conformists and Radicals

6 February 1967 (U)

Portrait of a Radical

Percy Dearmer

There can be no more relaxing way of spending an evening than to sit back in a comfortable armchair and listen to a programme about a well-known figure remembered by his friends and family. This year we are almost unnoticeably celebrating the life and career of a very distinguished editor of hymns and carols. Percy Dearmer (1867 - 1936) was the industrious compiler of *The English Hymnal*, *The Oxford Book of Carols* and *Songs of Praise*. His influence on liturgical worship was enormous. Cyril Taylor's personal compilation on the 'Home Service', *Beauty for All*, produced by Colin James, with Frank Duncan (reader), brought to radio an endearing portrait of a man who devoted his whole life to the promotion of English church music. The programme was enhanced by musical illustrations recorded by the St. Martin's Singers, directed by W.D. Kennedy-Bell.

These days, when the Church, for the older members of the congregation at least, seems to have lost its way, Percy Dearmer might provide refreshing relief from hymns sung by choirs of a thousand voices with full organ, a hundred-piece orchestra and celebrities reading the gospels. Even in country churches, villagers struggle to cope with unfamiliar chants and hymn-tunes and are forced to listen to the uninspiring everyday speech of the prayers and collects, not to mention the Lord's Prayer, that has come about in an attempt to woo countless disillusioned worshippers back to a state of grace.

Mind you, Percy would have approved of some of the new thinking if it meant bringing faith back to those who thought the ritual remote and incomprehensible. He was a socialist of a very special kind, who believed in 'a kingdom of art and beauty' that had to be shared by everyone, not just a privileged few. When he looked round at the society of his day, he saw only 'lamentable confusion, lawlessness and vulgarity' and blamed the Church for losing touch with the people. He had no time for 'a machine-made cross and a jerry-built altar'. He wanted society to provide employment for artists to supply the church with works of art. He wanted to reform the singing of hymns by increasing the active participation of the congregation. All this from a man who could not sing a single note, nor whistle a favourite hymn-tune. 'You must give people what is good and they will come to like it.' He went about looking for help and came across the young Vaughan Williams, then only twenty-three years of age, and asked him to act as editor. New hymns like Chesterton's 'O God of earth' were introduced, but the criterion for Percy's choices was ever the 'lovely effect of music and words' brought together to produce in the singer 'a naïve wonder and adoration'. By 1928, the success of *Songs of Praise* encouraged the editors to compile *The Oxford Book of Carols*.

After his ordination, Percy Dearmer began his life as a priest in the modest surroundings of the South Lambeth Road, moving on to St. Mary's, Primrose Hill. In 1915, he travelled to Serbia. His wife, Mabel, had gone out as a medical orderly and subsequently died there of a fever. In the course of time he remarried and set to work on his series of lectures, 'The Art of Public Worship'. For their content and manner they were highly regarded. 'Beauty, like goodness, is an end in itself.' 'We can avoid beauty as we can avoid truth.' 'Art is rooted in God.' Is it begging the question if we dare to ask what he meant by 'beauty', what he meant by 'art'? The answer perhaps lies in his crusade against the 'brutal materialism' of the age.

There must have been, one would think, some considerable disquiet on the part of the Synod at Dearmer's 'anti-episcopal complex'. It was because of 'those appalling bishops' that he found himself without a church of his own, which accounts to some extent for the neglect he suffered as a result of his outspoken views. His radicalism made him into a kind of 'honest-to-God' figure and led him to tackle many knotty problems that still confront us today. After his appointment as the first Professor of Ecclesiastical Art things began to improve, and for the last five years of his life he served as a Canon of Westminster Abbey.

Percy Dearmer 'left his mark on the fabric of the church', cleansing it of its impurities, repudiating the clerics in the process. When a small child described John Bunyan's *Pilgrim's Progress* as 'an alligator', Percy's reply was typical of his humour:

"An allegory is by no means without teeth, and teeth bite!"

His central belief rests on three great attributes of God: 'Truth, Goodness and Beauty', predominant realities which form the very foundation of his philosophy.

*

16 June 1967 (P)

Diplomacy and the Vatican

Adrian Johnson, in his 'Current Affairs Magazine' for 'Study Session', presented a timely analysis of the changing attitudes within the Vatican. Gregory Macdonald, Anthony Spencer and Emanuel de Kadt, with John Todd in the chair, discussed the new role the Vatican is taking as a mediating influence in coping with the ever-increasing problems between Church and State — in particular in the Communist world and the West.

There is also a wish to present a positive programme of help in easing difficulties in the developing countries. As the Pope has pointed out, the rich industrial societies of the northern hemisphere must come to the aid of the impoverished primary producers of the southern hemisphere. The Pope's diplomatic initiatives have reinforced his statement made when he was Secretary of State: 'Diplomacy is the art of establishing and maintaining international order; in a word — Peace.'

*

2 February 1967 (U)

The Life of a Saint — without the Shadow of a Doubt!

Paris 1909. A child was born to agnostic Jewish parents, a child unwanted perhaps and never baptised. The father may have wanted a male child. At all events they were saddled with a frumpish little waif of a thing with seemingly no talents, nor pretensions to greatness. In consequence, she grew up believing in what she later in life called 'the mediocrity' of her 'natural abilities'.

Her relationships were complicated by her childhood obsession with bodily cleanliness and her dislike of physical contact. In her maturity, still convinced of her unattractiveness, she encouraged the continuance of her self-imposed castigation by deliberately wearing severe tailored dresses. She even made herself join a women's rugby team! She became 'the categorical imperative in skirts.' Her condition was not helped by constant sinusitis pains and short-sightedness.

All this may appear to be almost comical if it were not in fact tragic. At university, she chose to study philosophy, which took the form of skipping lectures and spending most of her time smoking cigarettes in the boulevard cafés. That's philosophy for you! At this time, in Paris, she came under the influence of the medieval philosopher, Alain de Lille, nicknamed 'Le Docteur Universel', and learnt early in life that 'Doubt follows after certainty like a shadow.' The root of her solitude lay in her unshakable belief that she was unlovable, an expression of her 'blinding vulnerability.' A moment of truth occurred in wartime when a sailor tried to kiss her and the husband of a friend told her he must have been drunk to do such a thing, upon which she wept copious tears.

Barbara Bray's outstanding analysis of the life and spirit of Simone Weil gave an unforgettable portrait of a human being who found a way of triumphing over adversity through total physical and spiritual sacrifice. That in itself may be likely to deter us, for which of us wants to wallow in the suffering of others for its own sake, but in the case of Simone Weil it was for the suffering of the whole of humanity. Barbara Bray was joined in this stimulating discussion by Douglas Hankin, Brian Hewlett and Muriel McLean, and readings were movingly spoken by Patience Collier. Her recital of the metaphysical verses, 'Love Bade Me Welcome' was the most compelling broadcast this week.

Like Emile Zola, who went to live among the miners and their families in order to write *Germinal*, Simone spent ten hours a day potato-lifting so that she could be in among the workers. She associated with members of the trade unions to get to know their philosophy. In return, workers flocked to her lectures on Marxism and the social sciences and, though her experience in the factories made her even more hypersensitive, she converted her trauma into a significant treatise, *La Condition Ouvrière*, which Albert Camus described as 'the greatest and noblest book that has appeared since the Liberation.'

Gradually, by converting her own personal agonies, she grew more concerned about the wider sufferings of the world and succeeded in regaining, in her own words, the 'consciousness of my own dignity.'

Her remarks about the established Church were sharp and controversial. 'Our universe is peopled with myths and monsters,' she wrote and concluded that Christianity was 'the religion of slaves.' Yet in the end she succumbed to faith and found inspiration and solace in the poetry of the English Mystics (see p 172). The great moment of her conversion found its expression in the words of George Herbert, described by Barbara Bray as 'the encryptical embodiment of love':

> Love bade me welcome: yet my soul drew back,
>   Guilty of dust and sin.
> But quick-eyed Love, observing me grow slack
>   From my first entrance in,
> Drew nearer to me, sweetly questioning,
>   If I lacked anything.
>
> 'A guest,' I answered, 'worthy to be here':
>   Love said: 'You shall be he.'
> 'I the unkind, ungrateful? Ah my dear,
>   I cannot look on thee.'
> Love took my hand, and smiling did reply,
>   'Who made the eyes but I.'
>
> 'Truth Lord, but I have marred them: let my shame
>   Go where it doth deserve.'
> 'And know you not,' says Love, 'who bore the blame?'
>   'My dear, then I will serve.'
> 'You must sit down,' says Love, 'and taste my meat.'
>   So I did sit and eat.

'One can only be secure in the sphere of the spiritual', Simone wrote, but she was well aware that: 'To want to be understood before one can understand oneself is a fault.'

On 2nd November 1942 she sailed for England to join the Free French Ministry of the Interior and took a small room in Holland Park, spending her time preparing documents for the liberation of France. She loved the freedom of a friendly foreign city, the people, the parks, the pubs, even the policemen!

Now her writings, in her quest for spiritual purity, began to have that perceptive power of the mystic. For Simone Weil the things of the earth could never give that sense of spiritual completeness that led to her deep and abiding love for humanity.

Simone Weil died from malnutrition with resultant tuberculosis in a Kent sanatorium in 1943 at the age of thirty-four and was buried in the New Cemetery at Ashford.

She ever sought the end of human suffering, the coming of peace in the world, that universal love for one's fellow human beings so essential to our survival. The fact that she did not choose 'the primrose path of dalliance', as Hamlet says, but opted for the rough stony ground that Jesus trod on his way to Calvary is a testimony to the strength of her faith.

Barbara Bray, in her article in this week's *Radio Times,* sums up her view of Simone Weil's place among the mystics: 'Since her death she has often been acclaimed by believers as a saint, a 'witness of the absolute'....I want to suggest that the life of Simone Weil, illuminated by the same severe radiance as we know in Emily Brontë, has a meaning far transcending theology.'

17 February 1967 (U)

Holy Smoke!

Well, there's no smoke without fire, so they say, and I'm not talking about choosing the next Pope! It seems, according to 'Woman's Hour' that 'Women in Holy Orders', as a topic of conversation, is a hot potato! There's so much heat generated by the fanatics on both sides of the altar-rail. A controversial report has just come out on the subject, written by a body of 'prominent clergy' who appear to have minds of their own. If they should prove to be male, they would do well to remain anonymous!

Those against the idea of admitting women into the vestry and letting them loose in the pulpit think it's the absolute limit and just the thin edge of the wedge. If they can do it in Rome, why can't we do as Rome does here?

After all, in Russia, women are still kept separate from the men in church. It seems outrageous, does it not, that women in their monthly period should be considered 'unclean' and therefore unfit to enter the sanctuary? Anyway, one would think it was the last place they'd want to go in the circumstances!

I remember being uncomfortable with the separation of the sexes idea when I found myself wandering through the Venice Ghetto. I crept into a synagogue during prayers and saw the men wearing their black hats and coats, the women clustered together up in a gallery, hidden behind grilles. I felt sorry for those women, though I doubt if they felt sorry for themselves, having carried on the tradition since the days of the Old Testament.

Ann Cheatham, the presenter, reported that, at the much publicised meeting between the Archbishop of Canterbury and the Pope in Rome, only Catholic women were admitted. The rest were asked to leave. The official explanation was pure sophistry: 'To you [presumably non-believers], women are people, to us [Catholics] women are temptation.' In other words, as I said, it's all pretty hot stuff!

13 September 1966 (U)

A New Dawn?

With the approach of the Jewish New Year, it seemed appropriate for me to find out how it differs from anyone else's New Year, so it was fortuitous that a representative of the Chief Rabbinate of Great Britain and the Commonwealth, Dayan Doctor Myer Lew, happened to come on air this week to explain it all.

Rosh Hashanah is a 'personal and religious landmark' which holds, as it approaches the traditional day of Atonement, a deeper message not only for Jewry but for the rest of humanity. 'It bids us,' said Dr. Lew, 'pause and think of the mystery and meaning of life, of its purpose and destiny, its struggles and strivings, its sweetness and sadness.'

At all times of national moment in ancient Israel, the raw trumpeting of the 'Shofar' echoed across the land. It was this primitive instrument, fashioned from the horn of a ram, that silenced the crowd at the foot of Sinai when Moses proclaimed the 'Ten Commandments', 'a code that has remained the most cherished possession of mankind,' and will, Dr. Lew reminds us, 'announce the Messianic era'.

In essence, Dr. Lew's message to us lies in the bringing together of all the ends of our fragmented society under the umbrella of the 'collective consciousness' through bonds of 'brotherhood'.

As admirable as that aspiration may be, it does seem to me that the whole problem lies in the first place in a lack of purpose, a pointlessness, a dark sense of foreboding that undermines our lives today. New gods have replaced the old monotheistic beliefs. The beginnings of a shallow celebrity culture have begun to dominate our national life: pop idols and football stars are beginning to outshine the older heart-throbs of the post-war days.

New, more dangerous gods lure the youth of today to the clubs and rock concerts through the medium of a new kind of music. Isn't this what Matthew Arnold foresaw in *Culture and Anarchy*? The march of the Philistines of mass culture against the bastions of high culture, the plundering and rape of Mount Olympus by the art-hating Barbarians — are not these contributory to the final toppling of the throne of Apollo?

Eventually, the new craze for television will portray an image of England, the world even, that defies description. 'Imagination, Dead Imagine' as Beckett says. But this apparently is what 'the young ones' want today. Perhaps they're freer to express themselves in our more permissive age than I was in my school days in the forties when there was, I think, such a thing more clearly recognisable as the 'collective consciousness' that Dr. Lew is speaking of.

Is there a sense of destiny amidst the social and political tensions that face us all these days? He hopes that a new light 'will shine in Zion and the world at large.' I sincerely hope he is right. Something has to stop our decline and fall. But how?

Let us start, says the good Dr. Lew, with 'a call to repentance and reconciliation'. 'True penitence,' he says, is 'a return to God and fellowship with man.' He calls for a change of heart, but surely that cannot, short of a miracle of miracles, happen *en masse,* in the twinkling of an eye. It won't happen unless people want it to happen.

But I begin to like this man. He talks about a 'return' to basic values on a mass scale, a 'recognition of the Fatherhood of God and the Brotherhood of men' (and presumably he included also the sisterhood of women!), irrespective of race or creed. Out with selfishness, out with greed, out with envy and jealousy, out with suffering and poverty, out with all forms of hatred and cruelty, and, in the world-shaking words of Alfred Lord Tennyson's *In Memoriam*:

> Ring out the thousand years of war
> Ring in the thousand years of peace.

Tennyson wanted it. We all want it. Nobody's waiting for Orwell's 'Brave New World'. Or are they?

There is a terrifying perverseness about the way the modern world wishes to go: more crime, more drugs, more killing, more injustice, more suffering, and consequently more rules, more regulations, more laws, more restrictions, more house searches, more firearm checks, all of which can only lead to more government and in the end, totalitarian control over the minds and movements of every individual.

Dr. Lew believes in 'the sanctity and dignity of life' as Dr. H. M. King, Speaker of the House of Commons' believes in 'the worth of the human being....the right to think and believe....without persecution and with a respect for the law'. These are the deeply held beliefs of the courageous Winston, Orwell's principal character in *1984*, the last man left alive to carry the torch for the survival of human dignity.

Unfortunately, there is today a growing lack of respect for the old way of life. Things have gone too far. 'The centre cannot hold,' as Yeats says in his doomful poem, *The Second Coming*.

Dr. Lew asks for a 'universal renewal' in the midst of this chaos, a return to 'wisdom, love and compassion', but these are unattainable unless we start from the fundamental principles of upbringing and education. We have to start young to discover that those life-enhancing virtues are there for the asking.

From my notebook: *10 September 1966*

A Voice for Peace

The review of Dr. Lew's talk is too long. Shorten or rewrite (see p172).

Some broadcasters one warms to instantly. I like Dr. Lew. My one fear is that the perpetrators of cruelties and atrocities in today's world may not be capable of listening to his abstract language and miss the true heart of his message. He's a man of good sense with a deep understanding of the world's troubles, the torment of the nations, the need to hold on to tried and established values, the wisdom of the ages. He knows exactly what has to be done to bring about the changes that would make the world a better place.

Crime and Punishment

14 April 1967 (P)

Essay in Malice

Martin Freeman's marriage had not been a success. Marion, his wife, had carried on affairs with at least three other men, and he himself was desperately in love with his secretary, Lisa, whose religion would not permit her to marry a divorcee.

One day, Martin returned home to find Marion in considerable pain, but following a medical examination, the family doctor telephoned Martin to inform him that nothing was seriously wrong with her. Now, Martin Freeman saw his chance. He told his wife that she had not long to live and would probably have to undergo an unpleasant operation, carefully placing a full bottle of sleeping pills by her bedside and insisting that she should not take more than the required dose. Of course, she did take more and was later found dead. Martin told a deliberate lie and contrived a situation in which his wife would commit suicide. The question was: did Martin Freeman murder his wife?

After listening to the enactment of the crime, a panel of four speakers in Trafford Whitelock's production of 'Your Verdict', discussed the problem from the viewpoint of the man in the street. The qualified legal opinion of F. W. Beney QC always places the more personal views of the panel (of which I was recently a member) in perspective. In this instance, Mr. Beney added some interesting comments on the inadequacy of our laws of evidence.

Few programmes these days, alas, afford us the opportunity of hearing the evocative voice of John Snagge.* Mr. Snagge here succeeded in getting the maximum response from a panel of people who were making their maiden voyage into broadcasting.

* *The veteran commentator of the Oxford and Cambridge Boat Race. His deep, gravelly voice was immediately recognisable. On one occasion, he was unable to see the boats clearly and amused listeners by filling in with 'Well! It's either Oxford* (then cautiously) — *or Cambridge!'*

12 April 1967 (P)

The Smiler with the Knife

Unsolved crimes must of their very nature possess an element of the anticlimactic. There is no neat tying up of loose ends, no satisfactory conclusion to please the admirers of a Sherlock Holmes mystery.

In 1888, five prostitutes were brutally murdered and mutilated. The murderer was brash enough to carry on a sinister correspondence with the police.

> I'm not a butcher, nor a Yid,
> Nor yet a foreign skipper.
> But I'm your own light-hearted friend,
> Yours truly, Jack the Ripper.

The police seemed totally inadequate to the demands of the case. 'I'm down on whores and shan't quit ripping them until I get buckled.' Inefficiency, dilatoriness and confusion dogged the futile efforts of the police to sort out the many-faceted identity of 'saucy Jack'. Tony Van den Bergh's excellent documentation and narration built up the tension and the horror with particular skill by the use of fragmented voices, in appalling nineteenth-century glimpses of late-Victorian squalor and depravity.

13 April 1967 (P)

Habitual Criminals

Judging from Neil Durden-Smith's excellent programme, 'Habitual Criminals', I doubt if there is any degree of chastening for those criminals who continually return to prison for the security of the place. The remorseless clanking of the prison gates and the crunching of the warder's boots on the hard gravel of the prison forecourt must surely be a sinister deterrent for most, though there may be some to whom the sound is sheer relief.

Mr. Durden-Smith's interviews with the prisoners of Blundeston never once betrayed any note of condescension or unctuous sympathy.

For 'Alf', crime was a way of life. At the age of eight he had been put through jewellers' fanlights by his notorious father, and very soon, prison became for him simply an occupational hazard.

Neil Durden-Smith

'Dick' had always had a flair for impersonation: peers of the realm, and even a rural dean formed part of his extensive repertoire. Now, he seemed to want to find 'another modus operandi'.

'Bill' was frightened of being fond of people in case he hurt them. He never made any friends at all outside prison, just like the man who had been locked away for more than half his life in approved schools, Borstals and prisons, harbouring a deep hatred of himself and his life of petty theft, forgery and armed robbery.

'Bob' found nothing in what Huw Wheldon has called, in 'Home for the Day', our 'splintered society' that could offer him an adequate alternative to the security of prison life.

13 April 1967 (P)

The Hi-Jackers

The appalling truth that came out of Maurice Denning's enquiry into the world of the hi-jackers was that anyone could walk into a clearing-house, pass himself off as an accredited driver and get away with a load of valuable goods without as much as a routine check-up on his credentials.

The sinister figure of the informer lurks in the shadows, ready to pass on information to anyone who can pay the price; farmers and café proprietors stand by to act as clearing agents and 'nobody checks who you are'. There is a good deal of dirty work at the cross-roads in all this, drivers beaten up and dumped in Epping Forest, thousands of pounds' worth of goods stolen. The fear and the risk involved were pre-eminent in these interviews with drivers and hauliers in a programme that brought to life an aspect of crime that requires serious investigation and a further revision of the law. The English legal system is thought by many, especially Englishmen, to be the best in the world. But is it?

*

24 January 1967 (P)

No Offence, Mate!

'Focus' this week dealt with the problems of wife and children when the husband goes to prison. 'Why should they be penalised financially and emotionally?'

Edgar Lustgarten asked if such a disaster could have a permanent and damaging effect on their lives. Does 'the clear, cold, statistical voice of the law' provide enough protection for a prisoner's family? The problem might well be that the wife had never really had a good week's pay in her life. One wife had £12 free and 28/- family allowance, not to mention the constant fear of losing her home completely. All she wanted was her 'own street door'. Yet when her husband came home there would be just the same degree of misery, and fear that he might just be back inside within the month. Some children ended up undergoing psychiatric treatment. One child was burdened with guilt when her father went to prison.

Then there was the humiliation of 'the closed visit': the difficulty of talking through close netting and a glass partition; the hurt of not being able to touch, the lack of privacy, the nervous strain, the father degraded in prison clothes, the waiting for the wives' names to be read out, and so on.

A psychiatrist from the Tavistock Clinic asked some imponderables: Who suffers the most? The prisoner? The family? Or the children? At least the Mountbatten Report had moved forward by recommending private visits, the possibility of home visits and an extension of parole visits.

Mention was made of Pauline Morris's book, *Prisoners and Their Families*, in which she recommends more help to alleviate the resulting loneliness, despair and financial worry that families feel when deprived of the potential wage-earner. Some wives, it was admitted, actually had come to accept that their husbands were inveterate criminals. When the husband was 'out on the job', the family could live quite well on the 'easy come, easy go' basis, but the price was high, living all the time on their nerves, waiting for the long arm of the law to reach for the knocker on the front door.

6 October 1966 (U)

The Tottenham Outrage

Scene: A small factory in Chestnut Street.
Time: Saturday 23rd January 1909.

The factory gate was right opposite the police station. The car with the factory wages was standing outside the gate. So everyone had a 'grand-stand view'. Jacob and Hefeld, a couple of Russian anarchists, knew the place well. Hefeld had worked for a fortnight in the factory and was able to take a good look round. Everywhere was as quiet as a mouse, if, that is, the little furry creature had thought of anything so outrageous as a wages-grab right under the noses of the police.

'Hope we won't need the guns,' said Hefeld.

'Hope so too,' muttered Jacob under his breath.

Thus began the gripping account of 'The Tottenham Outrage', narrated by Edgar Lustgarten and produced by Joe Boroughs. Lustgarten's graphic rendering of this grim incident brought home all the drama and tensions of a crime novel.

The wages clerk, carrying the money-bag, walked towards the gate. The two Russians sprang out in the quiet of the morning. The snatch was made but the wages-clerk held on and made a fight of it. A gunshot rang out, a shot that changed everything. There was £80 in the bag, but the gunfire, 'Well!' said the narrator, Edgar Lustgarten, 'it transformed the crime.' They grabbed the swag and ran for it, spraying gunshot all over the place.

Sturdy George Smith sprinted after the thieves, tackled Hefeld and was gunned down by Jacob. 'After Smith, they'd less to lose and more to fear.' They covered each other to reload. A crowd formed, waiting silently till the guns were emptied.

Ralph Jocelyn was standing in the front of his house. He was twelve years old.

'He could pick us out. Shall we?'

'Yes?'

'All right!'

Two gunshots — and one small child is one small corpse. No more than 'a bundle in the road.'

A car chase started up, only to end with bullets in the tyres.

As if all this was not outrage enough, the real 'Tottenham Outrage' was yet to happen. A network of police set out on bicycles, motor-cycles and patrol cars. It was a rare occasion for guns to be issued. A constable, Tyler, pursued the gunmen only to be shot and killed in his turn.

The chase took them to Highams Hill and across the marshes. Then the Russians hi-jacked a tramcar. Holding the gun at the conductor's head, they ordered him to drive on.

'Faster!' they shouted. 'Faster!'

Jacob stayed to cover the terrified passengers. Their way obstructed by a milk-cart, the gunmen shot senselessly at the milkman. Then they commandeered a grocer's cart, but in spite of lashing and whipping the horse into action, the cart would not move. The grocer had put the brakes on.

Now they were at Epping Forest. Suddenly, a shot caught Hefeld, wounding him. It seems that he put a bullet through his head. At least if he did not, then it was someone else. Unhappily for him, it did not finish him. It is strange to think that he was rushed to hospital to have his life saved so that he could die on the scaffold.

Now Jacob was on his own. He came to a cottage with a young mother and her two children. He threatened them and ran upstairs. Soon the cottage was surrounded by a throng of people. Constable

Eagles burst open the door and fired. Jacob was dragged out and died within minutes. One of his shoes was missing, a fact that seemed to strike the onlookers as macabre.

Edgar Lustgarten

The telling of this story, the neat presentation, the dramatic intensity of the narration, the doom-laden voice of the narrator, the graphic script with all its twists and turns, the sheer terror of those who became inadvertently involved in the action, contributed to a compelling half-hour of radio — a tribute to the consummate skill which Edgar Lustgarten brings to these crime programmes — in this case, altogether, as he said, 'a chase which, in scale and character, must surely be unique in this century in England.'

One mystery remained. What happened to the bag with the swag! It was never found! Nor was Jacob's shoe!

England and the English

From my notebook: 30 June 1967

List of Scripts Received
For possible review in early July 1967

1. 'Is Britain being threatened by Over-population?' by David Eversley. Two talks on Third Programme on 9 and 12 July.
2. 'Visitors to Britain'. Seven readings as follows: Emerson (10 July), George Mikes (11 July), Hippolyte Taine (12 July), Chiang Yee (13 July), Karel Čapek (14 July)
3. 'Visitor to London'. Dr. Claire Weekes. Woman's Hour, 11 July
4. 'England is My Village'. Storytime. Home service 11 July.
5. 'Focus on Visitors to Britain'. Producer: George Fischer. 11 July 1966.
   'Private Schools in Poor Areas'. Producer: Keith Hindell. Third Programme. 11 July
7. Peter Ustinov. Three Conversations. Script + one playback.
8. 'House-hunting Safari'. James Norbury. Woman's Hour. 14 July
9. 'Every Survey is Checked'. Joan MacFarlane-Smith. 14 July
10. 'Partial Recall'. Sir Compton Mackenzie. Producer: Archie Lee. 14 and 18 July
11. 'The Industrial State'. David Dimbleby. Producer: Anthony Moncrieff. Playbacks.

Theme for this week? Visitors to Britain
Theme for next week? Looking back on 2,500 hours of listening. And two raconteurs: Ustinov and Compton Mackenzie.

11 July 1967 (U)

As Others See Us: The Popular View

The *Radio Times* this week informs us that, by the end of this year, three million overseas visitors will have stayed in Britain. The impression they receive of our country is depressing.

They find our hostelries not all that clean and very expensive. They find our accommodation 'broken down', threadbare and poorly decorated. There are no showers, no private bathrooms, no soap or towels provided — as a Danish medical student readily remarked : 'one for the head and one for the bottom!' We don't provide adequate heating and the beds are often damp, the wardrobes 'smelly'.

Whilst they praise our breakfasts, our system of regimented mealtimes means that you can't get a meal at any time of the day or night. They don't like our cold meat pies. They can't abide the coffee. No pepper and salt is provided at table, and it seems we have never heard of salads, though it must surely depend on where you stay — and by the way, Americans, and all Americanised Europeans, miss their iced drinks.

A Dutchman had the grace to admit that we were a 'polite' nation who could do with a clean-up and a wash-down, and it wouldn't be a bad idea, said a departing Australian, if we had decent Tourist Offices dotted around the country with informative brochures on places to visit.

But wait a minute! There must be something good they could say about us!

At last, a German was interviewed, who admitted that London was an 'exciting town' with 'something for everyone's taste'. After all, he said, 'London is the cultural capital of Europe'.

Well, you could knock me down! And, what is more, we have freedom of speech, and, he said, 'We boys like your mini-skirts! You see, English girls have nice legs!'

From my notebook: *10 to 18 July 1967*

As Others See Us: The Classic View
Notes for a possible article

Repeats of seven programmes of readings by distinguished visitors to England, are being broadcast daily this week. Selected from the Journals of the American essayist, Ralph Waldo Emerson (reader: Marvin Kanel), the Czech humourist, George Mikes (reader: Geoffrey Matthews), the French philosopher, Hippolyte Taine (reader: Allan McClelland),Chiang Yee, the Chinese author of the *Silent Traveller* books (reader: Frank Henderson), the Polish humourist, Karel Ĉapek (reader: Anthony Hill), the American writer, Washington Irving (reader: Peter Marinker), and the Indian novelist, Nirad Chaudhuri (reader: Preston Lockwood). The programmes were produced by Ronald Mason.

The 'Radio Times' gives leading quotations:

1. Emerson (from *English Traits*): 'If there be one successful country in the universe for the last millennium, that country is England.'

2. Mikes (from *How to be an Alien* and *How to be Inimitable*): 'If you want to become a true Briton, you must be fond of queueing. An erstwhile wartime necessity has become a national entertainment.'

3. Taine (from *Notes on England*): 'The English custom of reserve leads to a kind of stoicism. There is no confiding, no letting go, even with one's nearest and dearest.'

4. Yee (from *'The Silent Traveller in London*): 'Londoners have all kinds of worries, as we Chinese have, but it seems to me that they have one extra worry of which we have not dreamed — the worry of happiness.'

5. Ĉapek (*Letters from England*): 'In Czechoslovakia, Italy, France, the street is a sort of large tavern, a meeting-place, a play-ground and a theatre, an extension of home and doorstep: here, it is something which belongs to nobody, a gulley through which life flows to get home.'

6. Irving (from 'Old Christmas' and *Bracebridge Hall*): 'It is indeed the season for kindling not merely the fire of hospitality in the hall but the genial flame of charity in the heart.'

7. Chaudhuri (from *A Passage to England*): 'Englishmen are not

aware of their habit of tacitness, which they call understatement. They are even proud of it, and overdo it at times.'

Note: Abandoned the idea in favour of programme of interviews with foreign tourists on 11 July.

*

29 June 1967 (P)

Studying Contemporary English

English is an international language. On lecture tours both east and west of the Iron curtain, I have always met with unqualified enthusiasm for English Studies, in many cases prompted by economic or diplomatic needs, but often by a simple desire to communicate on a social or business level. Every year, thousands of overseas students from every quarter of the globe converge on London and our provincial cities, seeking tuition in one of the state colleges or in one of the many private schools which now thrive in the capital. ' English as a Foreign Language' then is one of our most valuable exports.

The first of five talks by Professor Simeon Potter, with the over-all title of 'English Today', dealt plainly with the work of Hornby, Gatenby and Wakefield, whose widely recognised *Advanced Learner's Dictionary of Current English* has an important place on every well-informed student's (and teacher's) bookshelf.

I was disappointed not to hear the name of Professor Daniel Jones, whose *Outline of English Phonetics* was regarded with nothing short of veneration by students and teachers alike and paved the way for A.C. Gimson's more recent *Introduction to the Pronunciation of English.*

Besides the authors of the *Advanced Learner's Dictionary,* Professor Potter paid tribute to the invaluable place the British Council publication, *English Language Teaching* (edited by Dr. W. R. Lee) holds in bringing together readers and contributors from many parts of the world in a common bond of mutual understanding and interest. The talks included accounts of ISV (International Scientific Vocabulary) as well as portmanteau words, acronyms and word registers.

11 July 1967 (P)

Focus on Visitors to Britain

It is at last becoming widely understood that tourism is not simply a business but also an effective means of understanding other nations. Three million tourists come to Britain every year and bring in a revenue of £400,000,000. What do they get for their money? Precious little as far as I could see from Edgar Lustgarten's view of the situation.

That we have 'very fine toast' doesn't say very much for our cooking. We serve far too many peas and carrots. As for our hotels, they are unattractively decorated. The hopeful visitor, used to eating meals at all hours, is regimented to fixed times for breakfast, lunch, tea and dinner. Have we not heard this before?

Would it be too diplomatic and British to mention the number of broken-down foreign *pensions* I have found myself staying in, with bathrooms three floors up, which always seemed to be occupied by harassed chambermaids battling with the in-house laundry? And what about the experience of a friend who went to Spoleto recently and stayed in a hotel with no water in the taps at all?

Well, after all that, we are found to be kindly and polite, and our policemen are still as helpful as ever.

29 June 1967 (P)

Corner of a Foreign Land

One evening, the director of a Bedford company counted nineteen languages being spoken in the local public house. Norman Evans interviewed many of those Bedford immigrants and proved fairly conclusively that people can live together amicably. Inter-racial dissension is not inevitable. England for most of them means money, security and a home of their own, but there are problems of social values and an uncomfortable division of loyalty.

The recent 'Home Service' repeat of 'Visitors to Britain' would have afforded immigrants some consolation in Emerson's words:

'If there is one successful country in the universe for the last millennium, that country is England.'

Like George Mikes, the new arrivals may even grow fond of the queueing, the reserve and the stoicism observed by Hippolyte Taine, and the tacitness and understatement lamented by Nirad Chaudhuri. They may even go so far as to identify themselves with what Chiang Yee referred to as 'the worry of happiness' — an especially Western preoccupation, perhaps the very source of our materialism.

*

21 July 1967 (P)

Anything to Declare?

The Thai lady in 'Anything to Declare?', and visitors and immigrants alike, may not approve entirely of contemporary Britishness or our neglect of old people, nor identify themselves with 'the current British obsession with sex'. But there are great changes taking place in our national life.

Bruce Angrave again cleverly caught the contemporary mood in his *Radio Times* cartoon, but this time, instead of John Bull reclining lazily in a hammock and dreaming of 'Swinging London', we now have the image of bemused tourists in traditional costume gazing uncomprehendingly at a Carnaby Street Miss in a Union Jack miniskirt. It's all part of the post-Beatles age, with flower-power, hedonism, and all that 'love and permissiveness' stuff, to say nothing of psychedelic light shows, wild clothes, stiletto heels, topless dresses and street happenings as portrayed a few weeks ago in Paul Stephenson's production, 'Anarchy in the City' in which Tony Aspler investigated the swinging London underground of the arts.

On the other hand, Pamela Hansford Johnson may well be right in claiming that we have to call a halt somewhere along the line in case our social health should be gravely affected.

Pamela Hansford Johnson

9 July 1967 (U)
Waving or Wavering?

Waving the flag these days seems to be on the wane, according to Alastair Cooke in 'Letter from America' this week. Now, I am deeply depressed to hear that, because I am from a generation of English children who grew up thinking that waving the flag for Great Britain was a genuine way of expressing our love, admiration — call it what you like — for the things we valued most about our country. But what did we mean by 'country'? Did we mean Britain? Did we mean England?

King George VI and Queen Elizabeth, with Princess Elizabeth and Princess Margaret Rose

I remember waving the flag for our King and Queen, and the Princesses Elizabeth and Margaret Rose at the Coronation Party in my little Elementary School in 1935. I still treasure the special book about our new king, presented to every schoolchild in the land. I was so proud of our flag in those days. I did not know as much, but the Royal Family and the Union Jack must have stood for most of us for stability, family unity, and even, in an abstract way, love.

The loyalty, admiration, call it what you will, that our mother and father felt towards the Royal Family was part of our childhood ethos. And now, thirty years later, I find I have had no reason to alter my view. When I hear 'Jerusalem' sung by a choir of thousands, I feel exactly as Ogden Nash puts it, 'all reticently thrilled and tinglish,' because, I suppose, I am English. And because I am English, my heart leaps to the spiritual call of Blake's words and the triumphant resonance of Parry's music.

After all, the Welsh have some good national tunes. What could be more stirring than 'Men of Harlech'? The Scots have 'Scotland the brave' and loads more. So we benighted Englishmen ought to be allowed one flourish of patriotism to ourselves. Those feet 'walked upon England's green and pleasant land,' and not on the wild Grampians, nor the barren slopes of Snowdonia.

Sad to say, there is a darker side to things creeping in now. National pride is beginning to break down. Since the war, class divisions have become more blurred, which is no bad thing provided we 'hold on to things that are good' as the saying goes. With our current 'permissive society' and its new (and some think questionable) freedoms, who knows where we will all go from here? All I know is, my old world is fading fast.

Sir Hubert Parry

Radio programmes these days reflect those changes right across the board. The range of broadcast talks show there is a good deal of concern about the upbringing and education of our children, the fashion for and influence of American values and lifestyle, the shortage of affordable housing, the threat of over-population, the decline in moral standards, the rising crime rate and, not least, the state of a nation that seems to be splitting at the seams. Well! The barricades are down. The heralds of this new society hold our future in their hands.

For the young and up-and-coming generations the real thrills are to be found on Radios One and Two — a thriving world of 'pop' music, disc jockeys, pop stars and starlets. As for 'high performance' plays, concerts, talks and feature programmes, we can be thankful for the abundance of creativity that characterises productions on Radios Three and Four, and long may it be so.

In the United States, as Alastair Cooke reminds us this week, the 'flag' is sacrosanct, a national icon, a symbol of unity in an incredibly diverse collection of peoples. Yet every single person swears allegiance to it. Every township is a-flutter on Independence Day, every car and truck sports the Stars and Stripes. It is inscribed on cushions, on chocolate boxes, on all manner of commercial goods. It is so sacred, says Mr. Cooke, that it must never be allowed to touch the ground and, should it be torn, it must never be mended.

Of course, Mr. Cooke suggests, perhaps we would prefer to be Russian and file past the tomb of Lenin to show our patriotism. But then, he concludes sadly, 'patriotism is not any more one of the cardinal virtues even among the older generation of democrats.'

*

18 June 1967 (P)

Achievements of a Lifetime

In 'The Time of My Life' series, Derek Parker interviewed some of life's high 'achievers'. Sir Adrian Boult created the BBC Symphony Orchestra and in the process came to know already famous personalities like Pablo Casals, Toscanini, Holst, Delius and Vaughan Williams. Sir Adrian modestly attributed his success to 'a fortunate life and good timing.'

I was impressed with the second of these programmes in which Kenneth Harris interviewed Baroness Burton of Coventry about her life and achievements (see p.246). Like Sir Stanley Matthews (see p. 279), Lady Burton had an encouraging father who guided her successfully through her early years as a sportswoman. Beset with financial difficulties, she went to the Rhondda Valley to teach and saw the poverty and the unemployment there — as Geronwy Rhys described it, she saw 'a world of stone.' Lady Burton's indomitable spirit was a vital factor in her ultimate achievement and, like one of her idols, Gracie Fields, success never spoiled her.

Julian Huxley

Robert Pocock's birthday tribute to Sir Julian Huxley, and Lesley Perowne's recording of a talk by Brigadier Sir John Smyth VC, in which he vividly remembered friends and contemporaries including Dr. Horace King, Speaker of the House of Commons, the war poet, 'Woodbine Willie' (the Rev. Studdert-Kennedy), and the Bishop of Birmingham — all deeply felt essays in courage, faith and determination.

August 1967 (U)
Collectomania!

The other day I listened to a programme about collecting things. Several people from various walks of life took part — a teacher, a banker, a solicitor, a housewife and so on. A politician talked about the amount of paper-work he had to cope with from the various parliamentary offices. He had collected a phenomenal number of files and documents over a comparatively short period of time and hardly ever had to consult one of them.

I am always thankful that I never became a politician for all sorts of reasons. I have no wish to have power over others and, not being a natural bureaucrat, I have a particular dislike of roomfuls of files and records — though I do tend to collect a monumental amount of books and personal papers at the expense of the normal comforts of life.

Of course, most people collect something of particular interest to them, whether it be stamps, Goss china, fountain pens, garden gnomes, or whatever bizarre item might obsess a collector. But where to store them? Put up a shed! Put up another shed! Rent a garage! Marry one of the off-spring of a man with a warehouse, perhaps! What about giving up collecting altogether? Never!

And what about cataloguing your collection? Before you can even find time to read the books or admire your belovèd trinkets and bric-à-brac, you are driven by an unseen power to sort them into some kind of order. Only then can you sit down in your favourite armchair — Oh! Just a minute! You have to remove the piles of old 'Picture Posts' first! — and relax. But no! You will never finish buying, storing, sorting and cataloguing — and worrying!

A friend, concerned about my magpie habits, sent me a postcard depicting a wastepaper basket full of discarded bills and bank statements, etc. The caption read: 'Before I throw these papers away, I must sort them from A to Z!' Perhaps I might think about starting some sorting tomorrow! Well, after the weekend — perhaps!

Now! I collect items to do with Napoleon. I have a napkin from the famous sale at the Tuileries in 1848 (we call it Nappy's nappy!), a framed collection of very nice plaster moulds of Napoleons's marshals and generals, a nice little portrait of the great man painted on enamel, numerous busts — porcelain busts, earthenware busts, Parian busts. You name it, I've got it! At home they say:

'Why on earth do you want to collect all this junk to do with Napoleon? It's taking up far too much space. We haven't got any room for our own collection of 17th century Mongolian handcrafts, our prize collection of medieval crumhorns, not to mention our family teddy bears and dolls, and umpteen other things. Why Napoleon, for God's sake? He was our sworn enemy?'

'Well!' I exclaim. 'What about my collection of autograph letters, my ephemera collection and my cockerel collection?'

Napoleon I

Now, this is the interesting bit. It is true that Napoleon doesn't get a very good press these days. In fact, apart from the besotted Lord Byron (who thought him a hero) he never has been with us English. Romantic as he may have seemed, he was aggressive, self-indulgent, perfidious, a megalomaniac, an obsessive, a suitable case for treatment — and very collectable!

And what about cockerels? Handsome as they are, they have nasty habits. I know because I have first-hand knowledge of the beasts. As a boy, on our farm, I used to have to clean out our chicken-houses once a week in my school holidays! Chickens are vicious, smelly, mucky, flea-ridden, horrid birds. They are also arrogant (especially the male of the species, as Chaucer well knew), aggressive and self-indulgent like Napoleon, and much more attractive roasted and served up on a dish. So why on earth do I collect images of them, on plates, on egg-cups, on beer-mats? But then, are not cockerels delightfully absurd, strutting and crowing about the place — the Napoleons of the farmyard?

By the way, I believe there's another programme coming up about clearing out the attic! If so, I may just listen in for a few tips. But I must hurry now because I don't want to be late for the bargain of the century down at the Portobello Road Saturday Market!

Entertainers and Performers

3 March 1967 (P)

'G. B. S.'

My first and last meeting with George Bernard Shaw was at Frinton on a hot summer's day before the Second World War. I was six or seven at the time. With the exuberance of youth, I came dashing round a corner and nearly butted him in the midriff. I think I was pretending to be an aeroplane at the time. I remember the long silent stare and the glint in the eyes. All this returned vividly to mind as I listened to the brilliance of Max Adrian's portrayal of G. B. S.

Max Adrian

In the beautiful and beguiling lilt of the Vico Road sort, Mr. Adrian gave a wonderfully convincing and sensitive portrait, with all the breathless verve, the whimsical self-analysis, the incorrigible philandering of this most delightful of *enfants terribles*. Of course, so many good things had to be left out of the original production. The result was sometimes too rapid a telescoping of time, but Michael Voysey, who devised the biography for the stage, overcame the larger problems of compression, helped by Mr. Adrian's mastery, full of sly chuckles and private confidences, a *tour de force* that made one of the most enjoyable broadcasts you could hope to hear.

3 March 1967 (U)

'Corno di Bassetto' — Behind the Mask

He was a pest at public meetings, joined *The Star*, as an independent journalist, wrote unprintable articles that gave the editor goose-pimples, and found a timely outlet for his rebellious opinions on things sacred to the upper crust by joining the Fabian Society. Well, have you guessed? Who else but George Bernard Shaw, the critic with a twinkle in his eye, as exposed in all his infinite variety in Charles Leffaux' brilliant production of 'G.B.S', Michael Voysey's clever portrait, starring Max Adrian.

The benighted editor of *The Star* knew how to turn base metal into gold — by bringing the young Irish upstart down to size with an offer of a music column, under the pseudonym of 'Corno di Bassetto'.

'I wrote about anything I pleased.' bragged the cocky 'Corno'.

Writing of Madame Adelina Patti, whom he heard sing in a concert at Covent Garden, he described her as a combination of 'an Adelina Jekyll and an Adelina Hyde' in a performance 'that made *God Save the Queen* sound fresh and noble'. But with encore after encore, he couldn't resist an opinion that she was 'too big for that sort of thing! The Queen of Song should leave the *coquetterie* of the footlights to the *soubrettes*.'

G. B. S.

Shaw is recorded somewhere as remarking that there was only one place worse than prison and that was the theatre! When audiences are sparse 'the theatre is a place where two or three are gathered together'. He was arrogant enough to claim that the theatre was 'the apostolic succession from Aeschylus to myself.'

When 'Corno' was a child, he could remember his father giving him his first dip in the sea at Killiney Bay. Of course at that time he would have been a mere 'cornetto'! His mother was fond of animals and flowers but she could not cope with human beings. She took up spiritualism when his sister Agnes died and became even more remote.

On seeing Isadora Duncan for the first time, Shaw could only comment: 'Her face looked as if it was made of sugar and someone had licked it.' She promised to dance 'without draperies' — a not-to-be-missed spectacle he forgot to go to!

There is always, with Shaw, a feeling that behind the mask there is an impish leprechaun taking a wicked delight in deceiving his innocent readers.

'I am,' he said, 'one of my most successful fictions.'

At the age of ninety-three, he is said to have fallen out of a pear-tree! Defiant to the end, he must somehow have recognised that God finally existed, but the aged *animal méchant* was going to have the last word:

'If He [God] starts giving me examination marks for any of my activities, there will be serious trouble between us.'

Three-quarters of an hour passed by in a matter of minutes as one anecdote after another crowded the mind with images of the extraordinary life of a man who invented 'the theatre of ideas'. A keen intellect combined with a ready wit must surely be the perfect recipe for the lasting success of the man behind the mask — 'Corno di Bassetto'.

22 January 1967 (P)

Nijinsky's Diary

Nijinsky

Few human beings have suffered more anguish and self-searching than Nijinsky. We were given a second chance to hear his widow present excerpts from the great dancer's *Diary*, a most inspiring experience for a quiet Sunday evening. Here were all the mental and spiritual meanderings of a frightened and tortured soul. 'Every person has feeling but they don't understand what it is....I am a madman who loves mankind...my madness is my love toward mankind.' Paul Scofield's readings were very moving, even beautiful and serene in the agony of it, a marvel of voice and feeling, in the words and thoughts of the most gifted of men.

From my notebook: *28 January 1967*

Madame Nijinsky

My Nijinsky piece last week was severely pruned owing to lack of space. I have now received a letter from the producer of the programme with information I did not possess at the time of writing:

Dear Mr. Thorogood,

I was happy with your notice of the Scofield reading of the Nijinsky Diary. As to your point that it was 'his widow's memorable presentation', may I point out that the diary (as published by her) was selected, abbreviated for broadcasting and produced by me. Mme Nijinsky wrote and recorded her introduction (which was produced by Carl Wildman) only after the Diary and the music had been recorded, put together and recorded on the Third Programme.

Yours sincerely,
H. B. Fortuin, Drama Producer (Sound)

*

22 January 1967 (U)

A Tortured Soul

Mme Nijinsky's translations of her husband's *Diaries* are not only wonderfully articulate but also intensely moving. 'I am Nijinsky. I am one who dies when he is not loved.' By the time he wrote those words, Nijinsky had left Diaghilev's Russian Ballet and gone to live in Switzerland, during the last years of the First World War. He was, by this time, not only 'le Dieu de la danse', he was, writes Mme Nijinsky, 'a humanitarian, a seeker after truth, whose only aim was to help, to share, to love'. This much I could glean from the note in the *Radio Times* by the programme's producer, H. B. Fortuin.

Not until you hear the words of the great master can you possibly realise the immensity of his suffering, his total immersion in his art, and the breadth of his thought. His preoccupations about art and life, beauty and God, carried him beyond the limits of his reason and dangerously near to madness. To listen to this painful process through the personal diaries is to enter the innermost depths of his sensibility, to experience almost at first hand, the trauma and despair of the true and consummate artist.

Nijinksy and Karsavina in Giselle, *Paris, 1910*

Nijinsky could write feverishly, hour upon hour, through the night. Ironically, he believed that Nietzsche lost his reason because he thought too much! 'Scientists think about me and break their heads.' When he thinks of the state of human understanding, his heart is torn apart. 'Every person has feeling but they don't understand what it is.'

Paul Scofield's reading of Fortuin's sensitive selection of these extraordinary diaries was impressive, bringing through the unique *timbre* of his voice a haunting poignancy, guiding us through what seemed to be the whole scale of human thought and emotion.

1 February 1967 (P)

Diva Divina!

The room was crowded with members of an exclusive ladies' club. The place? An upper room in a palazzo in Via Manzoni, Milan. The year: 1958. The guest of honour: Madame Maria Callas. There had been serious criticism of her behaviour in the press: fits of temperament, angry scenes, walking out during rehearsals at La Scala. All this was on an essentially human level. To her adoring public she remained their goddess: 'La Divina', and it was in this guise that she appeared in the talk by Stelios Galatapoulos in 'Home This Afternoon'.

In that upper room, Madame Callas, in defending herself against all the criticism, addressed the ladies with a philosophic calm that was completely disarming. Mr. Galatapoulos, her most recent biographer, perhaps rightly in a short talk, chose to gloss over those events to present us with Callas, the great 'diva' of Italian opera.

I remember her last in the great amphitheatre at Epidaurus. We had come in small boats from Piraeus, over a translucent azure sea, and climbed the twisting road through a grove of cypress trees, alive with the sound of cicadas. In this ancient setting, under the star-studded sky of the Peloponnesus, 'La Divina' gave a tempestuous performance as the sorceress Medea that seemed wondrously close to the reality of her own life.

But then, ah, then! On that memorable far-off day in Milan, we joined a queue of elegant adoring Milanese ladies of a certain age. They had come to pay homage to the greatest prima donna in the world. I watched her quietly conversing with her fans as we slowly edged forward to be presented. She was wearing a simple black dress and wide-brimmed black hat — and no jewellery to detract from her incredible beauty! As I moved forward to greet her, I was momentarily struck by her radiance, entrancing, enchanting. Like some hopelessly dumbstruck medieval lover, I struggled to find appropriate words. Hardly a minute — a snatched, precious exchange of greeting, and we had moved on towards the *thé al limone* and elegantly served *pasticceria*. The magic was with us in that silent temple of adoration — tranquil, yes, but the heart still beat fast.

Maria Callas

*

27 May 1966 (U)

Gay Paree!

To a young man used to the strict proprieties imposed by the Lord Chamberlain on what could or could not be done or said on the London stage, my first visits to the *Folies Bergères* and the *Casino de Paris* in 1947 were etched forever on my memory. I still treasure my illustrated programmes, and I believe, if you asked me, I could root out from a dusty corner my first ticket. The sight of so much nudity on stage, in fantastically elaborate *tableaux vivants*, was beyond my wildest dreams. At first, I felt uncomfortable, watching so much alluring female shapeliness parading past me overhead, so close to me, in full unfettered view, along the daringly transparent walkways.

I was just nineteen and almost totally untutored in things of the flesh. As a country boy, brought up on a farm, then grammar-school and university educated, I had led a pretty sheltered life. To make matters worse, I was shy and inhibited. So my first feelings, sitting there on my own in the stalls of the *Folies Berg*ères, were ones of guilt. What would they say at home if they knew? And now, here I was in post-war Paris, seeing the sights!

So I could recall those early pleasures while listening in to Robert Nesbitt's nostalgic look at the good old days in 'gay Paree', as they used say. I need not have worried, according to Mr. Nesbitt, because the lavish entertainment was not at all intended to be salacious. One had to get used to the idea that nudity was not 'naughty'. Difficult for an English grammar school boy newly released into the wider world of sex.

After all, the very attractive girls up there on stage, doing their fantastic high kicks, were mostly British. Even the French had to admit that the British girls were better dancers, better trained and better looking! — at least according to the Folies founder, Paul Duval. Yet here (I tried hard to convince myself) was 'a traditional indigenous French form of entertainment deriving from the old 'Follies' of the music-hall days and much enjoyed by English Victorian and Edwardian gentlemen escaping from the restrictions of the home for a gay* weekend on the Continent.'

On many nights afterwards, I went to see the high-kicking 'Bluebell Girls' and revel in the delights of star attractions: Maurice

Josephine Baker

Chevalier, the Dolly Sisters, Mistinguette, and the glamorous black American dancer Josephine Baker. Thank you, Mr. Nesbitt, for dwelling for a while on these treasured memories.

i.e. 'carefree', 'entertaining', in 1960's parlance

*

29 May 1966 (P)

Round the Horne!

Kenneth Horne

Amidst the sparkle of outrageous innuendo, 'Round the Horne' pursues its reckless course. With amused tolerance, announcer, Douglas Smith, is allowed to get in his party-piece and, in a flash, this delicious band of English eccentrics is careering over the pages of the script in a rush of preposterous word-play, half-allusion and remorseless punning. Kenneth Williams is wildly funny with his rustic ditties, rife with double meanings. Betty Marsden's fruity contralto sets us bewilderingly between tears and laughter, as all good comedy does. The versatile impersonations of Bill Pertwee and Hugh Paddick leave us tottering on the precipice of complete abandonment.

Kenneth Horne leads us with urbane aplomb through this zany world. Waxing sentimental over the good old days 'when Lord Moran* only wrote prescriptions', he introduced a clever parody of the Sherlock Holmes stories. It seems that 'Julian and Sandy' can get away with anything, too. Judging by the highly infectious laughter from the direction of the audience, there seems to be no likelihood of the hilarious troupe losing popularity because of theatrical 'camp'.

Between the high goonery and low humour, the Fraser Hayes Four soothe us back to sanity, but if we fall into stitches after Sunday lunch it is all the fault of Barry Took and Marty Feldman (who write the scripts), not forgetting John Simmonds, the courageous producer.

* The Queen's physician

24 January 1967 (U)

Rule Britannia!

Though it was beyond the confines of my remit as critic of 'The Spoken Word', I could not help myself laughing at the comical portrayal by Derek Francis of His Excellency Sir Jeremy Crichton-Buller KCMG, ambassador to the decidedly chilly country of Tratvia. Aided and abetted by his First Secretary, Henry Pettigrew (Frank Thornton) and the dizzy Lady Daphne Crichton-Buller, who is engaged in putting up a poster for the wine festival ('the local booze-up to Bacchus'), Sir Jeremy is more concerned with getting central-heating installed in the Embassy. Whitehall has not responded to his entreaties ('Tell them to get a blasted move-on!').

The Russian Ambassador, Comrade Sergei Ivanoff (Michael Spice) is concerned that news should not get out about a top-secret system, so the King of Tratvia, Hildrebrande the Third (Francis de Wolff) ('I can't help it if I'm a power-failure!'), has the Embassy bugged. The late arrival, or as we understand, 'rate allival' of the Chinese Ambassador, Wong Hi Wong ('Old Sweet and Sour') complicates the matter even further through his mispronunciation of a vital message.

Thus begins Lawrie Wyman's 'The Embassy Lark'. Unfortunately the promising beginning was not matched by the remainder of the programme and I began to mourn the passing of 'The Navy Lark', the programme's brilliantly funny predecessor, with its sparkling humour. This unlikely tale ends with the saving of Tratvian pride by the King consenting to be weighed against bottles of wine, and due to bureaucratic incompetence, Whitehall mistakenly buys 56,000 gallons of wine. No doubt the producer Alastair Scott Johnson and his cast had a great deal of fun recording the series — and no doubt a few sizeable hangovers!

2 September 1966 (U)

Frankie Howerd: A Man of Parts

Some years ago, on a morning visit to the Derry and Toms roof-garden, I found myself going up in a rather crowded lift. Suddenly, it stopped. We all displayed, for a few moments, some of that natural English composure. As we stood transfixed, prepared at any moment to plunge to ground level, a small oddly familiar voice uttered the famous words: "Oh! Calamity!" We laughed, and the lift started to move again, upwards fortunately. So it was a pleasure to hear again the distinctive voice of Robertson Hare, who joined June Whitfield and Wallas Eaton to discuss the humour of Frankie Howerd.

Apart from technique, which can vary in so countless ways between comedians, there is no doubt that timing is the key to really successful comedy. Clever word-play goes some of the way and some tricks of rhetoric may help. In the case of the pun, Freud tells us that much depends on the distance between the two contrasting ideas. The connection between the name of a popular dance at the *palais* and a world-famous dog-show might stretch the imagination, but when Frankie made the throw-away remark: 'My 'St. Bernard's Walk' was the talk of Cruft's', it brought the house down.

Frankie Howerd

Of course the script of this programme was by Charles Hart and John Bishop. Knowing their propensity for 'corn', we might expect the 'dancing' theme to extend to that much-maligned town of Slough. Yes, wait for it! "Slough, Slough, quick, quick, Slough!" A dance-instructor with a name like 'Jonquil' might be expected to come up with a crack like that.

'What would you do if I asked you to be my partner?'

'Run the four-minute mile!'

The ice-run of one pathetic joke after another in any other comedian would have made the audience go stone dead. But not with Frankie Howerd. As June Whitfield said: 'He is a man possessed.' He can always get a laugh from a simple introduction like: "A funny thing happened to me last week." (Pause — funny look — followed by widespread titterings). With all this amiable silliness, he can reduce his adoring audiences to helpless laughter. When he is called up for an identity parade after a woman has been assaulted, he even got a ripple of laughter with a mitigating remark: 'They all look so different in the daylight.' This immediately followed by:

'I've got influence, you know. I've done a police concert!'

And he was walking-out with Policewoman Primrose. 'She was really hot-blooded. I had to blow her whistle for half-time! 'First offence Francis', that's me!'

President of the Angling Club on the pier: 'I'm sorry sir, this is as far as you can go.'

Angler: 'It's usually the girl who says that!'

Like many comedians, his stock-in-trade is the innuendo. At the end of the pier he meets the girl selling souvenirs: 'I've come to have a look at your novelties.' This produces loud guffaws from the front row. The scene continues:

'Do you have any favourite beauty-spots?'

'I do have one, but you can only see it when I'm in my bathing-suit.'

Of course there is the private Frankie — not always to everyone's liking — temperamental, sharp-tongued, cynical, and perhaps, for all that, curiously likeable, if the mood and the moment are right.

Frankie Howerd is a man of many parts. When interviewed by a psychologist in one of his acts, Frankie was told:

'You have the I. Q. of a sensitive, highly-developed aborigine.' To which Frankie's reply was: 'I knew I was different.'

6 March 1967 (U)

The Spice of Life!

When we were children from the 1930s on, Father used to take us to 'Variety', which for him was the spice of life as far as the London theatres were concerned. Locally, we could go to see Billy Russell at the Ilford Hippodrome, Max Miller at Stratford Empire and, on grander occasions, the Crazy Gang at the Stoll and Tessie O'Shea at the Palladium. We would drive up to town in our new Ford V8 and park in Father's favourite spot near the Savoy Hotel in the Strand, where there were in those halcyon days no parking restrictions and plenty of spaces. On our birthdays, he would treat us to a pre-theatre supper at the Trocadero in Shaftesbury Avenue, where we were elegantly served by waiters in white bow tie and tails.

One of Father's very favourite comedians was Freddy Frinton. Watching Freddy on stage invariably reduced us to laughter, we rolling about in our seats, holding our aching sides, our eyes brimming over with tears of merriment. I don't believe I have ever given myself up to such uncontrollable laughter since, not in the way we did then. So what a delightful surprise it was when the hilarious Freddy appeared on the 21st anniversary programme of 'Housewives Choice' this week.

The *Radio Times* has provided readers with a rare photograph of him to cherish. There is something undeniably melancholy about the eyes, something that holds a sign of deeper things than we shall ever know. The thick eyebrows have a comicality about them that is decidedly George Robey-ish. The generous mouth and cheekiness of expression suggest an innate clownishness, ready to burst upon us at any moment. The knowing smile seems to be telling us to watch out because he has some prank up his sleeve we are least expecting.

Freddy was born in Grimsby and eventually joined a concert party in Cleethorpes, where he enjoyed great success. He starred in pantomimes, farces and revues, and kept everybody laughing during the grim wartime years. His television show, *Meet the Wife*, with Thora Hird, which ran for forty episodes, marked him as a favourite with wider audiences. If you missed this unmissable treat and live within a stone's throw of Bradford, then do not lose out on a rare opportunity to see the inimitable Freddy in action in the current production of *Cinderella* at the Alhambra Theatre.

*

From my notebook: *Christmas 2002*

The Fabulous Freddy Frinton

A friend has lent me a hilarious video of a short sketch by Freddy entitled 'Dinner for One'.

Miss Sophie, a lady of refinement, played by May Warden, is having her 90th Birthday Party on New Year's Eve. James, her aged retainer, is, as is customary every year, serving the traditional three-course dinner. Each course is accompanied by its specially chosen wine. In keeping with tradition, places have been laid for four old friends including an admiral, but since they have all died, she sits at the head of the table in solitary splendour. At each course James asks for permission to serve the wines, to which Miss Sophie replies, to the increasing hilarity of the audience: 'The same procedure as last year, James'. In the absence of the sadly-departed guests, James, in the true spirit of the occasion, is required to impersonate them, drinking their wines himself whilst serving the various courses. The comedy increases as he goes from tipsy to blotto.

Freddie Frinton with May Warden

In a surprising *dénouement*, the farcical situation is brought to its sublime conclusion by James taking Miss Sophie's arm and, with a suggestive wink at the camera, accompanies her to her boudoir, saying: 'The same procedure as last year, Miss Sophie?', cautiously adding:

"Well, I'll do my very best!'

I am sure Father would have collapsed with laughter at this sublime piece of farce, acted out with such consummate skill by his favourite Freddy Frinton.

*

From my notebook: *20 March 2004*

Herr Frinton of Hamburg

I have just been shown an article from *The Telegraph* some years ago about Freddy Frinton by Roger Boyes. It seems that Freddy has, over the years, become the centre of a cult in Germany. His comedy sketch is watched by 13 million Germans, glued to their television sets 'as New Year's Eve lurches towards an inebriated climax.'

The first performance on stage was such a success that a German producer filmed a definitive television version in Hamburg, which is the reason why British audiences have not seen it and the name of Freddy Frinton is remembered only by a select few, old enough to remember him.

The sketch regularly appeared in music halls throughout Germany in the 1920s. Crowds still gather round the television in every *bierkeller*. Restaurants offer a menu exactly as served in the sketch.

Freddy Frinton died in 1968. It is sad indeed that *Dinner for One*, the one remaining example of his rare talent, is not available to British television audiences, and that he is only revered and remembered outside the country of his birth.

*

Gardens and Countryside

12 May 1967 (P)

'Down the Garden Path'

Roughly 2,000,000 people visit gardens every year and on average some 2,000 gardens open to the public. In addition, over 1,275 private gardens open their gates every summer on behalf of the National Gardens Scheme.

There is an enticing visual effect in the free-flowing lines of the English garden, not found in French and Italian gardens, even Monet's. But such 'free-thinking' is not always to be found. Lord Aberconway's father grew formal gardens carved out of terraces at Bodnant, with its array of rhododendrons, camellias and magnolias.

Sir Frederick Sterne, on the other hand, had to cope with fierce gales blowing up the Channel to grow his chalk garden on the Downs above Worthing, and how charming it is to wander about his colourful floral plantings, high over the town with views of the sea beyond.

In the garden of Beverley Nichols, with its enchantingly informal formality of design, a liberal sprinkling of classical names of flowers and herbs nestle in the borders. In 'The World of Sound', produced by Denys Geroult, the voice and memories of Beverley Nicholls, author of *Down the Garden Path,* evoked an old world Proustian charm. There was something of that strange admixture of nostalgia for an innocent past and the subsequent disquietude of age and experience.

Vita Sackville-West

But can there be a more captivating garden than Sissinghurst? It is surely the perfect example of the union of the classical and the romantic, and who better to represent those two aspects than Nigel Nicholson and the incomparable Vita Sackville West? I suppose, in its deceptively informal drifts of colour and its consciously haphazard but happy marriage of shades and hues, it is a glorified form of a simple cottage garden.

Nigel believed in a combination of

expectation and surprise. There is everywhere exquisite taste. There are no rhododendrons, no hybrid tea-roses, no herbaceous borders, hardly a straight line anywhere. The beautiful white garden is a tapestry in greys, whites and silvers, a misty mirage of foliage and flowers.

*

26 April 1967 (U)
Hedging Our Bets!

April is the month for hedgerows, and the contributors to Freddy Grisewood's edition of 'Any Questions' wholeheartedly deplored the destruction of hedges currently taking place around our countryside, with consequent loss of wild-life. Did I say 'wholeheartedly'? Not quite, for Lord Waldegrave, a farmer and Chairman of the Country Naturalists' Trust, admitted that some hedges had to go if we want to make ourselves more efficient in farming. A Bill is going through the House of Lords and we can expect to hear of some protection at least (The 'Lords', he claims, is the place where the more sensible bills are presented!). It is all, apparently, 'a question of balance'

Anthony Hopkins reminded his Lordship that America used to have vast lush fields — now they had vast dust bowls, to which His Lordship retorted that there are, even so, no hedges to speak of in northern France.

Rosamond John completed the discussion by remarking: 'It isn't only the wildlife that suffers; there are lots of other things that go on in hedges in the summer time', to which there was a roar of laughter and an enthusiastic round of applause.

*

December 1967 (U)

The Raggle-Taggle Gypsies O!

'Country December, and the ridges of last ploughing shining like new chocolate under thin sunlight, lap-winged still, sometimes flaked with the white wings of inland feeding gulls. At dawn and dusk, at the cold margins of the short days, the rooks trail outward and homeward, against sullen sunsets or under low clouds that blow and trail like cobwebs across the winter horizons.' So begins C. Gordon Glover's introductory article in the *Radio Times* this week.

Whatever one thinks of the flowery poetic language, it is still a very emotive way of reaching listeners, many of whom are confined to narrow city streets, or live in one of millions of flats in vast sprawling suburbs. The words are married to the voice, whose rich soft tones lull us into a state of sweet repose and contentment. If 'we have no time to stand and stare', or are too homebound by daily routine to bring ourselves to board a bus to Kew or Hampstead Heath, then C. Gordon Glover is the man for us.

In his style he is a kind of prose Patience Strong. While visiting Oxford in the company of Arthur Phillips, he admires the 'waters of an ancient weir, winter brown and fleeced with white.' In the Thames Valley he enjoys, in the words of Matthew Arnold's *The Scholar Gypsy'*, 'the brotherhood of open countryside'.

Dark December brings 'the shortest days and longest nights of the old year'. This is the time when the blackbirds come out well before 7.30 in the morning, accompanied later by starlings, sparrows and blue-tits. 'Jackdaws and rooks go trailing across the dark sky.' This time of the year can be 'fraught with fearful sounds — the yelps and squeals of foxes' in their December courtship.'

Bob Danvers-Walker spoke about all kinds of 'bizarre rural observances', 'things that go bump in the night', along the Northamptonshire byways around Kettering — rudely disturbed by a great banging and rattling of tins, cans and cooking pots to frighten off the gypsies.

26 May 1966 (U)

Rustic Idyll!

Ian Watkinson's 'Morning Story', *Beside the Cottage Door*, was announced to the nostalgic strains of the band of the Royal Artillery playing, as I remember, Percy Grainger's *Country Gardens*. Read by Marjorie Westbury, in the russet tones of the countryside, the story tells of Alice Barton, who lives in a cottage with her little grand-daughter, Maggie. 'The underwear she put on had seen better days.' Her face was 'wrinkled and sweet as a russet apple.' A tarnished barometer hung on the wall. Below the thatched roof were low casement windows, roses grew over the door and hollyhocks had found their rightful place in this English scene that would have done justice to one of those nostalgic watercolours by Birket Foster.

'Has my chair been put out?' Alice would ask.

A procession of tourists would pass by to see the quaint and timeless image of the old lady sitting outside her cottage door.

'I'll be ninety come Michaelmas,' she tells a lady tourist. "I've had nine little ones and I buried five of 'em.' (All fibs, of course!)

The questions from the mesmerised coach-party only show how far their own lives are from this ostensibly charming rural English scene. Alice is so grateful for their tips as she holds out her hand, whilst little Maggie protests at her stories.

"Well," says Alice, "that's what they want me to say." She gives Maggie the money to buy the village children sweets.

Behind this idyllic scene is the reality. Through the door, with its canopy of roses, is only squalor and filth, a pig-sty. "None of us likes work, that's for sure,' says the wily Alice.

An American sports car comes cruising round the corner. The driver stops for a photograph to take back home. Alice is sitting in the sun. She smiles, untouched by the changing modern world. The deception is complete!

Typical of the 'Morning Story', a feeling of discomfort, even apprehension, builds up as the story proceeds. In *Beside the Cottage Door*, cliché after cliché of the 'roses round the door' kind are turned back on themselves with the final snip of the pruning shears.

6 January 1966 (U)

Fairies at the Bottom of the Garden?

It was a relief from the cares of the world to go with Mr. Pennethorne Hughes into the realms of fairyland — through the magic door of the Home Service!

Now, before you have a laugh at my expense, I suggest you reserve judgement and have a serious think about this 'fairy' business. You see, it is all tied up with 'primitive science' and witchcraft. Yet we find all this fairy nonsense in great dramas and comedies, and even, God save us, the sudden appearance of a large family of gnomes on the neighbour's rockery.

What do they really look like, these insubstantial beings? Do they wear little green hats and little green jackets? Do they all have horrid little wizened faces and cast wicked little spells around the place?

On my return from Ireland once, a little nun with a wizened little face asked me if I had seen a leprechaun there, and I rather fancied at the time that I was looking at one.

Let us be serious about this fairy question, if at all possible. I was  taught to believe that fairies were sweet, decorative little creatures that sit on toadstools all day and make nice things happen to children that bossy grown-ups couldn't even dream about. In my sister's book of Scottish fairy tales, I once read that fairies were 'pretty ugly', which is a bit of an oxymoron to start with. Not only are they ugly, but worse still, they can wreak terrible vengeance on whoever gets in the way, especially humans! So be careful to stay at home on Midsummer's Eve, for the 'little people' will have plenty of nasty tricks up their little green sleeves that might just catch you unawares. It is highly unlikely that you would ever catch sight of them dancing their horrid little witch capers and furtive little fertility dances down by the compost heap at the bottom of your garden. Nevertheless, discretion is supposed to be the better part of valour, so it might be wise to keep well out of their way. And don't think you'll be able to snatch some of their fairy gold, either, because, as Mr. Hughes tells us, it is magically changed into rubbish when you get back to normal life — whatever that may be in the circumstances! Now, Mr. Pennethorne Hughes hasn't been translated into anything yet, so he is able to tell us a true story

On one occasion, an Irishman was apparently 'fairy-struck'. He was convinced that he had been spirited away to a-place-he-couldn't-remember for two whole years! When he walked back into the house he said to his half-demented wife: 'Here's a dress for you!' He opened the parcel only to find all his fairy dust had turned to horse manure! I can't believe she didn't give him a jolly good box round the ears for his pains.

Of course, it's no use trying to be rational if you're 'pixilated'. After all, the man was 'spellbound'. He made no attempt to explain himself. How could he? Perhaps he had been playing with the Queen of the May for all I know, or was beguiled by the wicked little green people to go stealing horses which, apparently is a fairly common thing in Ireland! Either way he was up to no good and was incapable of explaining himself. You know, it seems to me that he had only been a guest of the fairy kingdom because he actually 'believed' in it.

If you ask me, it's best not to have any truck with pixies and gnomes and trolls and goblins and the like. You may very well run the risk of being sprinkled with fairy dust, and, like our Irish friend, have an attack of amnesia. Just be very careful! Fairy dust makes you invisible!

Now, where do you think our presenter, Mr. Pennethorne Hughes, has disappeared to?

2 June 1966 (P)

The Countryside in May

In a month which gave us the Festival of Flowers at Westminster Abbey, the Wild Life Exhibition at the Alexandra Palace and the Chelsea Flower Show, 'The Countryside in May' looked back to refreshing glimpses of life outside the city and the town. If you have smelt the 'wild astringent flourish' of cow parsley, heard the song of the blackbird, seen the banks of thrift and campion in Devon lanes, then you will have observed what C. Gordon Glover called, with a certain deference to word-play, 'the forward march of May'!

In the city, we view the vicissitudes of the seasons passively from the top of a bus, but villages like Padstow in Cornwall actively celebrate the coming of summer with hobby horse and maypole, as Bob Danvers-Walker told us.

If you weren't sure where that bad chill came from in early May, you perhaps heard Bill Douglas describing the weather — the first days in the eighties, gales on the 7th, heavy rain on the 8th, fog on the 9th, ground-frost on the 10th, and then temperatures back to the seventies.

C. Gordon Glover's introductions to these popular 'Countryside' programmes set the scene perfectly. Few homesick Englishmen could resist the urge to return from arid deserts and steaming jungles to ' apple blossom falling like incense on the altar of approaching June'.

History and Ideas

26 May 1966 (U)

The Nature of Contemporary History

Rachel Wall, in her talk on 'The Nature of Contemporary History' seemed at times to be stating the obvious in a highly baroque style. Her question, 'What do we mean by contemporary history?' failed in my view to provide a recognisable solution. It is clear that 'history' is concerned with the past; it is clear that the world of today is one world, that contemporary history is world history, but since future historians will have to be selective in their choice of significant events, which of the happenings of our world are to be preserved and remembered?

Miss Wall infers that 'fascism' and '1914' are not fit subjects for inclusion in the pages of a recently-published journal on contemporary history, but there are some who fear that fascism has not died and that what may seem deceptively like *rigor mortis* is in fact a revitalising of the blood. It is undeniable that 'most people studying history today weren't even born on VJ Day' but it is equally true to say that the lessons learnt in Flanders in 1915 are indelibly printed on the memories of a considerable number of veterans still alive in the 1960s to tell the tale. It was, after all, only fifty years ago.

Rachel Wall, in her analysis of 'contemporary history', begins by suggesting that contemporary history puts the world of today in the contemporary situation. Simple enough. With the past, we are able to select the material after it has happened. With the present, we cannot know the outcome of contemporary events. For example, most problems today have their origins in the 1940's. If we look however at the rivalry of British and American interests in Asia, we have to go back to the Russo-Turkish War of 1853 to be aware that events are not necessarily irrelevant because they are recent.

So where does Miss Wall go next with her argument? If the world today is one world (see p. 284), then contemporary history means world history. For example, China, Russia and the U.S.A. are all concerned with events in Africa. So the contemporary historian does not look at nation-states. 'Ideologies,' she reminds us, 'have crossed frontiers.' There is much more interaction between regions. Contemporary design in buildings, mass entertainment and acceptance of new ideas and attitudes are common to all countries.

In Orwell's bleak novel, *1984*, the principal character, Winston Smith, is made to repeat the Party slogan: 'Who controls the past controls the future: who controls the present controls the past.' When Winston later asks: "But how can you stop people remembering things?', we understand the difference between the recorded past and the living present enough to know that 'contemporary history' is, in itself, an anachronism.

2 February 1967 (P)

The Mass Portrait Gallery

Professor George Rudé made a claim for 'mass history' as being likely to supercede, though not supplant, the history of 'Great Men'. It is the 'nameless and faceless people of history' who have become the active agent in the historical process. Unfortunately, he left many questions unanswered, remarking that Great Men may now begin to see their fellow-mortals as partners in the common task.

8 January 1967 (P)

The Biography and Inner Life of Ideas

The English are not generally speculative as a nation, which may be one reason why we have not taken kindly to the fact that ideas may have a history of their own, as Peter Burke endeavoured to explain in his two talks on the 'biography' and 'inner life' of ideas. He spoke in a terse, almost aphoristic style and assembled some fascinating theories for our consideration.

History could be said to be a series of bitter lessons, not always assimilated and remembered. However, the ideas of such widely diverse thinkers as Luther and Freud might be seen as 'attempts on the part of gifted men to understand and control some part of reality.'

Burke points to a vital change in our attitude to ideas over the last century. Our impression of the Victorian idea of progress was, and to some extent still is, if we care to take a look at our school syllabuses these days, political. Nowadays, we have invented new names for a new kind of professional in our midst. We have historians of ideas. We have economic historians.

If we think we are terribly progressive in these new professions, then we should think again, for they have already existed in Germany and America for many years. We move into a much more abstract world where ideas have been separated out and analysed historically under abstruse titles like 'the history of thought' and 'intellectual history'.

And do not make the mistake of thinking only of 'educated' people; even the 'uneducated' are allowed to have 'ideas' in their way too. But, says Mr. Burke, because it is patently more difficult for the historian to find out what the uneducated actually thought, we can fortunately turn to masterly works like Professor Norman Cohn's book, *The Pursuit of the Millennium*, for answers. 'It is not enough,' says Mr. Burke, to describe what men believed at one particular moment; we have to relate their beliefs to the changing world around them.' By way of explanation, he quoted the American historian, Arthur Lovejoy:

'Landscape gardening....seems a topic fairly remote from philosophy; yet, at one point, at least, the history of landscape gardening becomes a part of any truly philosophical history of modern thought.'

Now, I must warn you, this is a very dense and complex subject. We have already got ourselves into difficulties and we have still to tackle the effect of changing tastes through the ages, changes to morality and sexual behaviour, a consideration of Aristotle's 'categories', the influence of humanism, the Christian ethic, technological advances, all in an effort to define the biography of an idea.

I gave up, dear reader, when I was asked to consider who was enlightened by the Enlightenment? Well, we are told that ideas reappear in different guises. Shall we roam over the radical ruminations of Rousseau? Shall we dwell upon the daring deliberations of Darwin? Shall we mull over the momentous murmurings of Malthus? Shall we fumble fruitlessly over Freud and meditate morosely over the maxims of Marx?

I am not at all surprised to hear Mr. Burke confess that 'the historian of ideas is in a dilemma' and that 'explaining ideas is a hazardous business.' I was left in utter confusion when I heard that 'an objection people sometimes raise is that the history of ideas is nothing but the history of errors.' This is the point when I poured myself a strong Scotch-and-soda and retired to bed!

2 July 1967 (U)

Planning for What?

Why do we need a planned economy?

At the end of my one-and-only year at the London School of Economics I failed an examination on the strength of this arcane question. I naively rebelled against any suggestion that people should be the prisoners of any rigid social or political system. My views on the dangers of uncontrolled technological advances without moral back-up were not well formulated at that time, so my dismissal from that sacred temple of economic science was inevitable.

Mind you, that was not the whole story. I was much more suited to the more seductive pursuits of music and poetry to ponder the fate of the economy and the nation. But now, forty years on, I find myself this week listening to a distinguished scholar on the subject, David Worswick, Director of the National Institute of Economic and Current Affairs, making important statements about a 'planned economy' as proclaimed by the eminent economic theorist, Professor John Kenneth Galbraith.

My recent visits to Poland, Bulgaria and Israel, might have told me that there are wide differences in types of planned economy. Political circumstances can influence the local approach to economic efficiency. Yet everywhere nowadays industrialists widely recognise the necessity for planning. The trouble is that elaborate state planning necessitates a heavy increase in the bureaucracy and controls, and that could quite easily slip into totalitarianism. Capitalism, free trade policies and democratic socialism have no satisfactory answers to the question, either. Clearly, there is a weakness in the system which demands some radical thinking. As Mr. Worswick says: 'The industrial mechanism requires us to acknowledge that technology is always good, that firms must always expand, and that idleness is rather wicked as an alternative to work.'

In any case, Galbraith agrees that the economic system does serve man's physical needs (only in the richer countries, surely!), and that it is not entirely 'consistent with man's liberty or happiness.' For 'industrial planning is necessitated by developments in modern technology.' Soon the State is 'obliging' with research and development contracts. Before long, the planning of the industrial corporations merges with the planning of the State. Here, in my view, Galbraith loses touch with what he means by 'planning'. It is all very well, but it does seem to me that the more efficient we become the more the standard of living for many people will decline. It may come to a point where manufacturing is phased out in favour of the service industry. The most disturbing message from the Professor is that we can expect an all round fall in our values.

2 July 1967 (P)

Divided Opinion

Business is business, or so the saying goes, but there seems to be a fairly wide gulf between the American theory and the British practice, according to David Worswick, who, in a discussion with the Rt. Hon. Keith Joseph MP, set to rights some common misconceptions about Professor Galbraith's recent book, *The New Industrial State*. The main message is predictably simple: the future of our economy is one of inevitable change. 'We have no choice but to grow more efficient,' Sir Keith concluded.

26 April 1967 (U)
A Savage Judgement

During my wanderings through the mysterious byways of BBC Radio, I occasionally weaken my resolve to stick to the appointed task and find myself idly turning on 'Any Questions' for the sheer pleasure of listening to Freddy Grisewood. Everybody knows and loves Freddy. He's been around so long he is part of the fabric. Today he was sitting round the microphone with some distinguished guests: Lord Waldegrave, actress Rosamond John, musicologist Anthony Hopkins and writer and broadcaster Malcolm Muggeridge, so I knew I was to be entertained with some stylish discussion on a number of controversial topics. It doesn't come under my 'Spoken Word' brief so I have to regard it as an indulgence on my part, knowing that the Editor might put a blue pencil through the piece!

Poverty under the Welfare State does seem an anomaly but it appears that one in six of us are suffering from malnutrition. Since the influx of poor West Indian families in the 1950s, poverty as a theme in the press has not caught our notice, though we have shamelessly ignored it in London and our major cities.

Malcolm Muggeridge

Malcolm Muggeridge believed many families were poor because they had too many children. Rosamond John works as a 'liason officer' for the Schools Care Service between school and parents in what she referred to as an 'affluent' area. She pointed to a number of causes, not least a 'missing' father and the fact that family allowances are inadequate and urgently need to be increased. 'I do hope James Callaghan is listening!' she said. 'Happiness,' she added, 'is beyond rubies!'

Anthony Hopkins wanted allowances to come not in cash but in kind, which remark was greeted with applause from the audience. 'There is no guarantee that the money will be spent on the children.'

Rosamond John disagreed. She believed there was a good deal of wrong-thinking about the poor being 'poor because they deserved it', and that poor children were 'deprived children'. Poverty was a grim reality and a disgrace in a wealthy society like Britain, and 'let's have no more mention of alleged poverty,' when the real thing was just beneath the surface.

Malcolm Muggeridge was concerned about the population explosion getting out of hand. If we were to use the available resources, he said, we would have no need to talk of too many people. There was 'too much selfish use of what we have' and countless millions being spent on weapons of mass destruction.

All of which confirms my belief that a knowledge of history, the study of which should be compulsory in our schools, has one important value for us all — it shows us the errors of our ways.

*

26 April 1967 (P)

'English People are Sweet'

The question as to whether the English eccentrics were engendered by the 'eccentricity' of the English weather was dealt with in a suitable mood of levity. Anthony Hopkins reminded us of the relationship by referring to the recent cartoon in which a flash of lightning came out of a thunderous sky and someone said: 'Mr. Wilson* must be angry!'

Lord Waldegrave decided that our best eccentrics are peers and clergymen. No one on the panel mentioned any names!

As for the Common Market, well! — the English are incredibly insular. We love our barriers and we are constitutionally incapable of entering into the spirit of the thing. Anyway, whatever side we take we usually manage to come out on top. To quote Ogden Nash: 'I think the English people are sweet / And we might as well get used to them because when they slip and fall they always land on somebody else's feet!'

*The Prime Minister

Kings and Queens

17 February 1967 (U)

Pomp and Circumstance

Queen Elizabeth I

Listeners to the 'Home Service' today were entertained to a slice of history that has become a part of the nation's folklore. Noel Howlett and Beth Boyd presented us with a rattling good tale, ably produced by Nesta Pain, about Queen Elizabeth and her defeat of the Armada.

'Not that old story again,' I thought, but my fears were unfounded.

On 29th May, the Spanish fleet sailed out of the Bay of Lisbon. Pushing through raging winds, then slowed down by almost impenetrable fog, the storm-battered ships hovered uncertainly off the Lizard Point. No doubt there were rumours about the strength of the Spanish ships, a hundred-and-fifty sail with their 'lofty turrets like castles', lying at anchor, biding their time, 'the ocean groaning with their weight'.

Here were Drake, Hawkins and Frobisher to defend the day, and the crew of the Ark Royal, shouting for joy when the news of the Armada was announced from the topmast. A landing was feared. To avoid false reports, *The English Mercury* (the first newspaper in England) was published on 23rd July 1588.

The Queen took up residence at her palace at Havering-atte-Bower, where she received disturbing letters from the Earl of Leicester:

'My most dear and gracious lady,' he began, 'for your army, it is more than time you gathered them about you.....there is no dallying at such a time.....gather as many good horses, above all things, as you can.'

For all his propensity for flattery, Leicester was a highly competent strategist and the Queen wisely accepted his advice. An army was assembled at Stratford and East Ham. Fourteen miles down-river was Tilbury, a convenient resting-place for the Queen. A bridge of barges was drawn up across the Thames to impede the opposing forces.

Elizabeth emerged in royal and marshal pomp, mounted on a 'stately charger', 'the sacred goddess of the English soil.' Leicester was waiting to receive her, with two thousand horse and two thousand foot-soldiers. She appeared before her troops on Tilbury Hill in 'a monstrous farthingale of great amplitude' and a polished steel corselet.

With predictable grandeur, Beth Boyd read the Queen's rousing speech before her assembled troops, ships at the ready on the river below. Her words have come down to us through the ages and reached the ears of every schoolboy in the land: 'I know I have the body of a weak and feeble woman, but I have the heart and stomach of a king, and of a king of England too.'

With the rumour that the Prince of Parma had landed, there followed fierce engagements between the ships of the opposing sides in the Channel. A violent storm struck the Armada and swept it towards the coast of Holland and thence up the English coast. Thunder and lightning raged as Howard chased the Spanish ever northward. It was said even the winds and the waves 'fought mightily for England' and Leicester added in a letter to the Queen: "God hath also fought mightily for Her Majesty."

Great were the celebrations at Whitehall — tilts and tourneys, singing and dancing. Medals were struck with the Latin motto: 'Venit, vidit, fugit' — 'He came, he saw, he fled', an ironic echo of Julius Caesar's words on conquering the Celtic Britons.

Mr Howlett's programme succeeded in bringing out all the drama, the tensions, the fears and anxieties assailing the participants of both sides, and I for one was yet again beguiled by this presentation of one of the most turbulent episodes in European history and could have listened to it all over again.

17 February 1967 (P)

Queen of Hearts

Mary Queen of Scots was the Catholic Dowager Queen of France, cousin to Protestant Queen Elizabeth the First and heir to the English throne. In all these roles, she was seen as a danger to the English people. Her inevitable death at the hands of the executioner in the Great Hall at Fotheringay Castle in February 1587 was undoubtedly reprehensible. Catholic plots to assassinate Elizabeth had failed and Mary was, by her own complicity, drawn closer into the net by her ambitious sycophants, and thought by many to be the innocent victim of cruel political intrigue.

Alison Plowden's consummate compilation, *My End is My Beginning*, ably caught the spirit of the age and drew from the known facts, with the help of contemporary records, the true historical significance of Mary's plight.

Such a programme would normally be outside the area of 'The Spoken Word', which largely concerns itself with talks, but this piece had much that was factual enough to merit comment.

The Throckmorton* plot to murder Elizabeth, unwise as it turned out to be, was tinder for the terrible events that followed, making Mary the most 'unwelcome guest' in England. Early in the sorry history of this affair, the Jesuit, William Crichton, was arrested with incriminating papers in his possession. A Bond of Association was introduced that made it law 'to prosecute such person or persons unto death'.

Amyas Paulet

In 1585, the Parry plot brought negotiations with Mary to an end. The Queen appointed Sir Amyas Paulet to her service, who wisely recommended 'plain dealing' as the best policy. However the screws began to tighten and, as far as Paulet was concerned, it 'behoved him to eat with a long spoon'. With considerable astuteness, he ran an efficient secret service, though with instruction from Sir Francis Walsingham. A letter was given to Gifford which came into the hands of Walsingham and thus it was said: 'The honest man playeth the harlot with these people egregiously.' Mary became the unwitting victim of Walsingham's wiles. One of the conspirators, Babington, offered Mary a hundred well-wishers, but was caught re-handed in the thickets of St.

150

John's Wood. Paulet's supporters were reduced to 'conferring in the open fields as a protection against eavesdroppers.' Burghley — no sympathiser of Mary — wrote 'a grimly prophetic' letter with the much quoted sentence: 'I am constrained to scribble in haste' with the viewpoint that, shortly, 'the blow fall upon their mistress betwixt her head and her shoulders'.

Mary wrote: 'It grieveth me that the Queen, my dear sister, is misinformed of me,' but Elizabeth's reply was to the point: 'You protest yourself to be innocent but the Queen of England thinketh otherwise.'

Alison Plowden has chosen letters that reveal a certain self-protective formality on Elizabeth's part. On the other hand, one can only marvel at the felicitous expression and the neat, aphoristic style.

Francis Walsingam

Similarly, Mary has her Baconian epigrammatic moments:

'Spies are men of doubtful credit which dissemble one thing and speak another.'

'Circumstances may be good, my lord, but not the effect.'

The exchanges between Elizabeth and Mary are poignant. As her fatal day drew near, when things were at fever pitch, Mary wrote:

'I beg not to be executed without your knowledge' — a letter which brought tears from Elizabeth, who was increasingly pressurised by her Privy Council to make a decision.

On 1st February the warrant was signed and sealed. There were still fears that the Queen might change her mind and forbid the warrant. Paulet wrote that this was 'the shipwreck of my conscience'.

Mary was allowed six of her servants around her. The Privy Counsellors, together with a hand-picked audience of two hundred knights of the realm, were assembled in the Great Hall. Mary was now forty-four years of age, and a woman of strong faith. She refused to join the Protestant Dean of Peterborough in prayer.

'I am born in this religion, I have lived in this religion, and am resolved to die in this religion.'

She made an impressive appearance in her crimson petticoat of satin.

The horror and cruelty of the moment were heightened by the need for two strokes of the axe. The executioner held up the severed head. The elaborate wig came away in his hand, revealing Mary's hair, grey from grief.

A new era had begun.

Elizabeth, however, was less optimistic about the outcome of these troubled times, fearing a public uprising and the increased enmity of foreign powers. She wrote to King James VI of Scotland of the 'extreme dolour that overwhelmeth my mind.' Detailed accounts of her rage and sorrow circulated through the courts of Europe.

Had Mary ascended the English throne, England would have become once more a Catholic country, with ever closer ties with France and Spain, and subject to the power and influence of Rome under Pope Sixtus. Thus, by the stroke of an axe, the realm once more stood secure.

Alison Plowden is to be congratulated on her vivid production enhanced by the excellent performances of David March (Sir Amyas Paulet), John Pullen (Sir Francis Walsingham), and Douglas Hankin (Babington). Mary Wimbush as Elizabeth and Joan Matheson as Mary gave two very fine performances worthy of all that is best in BBC radio drama.

Mary Wimbush

*Nicholas Throckmorton (1554-1584) conspirator. Arrested while organising the plot between Mary and Catholic supporters of the Duc de Guise. Executed at Tyburn.

*

17 February 1967 (P)

'My End is My Beginning'

Alison Plowden's production, concerning the last two years in the life of Mary Queen of Scots, was both beautiful and touching, and meticulously narrated by Richard Hurndall. The part of Elizabeth was played by Mary Wimbush, who gave to it that complexity of defiance and remorse which contrasted touchingly with the lonely, pathetic Mary, played by Joan Matheson. The sinister figure of Francis Walsingham (John Pullen) loomed ominously over the conspirators' every move. 'Queens should be cold and wise,' wrote Marion Angus in a poem on Mary Queen of Scots. But 'She loved red-legged partridges, And the golden fishes of the Duc de Guise.' After the execution, Elizabeth wept. Perhaps the *Book of Ecclesiastes* might have given her the solace she yearned for: 'Better is the end of a thing than the beginning thereof.'

30 January 1967 (U)

The Merry, Merry Monarch!

My alternative title for this piece was: 'Through the Keyhole!' because Professor J.F. Kenyon has enabled his listeners to gain a private view of a king's bedroom and to make the acquaintance of some of the 'visitors' who frequented it!

We were entertained to an interesting compilation of anecdotes about King Charles the Second, as seen by his contemporaries. Produced by the ever-reliable Nesta Pain, the programme gave poor Charles a rather mixed reception as a man who 'never did harm to any living thing willingly' and held the view that 'affability was not necessarily tenderness'. He could be sexually ruthless. The barrenness of his marriage to Catherine of Braganza led in time to his taking a whole string of mistresses. In the 1660s, he took on the magnetic Barbara Palmer, Countess of Castlemaine, described at the time as 'that lewd imperial whore'. Without doubt she was a great beauty, but she was foolish, imperious and capable of great duplicity, carrying on countless intrigues with other men whilst, at the same time, appearing to be jealous of the King. This greatly affected the King's powers of concentration when it came to dealing with the business of state.

Charles had a fund of amusing stories with which he would regale the Court. How well he could tell a story and with what consummate wit! Everyone 'forgave him as if he were a saint'. Was it Halifax who called him 'our pretty, witty king'? 'My words are my own, my actions are my ministers',' he once said. But he was not a deep-thinking man and could no more employ himself in deep study than fly. He knew all about ships, though, and all about the architecture of ships, and understood the principles of navigation.

King Charles II

Charles's reputation at court was certainly tarnished by the sensational arrival of the Cockney 'actress', Nell Gwynne, a wild, reckless creature who had no regard for protocol or Court etiquette. She promptly asked him for £500 a year and in the end received some £50,000, a massive fortune at the time. The King's relationships were rarely sincere to the point of even minimal fidelity, for, whilst he had 'inclinations to love', 'his passions remained ever in the lower regions!' It was scurrilously remarked that 'his sceptre and his prick were of such a length!' He would spend hours 'sauntering' from one room to another, visiting mistresses in turn, in one long pleasuring of the senses. Whilst his infidelity to the Queen was plain for all to see, he spent much of his time with his French mistress, the Duchess of Portsmouth. In time, tiring of such frivolity and self-gratification, he became a country gentleman, relaxing at the horse-races, play-acting in the barn.

Professor Kenyon's portrait of Charles gave a truly picturesque account of the gaiety of the Restoration court, and yet underlying all the often joyless pleasure-seeking, lay a darker side. A hint of turbulence ran through the Court, reached out to those in government, into the market squares and beyond— a sense that all was not well in the land.

As the King lay dying, it became clear that he had disguised his true leanings towards popery and, following a stroke, a Catholic priest was called, Father Huddlestone, the very same who had saved the King's life on an earlier occasion. In truth, having saved him in body, he had now come to save his soul. Disguised in wig and gown, for fear of detection, Huddlestone performed his sacred duties perfectly. The King received absolution, took communion, and lastly, extreme unction.

Afterwards, the Catholics gained some small ground under Charles' younger brother, James, but only for a short time. The 'Glorious Revolution' would pave the way for more sober and sombre times.

*

29 January 1967 (U)

America's Last King

I could not resist listening in to Robin Hughes' production, 'The Insanity of King George III', a reconstruction based on the recent researches of two psychiatrists, Dr. Ida Macalpine and Dr. Richard Hunter, who, according to the preview in the *Radio Times*, 'exploded the myth of the King's madness' and finally led them to the correct diagnosis. *

The programme included readings from contemporary diaries, letters and reports, including the journals of the King's own physicians. But what was it that brought about the appalling sufferings of the king's person? Was it really insanity, or could it have been a serious physical disorder? Endless 'political' discussions failed to come to any satisfactory conclusion.

King George III

When Fanny Burney observed the king talking to trees in the park, was she witnessing a fit of madness, some strange delirium that was affecting his mind? Certainly it was very odd behaviour. People have been known, in a moment of whimsy or distraction, to address inanimate objects, but no-one can say by any stretch of the imagination that a tree is not a living thing, though it will certainly be considered by most of us as 'inanimate'. Even botanists admit these days that flowers shrink when we approach them with a pair of pruners.

The study by Dr. Isaac Ray in 1851 and another by Dr Guttnacher in 1941 failed to give adequate answers to the King's distress. Accusations of schizophrenia and manic depression only succeeded in confusing the issue.

On the positive side, George was abstemious in his daily habits, took plenty of regular exercise, was fond of the out-door life and was a devoted father and family man. He was a sensitive musician, a patron of the arts and sciences, and a discerning book-collector. His mystery illness therefore could be accounted for neither in physical nor in intellectual terms. There could be no other interpretation than that His Majesty must be 'mad'. The trouble was, no-one was permitted to examine him. No-one thought that the agonising treatments that caused him to howl so had anything to do with his abnormal behaviour.

One theory claimed that the King was suffering from a rare hereditary disease known as porphyria, caused by the body failing to break down haemoglobin. The symptoms included extreme sensitivity to light, severe mental disturbance and the excretion of dark pigments in the urine of the sufferer.

13 February 1967 (U)

A Spontaneous Reply from Queen Victoria

The secrets of life at the manse were revealed today by the refreshingly irreverent Reverend Robert Taylor, in conversation with Alastair Burnett, on 'Home This Afternoon'. In anecdotal frame of mind, they wandered through a royal maze of apocryphal stories, several about Queen Victoria.

The Rev. Taylor, pointed out that, on occasion, the Minister at Crathie was frequently called upon to leave the comparative safety of his home to brave the *terra incognita* of the royal dinner table. The strain was sometimes almost unendurable. One such minister was asked what he would like to drink.

'Port wine,' suggested the butler, *sottovoce*.

'Port wine, if Your Majesty pleases.'

To his surprise, the Queen leant over and whispered: 'Are you ill, sir?'

Now, times have changed, said Alastair Burnett. 'The royal family have very close ties with the locals round about.'

Robert Taylor reminded us that Queen Victoria, during her summer and autumn stay, would often visit the families in the cottages. In one of these dwellings lived a special friend:

Queen Victoria

'Now, Betsy!' said Her Majesty. 'You must come up to the castle for tea.'

Betsy politely refused.

'Well, Betsy,' said the Queen, 'are you afraid of me?'

'No, Ma'am,' came the reply. 'Not of you, but I am afraid of the man with the brass buttons who stands at the door.'

The Rev. Taylor, uncovered a further fund of delightful anecdotes from in and around the manse.

I liked the story about Queen Victoria, who, wearying of the rather long sermons at Crathie, was once asked by a zealous minister: 'Ma'am, what shall I preach about on Sunday?' to which she quickly replied: 'About ten minutes!'

12 February 1967(P)

Letter from America

The modern world is largely composed of democracies, republics and what some think of as anachronistic monarchies. Alistair Cooke spoke of the follies of pomp and circumstance in such a world. I always admire Mr. Cooke's hawk-eyed observation of American life, his urbanity, his cool detachment. Yet I detected an unusual note of cynicism seeping into his account of the recent arrival in New York of a monarch from the Old World, a diligent monarch who, dissatisfied with the futile debates of his parliament, suspended it and ruled the country by himself from his ten palaces. His opulent arrival in the New World was, to say the least, untimely.

Alistair Cooke

In a week, therefore, in which Mr. Kosygin dined at Buckingham Palace in a business suit, and Haile Selassie, King of Kings, appeared in New York looking rather like 'a professor of theology on holiday', King Hassan II of Morocco arrived in the United States accompanied by a *maître d'hotel*, a royal chef, four assistant cooks, a guard of honour and a vast retinue of over a hundred and thirty staff, occupying one complete floor of the Plaza Hotel. After all, the King of Morocco was hoping for a loan, at a time when the United States is attempting to dispel the notion that dollars are to be had for the asking.

Mr. Cooke's sarcasm reached its peak in recounting the tale of the wine-red carpet which did not arrive in time to 'ease the strain of His Majesty's placing his foot on American soil'. The subject gave Mr. Cooke an admirable opportunity to show his mettle in the sense of form, balance, accuracy, and a refreshing sprinkle of peppery humour that go to make an original and engaging political commentator.

*

Life and Beyond

27 May 1966 (P)

Measuring Time

'Breakfast Time Magazine' considered among other topics the question of the calendar. Dr. Willard E. Evans has campaigned since 1922 to revise the present system. Under his revised calendar, every year would begin on a different day of the week. There would be 91 days in each quarter, plus New Year's Day, which would be a world-wide holiday. I am amazed that, neat as the scheme may be, an enthusiast and scholar on the subject, such as Dr. Evans, could not see that, after so much 'timely' research, the scheme was unworkable.

26 May 1966 (U)

Happiness is Egg-shaped

Ruby Taylor presented 'Our Age', a programme about growing old. Pamela Muffin from the hotel business, Paul Thomas from industrial training, and Paul Russell, a law student, were asked a number of questions.

From my notes they went as follows:

Does the thought of growing old frighten you?

P.M.: Yes. Losing one's faculties. Awful!
P. T.: No. The prospect of a good pension helps.
P. R. It scares me. The loneliness, the lack of money. The only answer is to get married and have masses of kids. Then they can keep you.

What do you think about church-going?

P. R. The Church has to move with the times.
P. M. It gives you all sorts of guilt complexes. We're more educated now. We don't need a god when science compensates.
P. T. I believe in God when I need to. It is not necessary to go to church to do that.

Who do you think are more out of touch, the old or the young?

P. R. The old are the mainstream of life, politics and fashion. Young people look to the Labour Party for new ideas.
P. M. The old are in touch with human relations in general, but not in touch with the young.

What do you think about outlandish views and styles?

P. R. I don't mind the long hair as long as they wash it. Their shirts could get a bit shorter.
P. T. As the girls' tops get lower and the skirts get shorter, I do wonder when and where they're going to meet!

One contributor claimed old age came when you could remember the avuncular voices of Flotsam and Jetsam with their homespun advice in the early days of the BBC. The worst thing about old age is its unpredictability. You just have to be sure to keep your enthusiasm for life, keep your energy, be tenacious and, above all, keep a sense of humour.

Actress Patricia Hayes had a word or two to say about old age too: 'I don't enjoy it when I look forward but I do enjoy it when I look back....'appiness is egg-shaped'!

From my notebook: *16 May 1966*

Too Much Choice

It has been suggested [there was a scribbled note on my desk when I arrived this morning] that I should review the programme on 'Comprehensives' with Secretary-of-State Crossland. It is all about long terms, lack of money and selection at eleven.

On the other hand, the next best thing would be to listen in to the Commonwealth Festival events (not my remit!) Then, there is a feature on royal couturier Hardy Amies and an intriguing piece about Aubrey Beardsley, who produced a series of illustrations, 'grossly indecent even by modern standards,' and died of consumption at the age of twenty-five. (Beardsley's work is currently on exhibition at the Victoria and Albert Museum).

But time is short and, at the Editor's suggestion, I have to tackle the programme on Boros's concepts: 'Death is the birth of volition'; 'Death is the place of total intuition and complete remembrance'; Death is 'an abyss of existential homelessness' — and so on. I have to grapple with these concepts by midnight tomorrow — my deadline — and I have little hope of achieving a satisfactory piece by then.

So I must not indulge myself in an appraisal of Amies' fripperies of fashion, nor the phallic propensities of Beardsley's art, and I am disinclined to leap into the murky waters of 'Comprehensives'!

I am afraid I shall end up writing nothing on Boros, or at least only a few lines. The whole thing has brought on an attack of writer's block.

17 May 1966 (P)

Death and the Philosophers

Anthony Kenny has written a penetrating analysis of the nature of death. His argument is taken from the writings of the Hungarian Jesuit philosopher and theologian, Ladislaus Boros, starting with Boros's first premise: 'Death is the birth of volition.' You need to have a clinical mind to navigate the twists and turns of Boros's theory as set down in his principal work, *The Moment of Truth*. Yet, as Dr. Kenny observes, there are fallacies behind some of Boros's argument, and he suggests illuminating comparisons with Professor Ryle's work on the same subject, *The Concept of Mind*.

*

31 January 1967 (P)

Time Considered

Human nature being what it is, recent critics of BBC talks may have switched on just too late to hear Malcolm Muggeridge analysing Time and Eternity. If that is the case, they missed a good piece of broadcasting. Of course, the poetry of his terms of reference was inevitable: 'Eternity cannot end because it never began'. 'Time is our prison and our habitat.' If it had not been for that persuasive voice, the statement that 'deeds belong to time, ideas to eternity' might have seemed suspect.

Archbishop Bloom and a Buddhist nun carried on the discussion: life forever renews itself (even Mao Tse Tung approves of the 'regeneration' idea), the ultimate end is Nirvana — 'the repose of individual feeling merged into the whole of being, like a drop of water that melts into the ocean'. Thankfully, 'condensation' came about unexpectedly when all three speakers unanimously upheld the sanctity of the individual.

*

20 March 1967 (P)

Living Longer

Some people believe life to be a long preparation for something more desirable. Others, like Sir Paul Dukes, are convinced that the span of life can be extended by philosophical media. 'Slowness and thoroughness are the keys to long life.' 'Yet, even in the most optimistic conditions, I am three minutes from the grave.' Judging from Sir Paul's meandering conversational style, he must mean that slowness and thoroughness are synonymous with tedium and repetition, which may, alas, be the very stuff of life for some. I have no bone to pick with Sir Paul. He is a venerable thinker and a relaxed broadcaster.

Unfortunately, those of us who want to give more to life than just the humdrum nine-to-five routine will never be satisfied with a life that is not, to some extent, a race against time, a struggle against the impedimenta of philistinism and mediocrity. Sir Paul has won that battle, but for most of us the conditions are never completely optimistic. Success is an elusive commodity and the effort required to achieve it is difficult to sustain.

18 March 1967 (U)

What is Life?

This week I have been reminded of some uncomfortable truths in the words of a number contributors to 'The Spoken Word'. Sensible advice about growing old was delivered straight from the shoulder by that veteran diplomat, Sir Paul Dukes, who emphasised the importance of 'slowness and thoroughness'. 'Do the right thing slowly' seems to have been his principal motto, though in real life circumstances rarely afford us such an opportunity. The realisation that every moment of our lives we are a mere three minutes from the grave is startling, to say the least. The problem as Sir Paul sees it is how to extend our lives beyond our three-score-years-and-ten and still retain the quality of our allotted time. 'As age advances, let speed

Winston Churchill

diminish' he calmly advises us.

Few of us are likely to have a chance to shine in old age, but why shouldn't we have our moment of glory? Ellen Harris, recently retired from Reuters, gave a graphic account of Winston Churchill's famous walk from Downing Street to the Houses of Parliament on his way to announce the end of hostilities in 1945. He was just over seventy years of age. As he entered the House, MP's threw their order papers in the air and cheered. Ellen describes the emotion of that stupendous moment in history. She remembered having to give in to tears as she looked down on the scene from the Press Gallery, and how, on Winston's way out, the crowds surged forward to touch him as if to receive his blessing. He waived the police cordon aside saying: 'Leave them alone. It's their day.'

Small moments, too, can stay with us for a lifetime, as 'Sports Report' revealed when Leary Constantine described growing up in Port of Spain. In his courting days he had to walk two miles to the station and back, down a quiet country road in the dark — and he was afraid of the dark! He always had the sensation of being followed, and always he had the shade of his dead brother, Rodway, walking in front of him.

I am left this week with a small cameo, an image of old Tom Phelps, a Thames Waterman since he was nineteen, retiring at last after the toss-up for the Oxford and Cambridge boat race. He could remember how it all was long before the advent of broadcasting, when it was 'a very quiet affair!'

*

6 February 1967 (P)

Science and Mysticism

Three religious thinkers presented a fine composite picture of that earnest endeavour that besets all who choose to isolate themselves from the common stream of life. Teilhard de Chardin, the French mystic, was the subject of a penetrating discussion by six eminent scholars, who answered questions put to them by Vernon Sproxton.

Teilhard had known anguish of the existential kind, just as Kierkegaard had. Out of the experience arose a positive vision in evolutionary perspective, concerning the *telos*, or 'end-result/end in view' concept of our future. Teilhard's great contribution to modern thought was a new association of the scientific, the political and the religious. In this sense, Christ's teachings are not necessarily inconsistent with those of Marx and Darwin.

6 February 1967 (U)

No Ease in Zion

Last autumn, London hosted the Annual General Conference of the Chardin Association. Vernon Sproxton thought it a good idea to bring together in the studio some of the speakers from the Conference, among whom were Claude Cuénot (Teilhard de Chardin's biographer), Francis Elliott SJ (Professor of Biochemistry at Leopoldville, Congo Republic), Roger Garaudy (Director of the Centre for Marxist Studies and Research in Paris and Professor of Philosophy at Poitiers), P.G. Fothergill (Senior Lecturer in Botany at Newcastle), Bernard Towers (Lecturer in Anatomy, and Fellow of Jesus College, Cambridge), and Andrew Dyson (Chaplain of Ripon Hall, Oxford). Judging from such an array of intellect, one could expect a fairly challenging hour's listening, which certainly proved to be the case.

Teilhard de Chardin, the only religious thinker to have a society named after him, was a French Jesuit scientist and a writer on religion. Such a combination of science and religion should certainly provide plenty of food for thought and perhaps even give a more identifiable impression of this great writer, as discussed by such a distinguished collection of luminaries on the subject.

Cuénot began by considering Teilhard's important theme: the reconciliation of mankind with itself. Elliott introduced the idea that Teilhard extended the boundaries of scientific knowledge by moving science onto theological ground. Fothergill referred to the pastoral influences of his writings and the nature of his appeal to the man in the street. Towers spoke of the English establishment's prejudice, though admitting that most eminent scientists did recognize Teilhard's work as being a vital contribution to our knowledge.

Dyson explained that English philosophers were suspicious largely because they came to Teilhard's work from the traditional empiricist and positivist positions. Yet, according to Cuénot, there was a strong influence of English pragmatism which sets him firmly in the stream of English thought. Garaudy had a more visionary approach, suggesting that Teilhard's philosophy provided us with 'a world vision for our time', appealing to the 'increasing metamorphosis of man', possessing the 'optimism of a true master of the *joie de vivre*' and seeing the world as 'a construction site for the future.'

A compelling part of the discussion centred on the concept of the *telos*, or 'end-view', which Christ placed as the *omega* of evolution — Christ the Redeemer, without whom man is unable to restore himself to his rightful place in the world. Teilhard's view was, in a sense, a 'naïve optimism' dominated by his powerful belief in the resurrection of Christ.

On the other hand, Teilhard's philosophy is realistic enough to foresee the possibility of the failure of evolution. His Davidic view of eschatology was tempered by the belief that, in spite of death, judgement and destiny, 'all manner of thing shall be well' — the very belief promulgated by Dame Julian of Norwich. There was, in effect, no escape from 'original sin' because of its cosmic and collective nature — 'we are all responsible'. All this makes 'evolutive creation very fragile', a thought which, as with Kirkegaard, led to terrible moments of 'existential anguish'.

For all this, the discussion seemed to me to end on a depressingly negative note. There was 'no ease in Zion', no positive comfort, since it was impossible to prove scientifically that the world was good. It seemed that the Teilhardians' greatest achievement was to form an alliance with the Marxists! At this point I lost my way with words, words, words, and, leaving my unfinished notes on the desk, went upstairs to bed.

2 February 1967 (P)

'Love Bade Me Welcome'

The mind and spirit of Simone Weil were discussed by Barbara Bray (see pp 86-89). Convinced as a child, of the mediocrity of her abilities, Simone Weil* progressed through a remarkable life of renunciation and asceticism to a vision of Christ that was close to that of the saint. She had a 'staggering insight into all kinds of human suffering.' Affliction, for her, was a way to God. 'Total refusal in saintliness.' She studied and learnt by heart the English metaphysical poets, so that when she recited George Herbert's poem 'Love', Christ himself came down and took possession of her.

Her feeling for human suffering was immense. At the last, she could not even eat the food given to her on her sick-bed, knowing that it might serve more usefully to relieve the sufferings of the French prisoners-of-war. Thus, her end seemed to me, at first, to have the mark of futility about it: to have starved herself to death at the age of thirty-four when she had so much to give to posterity. But the measure of her sacrifice remains forever a supreme moment of spiritual endeavour, of her overpowering love for her fellow human beings and of her immaculate devotion to a Divine Ordinance. Patience Collier's readings were often touching, even at times moving.

2 and 6 January 1967 (P)

The Meaning of Life

From the dawn of human history, man has needed gods. Some men have worshipped money or power, while others have sought less tangible gods, gods who could give greater meaning than man could to the sufferings and tribulations of this world.

Much has been made of Prospero's farewell and Macbeth's dismal soliloquy on the meaning of life. Certainly, few of us who have, at one time or another, come face to face with death, or suffered anguish or pain, can have failed to ask ourselves the unanswerable question: 'What does all this mean?' Whether we accept the existentialist or the Christian view of the hereafter, it seems that between these two extremes there are as many variations as there are people who ponder the question.

Great men of vision like Pascal and Blake found answers that were satisfactory in specific conditions. But what of the rest of us? We might discover solutions in any number of books: Thornton Wilder's *The Bridge of San Luis Rey,* in which love is 'the only survival, the only meaning'; or Voltaire's *Candide* in which, in 'this best of all possible worlds', we are advised to return from our travels (in his case 'travails') to 'cultivate our gardens' in the metaphorical sense. The *Book of Job,* perhaps, may teach us the ways of unquestioning stoicism.

The problem is not, however, solved in the mere classification of it, as those who listened to Professor R. W. Hepburn's talks on 'The Meaning of Life' might have felt. He discussed a number of answers that might satisfy us and how far they would count in a final assessment. Life, for example, could be meaningful if there is a resurrection of the dead. Life could be meaningful if it is also purposeful.

I was reminded of Thomas Huxley's analogy of life as a game of chess, and his disapprobation of the father who allowed his son to grow up 'without knowing a pawn from a knight'. In other words, to live well, we have to know the rules of the game.

The most stimulating and accessible part of this talk concerned Tolstoy's periodic sensation of the meaninglessness of life, its paradoxical deadness, which he called an 'arrest of time'.

At this point, I grew impatient. This listening business became very hard work. How can the problem be dealt with in a twenty-minute talk? I began to battle with the Professor's voice, for one thing. His soporific monotones and arid philosophical abstractions made me chary of his neat theories, which ultimately, in his second talk, I was convinced would fail to come to any satisfying conclusion. After the quotation from Yeats about life being 'a preparation for something that never happens', I found myself back at the beginning again, asking the unanswerable, like Blake's 'Tiger': 'What immortal hand or eye, could frame thy fearful symmetry?' and, as in his 'Auguries of Innocence', trying with all my human limitations: —

> To see a World in a Grain of Sand,
> And a Heaven in a Wild flower,
> Hold Infinity in the palm of your Hand,
> And Eternity in an hour.

I turned to Cyril Connolly's *The Unquiet Grave* with solace and relief to discover that the secret of happiness (and therefore life itself) is 'to be in harmony with existence, to be always calm', and to know that 'human life is understandable only as a state of transition.'

Well! If Professor Hepburn has posed a question about the meaning of life, then I doubt if philosophy can answer it. However, when at a loss for an answer, I told myself, try a few well-worn lines from Shakespeare: 'There are more things in Heaven and Earth, Horatio, than are dreamt of in your philosophy.'

'Cogito ergo sum!' Yes, if we humans are thinking creatures, then we must know by definition that we exist. At least that must have something to do with the meaning of life.

In my confusion, I was literally saved by the school bell when listening in to the Home Service programme, 'The Secret World of the Playground', which afforded such unexpected pleasures — in particular, the little girl at her lessons on the first day at school, who wistfully whispered to a friend: 'I got it all wrong 'cos I was thinking!'

6 January 1967 (U)

Further Deliberations on 'The Meaning of Life'

I thought 'The Meaning of Life' had escaped me after last week's talk by R. W. Hepburn, Professor of Philosophy at Edinburgh University, but this difficult subject cropped up again this week in a second talk.

The Professor began asking some perplexing questions: 'Is the will free?' and 'Is human life meaningful?' The answer to the first could possibly be in the negative. Some might answer the second by saying: 'Only if there is resurrection of the dead,' but this would be grossly oversimplifying the matter.

'Life is not a word or a sentence,' says the Professor. 'We cannot think about the linguistic meaning when we think about the meaning of life.' With all the claims about 'God' and 'the Hereafter', we find that religious statements cannot guarantee answers to the problem. 'For life to be meaningful it must be purposeful'. Having purpose involves a divine 'purposer'. So if man could be seen in such a role — he could be, and almost certainly is, 'the tool to be used in the working of a divine plan.' There is a need for some 'supernatural insight', and who can provide it but man, the quintessential link between planet Earth, 'God', and the universe.

In Russia, the peasants knew how to live out their lives, close to earth — and therefore nearer to God — in contrast to a great writer like Tolstoy, with his debilitating lack of purpose, lack of will and sense of futility. Life for Tolstoy was all 'vanity and brevity'.

No! Once we have arrived at an understanding of the meaning of life, then we can know how to live it. Some individuals try the psychological or imaginative approach, but many take the religious path towards a kind of faith, though sometimes a blind faith. By the fact of life that we are presented with when we are born, we enter the maze of life, and spend our whole time in this world trying to find our way out of it.

That is what the meaning of life is all about, and, in this second talk, Professor Hepburn has tackled the question and its solution with consummate skill and insight.

13 September 1966 (U)

Rosh Hashanah

I was initiated into the mysteries of the Jewish New Year with a most erudite analysis by Dayan Dr. M. S. Lew, a member of the Chief Rabbi's Ecclesiastical Court.

Dr. Lew poses a number of sombre questions. At a time when we have 'an all-embracing educational system' and 'widespread dissemination of knowledge', why is there so much violence, so much crime, so much killing? Our world is full of doubts and dilemmas. What has happened to 'the good life'? Why are the fundamentals of faith so challenged and called into question? What has happened to the spirit of man in a world dominated by materialism and technology?

Have we not heard these daunting themes many times before? Every now and again someone more far-seeing than ourselves, someone in our fast-moving world of getting and spending who has found a moment to reflect on this almost insuperable dilemma comes forward with a warning, stops us in our tracks and forces us to reassess the causes of our predicament.

Dr. Lew seeks to remind us of what, deep down, we already know, that beyond the 'enthroned science and technology', beyond the mind and the intellect, there is a world of the spirit that few of us have time to consider. Furthermore, 'the spirit craves for inward satisfaction and fulfilment.' What our age desperately needs is 'a fusion of knowledge of the heart with a knowledge of the mind', a place where 'the light of that wisdom, love and compassion' combine to 'inform and enhance life on the higher plane.'

This is all very well but how many of us can find the time for prayer and meditation, let alone think about 'the higher plane'? But this is what the Jewish New Year is all about: it heralds the advent of a time of 'universal renewal' and 'a fuller life....illumined by the spirit of God and enriched by sincerity and devotion, humility and honour'. The Jewish New Year greeting is a petition for 'a year of happiness, blessedness and peace.' For most Jews, 'Rosh Hashanah' is a time of personal renewal too, accompanied by 'a spirit of inward joyfulness and confidence.'

All the terminology of Dr. Lew's argument is disturbingly abstract for the average human being who is constrained to live by rote, coping in many places in our fractured world with poverty, disease and a decline in moral standards. Old Testament values, enshrined in the 'Ten Commandments' and 'The Sermon on the Mount', need to be restated if this 'wisdom, love and compassion' Dr. Lew speaks of are to be revived.

Mind and Body

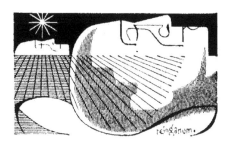

19 January 1967 (U)

Health and Science

In these days of relative freedom in sexual expression, it may well be unwise for parents to convey to their children the facts of life by drawing invidious analogies from the animal kingdom. Somerset Maugham wrote an instructive story about a son who turned out to know a good deal more about girls than his father had learnt in a lifetime. Nowadays, that seems rather the general rule than the exception.

For the sensitive child, growing-up can be a daunting process, as James Joyce suggested in his clever pun on Jung and Freud. The frightening and often traumatic phases of childhood and adolescence were never more vividly described than in those first memorable pages of James Joyce's *A Portrait of the Artist as a Young Man* and Somerset Maugham's *Of Human Bondage*.

Michael Smee's analysis of the relationship of health to science achieved a delicate balance between the psychological and the physiological aspects, giving just the right degree of friendliness and impartiality the subject required. His task was considerably eased by Dr. James Tanner, who spoke with a frankness and lucidity that would not have been possible when I was a child thirty years ago.

16 January 1967 (P)

What is a Freudian in 1967?

To learn that the *ego* is not master in its own house is frightening. Neurotic symptoms arise from the conflict between instinctual drive (the '*id*') and moral demands upon the self ('the *super-ego*'). It therefore seemed to me that Anna Freud's research into the 'conflict-free sphere of the ego' was at least one of the vital developments in psychiatric treatment which has come into its own since *The Interpretation of*

Dreams first appeared just over fifty years ago. Dr Penelope Leach has attempted to trace how far techniques in psychoanalysis have changed since that time. War in the mind will never, perhaps, be resolved for many victims of chronic neuroses, but Dr Leach provided gleams of hope in her programme. Alas, few specialists possess good voices for broadcasting but she spoke with such clarity that the complexities, the frustrations, the inhibitions and the fixations of the neurotic state seemed more deeply understandable than even the least informed layman like myself could have hoped.

Sigmund Freud - 'What's on a man's mind!'

The purpose of research and treatment must always be 'the relief of human mental suffering'. Part of the discussion centred on the crude and intense qualities of childhood longing, especially sexual longing, which frequently converts itself into a form of aggression.

In explaining the reasons for childhood depressions, Dr. Tanner had spoken of the rapid sweep of the emotions from ecstasy to gloom that mysteriously beset the child. Dr. Leach carried the question a stage further by telling us that 'depression' was aggression turned against the self. It was Jung who drew our attention to the *libido*, not, as Freud does, as an expression of the sexual instinct but simply as a will to live and survive.

*

16 January 1967 (U)

'Jung and Easily Freudened!'

Presenter Penelope Leach, of the Department of Social Psychology at the London School of Economics, writes in the current issue of the *Radio Times* that 'psychoanalysis is a living and ongoing theory, a dynamic treatment method, and a viable approach to an ever-changing society.'

However Freud intended his method to develop in the future, he certainly could not have imagined what critical scrutiny his theories would be subjected to in a time of mass culture and over-population. Dr.

Leach's excellent presentation, 'What is a Freudian in 1967?', was clear and precise in its detail, and was helpful in guiding the benighted listener through the labyrinthine paths of the Freudian canon.

Freud was a neurologist of the Viennese school and much of his work was concerned with the treatment of hysteria and the complexes, fixations, frustrations and inhibitions that assail the twentieth-century psyche. At least his theories brought a greater tolerance of the neuroses and psychological pressures in modern society.

Sigmund Freud

At a deeper level, Jung placed more emphasis on the 'collective unconscious'. In such a variable 'sea of troubles', mental symptoms appear to remain constant, whatever social changes come about. Childhood longings, however crude and intense they may be, still occur universally, and the libido will always be a force to contend with as long as human beings exist. In contemporary terms, the aggression that comes from a strong libido is frequently replaced by depression, which is, as Professor Leach points out, only aggression turned against the self — a condition of 'self-reproach'.

It seems that analysis does not necessarily guarantee cure; it can, however, help the patient to live with the condition. It 'attempts to pinpoint where the disturbance lies'. Most conflicts, it seems, have their origins in infancy — an aspect that came after Freud. Homosexuality was a case in point. The manner of 'the physical separation of mother and child' after birth has some oedipal bearing on the development of the child. Clearly, it is a misunderstanding of Freud's basic principles to attribute everything to sex.

All this discussion among distinguished scholars on the subject has after all served to show that Freud may be laughing in his grave. He would no doubt have been gratified to know that a group of distinguished psychologists and psychiatrists were willing to spare the time to talk about his theories in such a diverse manner. No wonder we're all confused! Do I hear you protest?

2 April 1967 (P)

The Doctor's New Dilemma

As far back as 1911, in an extended preface to *The Doctor's Dilemma*, George Bernard Shaw affirmed: 'I do not know a single thoughtful and well-informed person who does not feel that the tragedy of illness at present is that it delivers you helplessly into the hands of a profession which you deeply mistrust.' Much of the Preface echoes the thoughts of any prospective patient as he enters the ward, hands over his clothes, and signs away his body to the surgeon's knife. Unfortunately, we have not yet reached that blissful Utopia where pain and disease are unknown. There is no such thing as perfect health any more than there is a perfect health service.

A good deal of my childhood was spent in the sick-room and the ward. Our family doctor was the most amiable man alive. 'Well now,' he would say, 'shall we have the pink or the white medicine today?' I never had any confidence in his being able to relieve my suffering any more than my dear parents had. Year after year, and many sick-rooms later, he would come up with the same pink (camomile) or white medicine (zinc), just as if medical practice had not changed at all in the meantime.

War, however, begets research and leads to new discoveries in the ways and means of physical and mental survival. Almost overnight, technology out-sped time. No more 'pink medicines', nor any scrap of the medical practice they stood for. Today, with such rapid technological advancement, other more delicate problems have manifested themselves.

Thena Heshel's penetrating discussion on the new dilemma facing the medical profession these days delved deeply into the ethical considerations involved in the making of decisions about the welfare and even the life of a patient under treatment. Patrick Feeny's questions revealed a perceptive grasp of the subject and led to important statements from the panel on the use of new discoveries like the kidney machine, and the role of the community in medical welfare. A professor of moral theology came to the interesting conclusions concerning the ethical education of doctors, balanced against their technical education, which I thought to be of vital importance. Nevertheless, technological gain has, in the long run, to be balanced against biological loss. Not since Patricia Penn's documentary on 'War in the Countryside' have I heard anything quite so harrowing as the woman describing in detail the last weeks of her father's life in hospital, as the doctors struggled to keep him alive. But the prime aim is, and always must be, the good of the patient. The Professor put the matter very well by remarking that medicine is like grace: it is meant to co-operate with nature, not oppose it. The old adage about the functions of the doctor still stands: to cure sometimes, relieve often, and comfort always.

*

March 1966 (U)

Crisis in the Ward

That old investigatory stalwart, Edgar Lustgarten, has been going the rounds of our hospitals recently, trying to find out a few home truths about our downtrodden nursing profession. Tony Van Den Berg tracked down a few nurses and asked them some pointed questions in the process.

One thing is for sure: there is a real demand for nurses and more work than the existing nurses can cope with. Unfortunately, there is a serious 'wastage' problem since one in three drop out of the profession for a variety of reasons. A good many applicants have no realistic idea of what is likely to be demanded of them. A few (two per cent) left because the salary was too low, which suggests a change of attitude from the time when vocational considerations were paramount.

At first it is hard, since student nurses train on the wards and experience a pretty brutal encounter with death and disease. Unfortunately, only one in four who qualify intend to go on working in hospitals. After all, a nursing qualification is an international passport to travel. In the United States starting salaries are in the region of £2,000, and jobs are often located in exotic situations.

What is not acceptable is having to do the cleaner's work as well as acting as orderlies, making beds, checking laundry, serving meals and taking blood specimens. Many nurses dislike working in theatre and are disinclined to operate machinery when they could be dealing hands on with patients. And always there is the discipline, the exhaustion, and the gentleness required towards patients.

Apparently, there is a Ministry proposal afoot suggesting the idea of 'ward housekeepers' and 'theatre technicians'. But what comes out clearly in this programme is the desperate need to cut down on clerical duties, messenger services and sterilisation services.

Salaries come to £160 million per annum, a third of the total cost of the scheme. The system needs an injection of imagination and flair from the Body Politic if it is not to suffer a breakdown.

7, 15, 22 and 30 March 1966(P)

Biological Backlash

The impact of technology on the huge complexity of the natural world can sometimes be grave and irredeemable. Man can go too far too quickly and nature lashes back at him. In four documentary-style discussions, Gerald Leach questioned a number of distinguished biologists in order to assess our chances of what he chooses to call 'a dignified future'. The production by Mick Rhodes had a neat appreciation of essentials, drawing together the various threads of fact and speculation to a final vision of hope in 'Dreams and Goals'.

Professor J. N. Morris emphasized that preventive medicine, though highly speculative, was by no means a piece of science fiction, but the only means of using technology as a long-term answer to chronic diseases and their cure.

Dr. Alex Comfort was for encouraging emotionally-informed spontaneity as a means of achieving greater mental and physical stability. Man must learn to control himself, but not deny — a statement which seemed to me to require further qualification.

8 March 1967 (P)

'Things Fall Apart'

Anne Owen's touching programme about the plight of schizophrenic sufferers was touching because there was poetry in the self-searching of those fragmented minds: the woman from Birmingham who saw hallucinatory tigers prowling about her room when she gazed into the mirror, the man who felt a woman's face trying to push itself though his features. Then there was a man who suddenly knew of the existence of a horrific force at work, a mental telepathic wave that could split the brain. It fills one's heart with feelings akin to grief to hear of such sufferings.

'Things Fall Apart.' What more apt title could be found for such a condition of the mind? The quotation, from 'The Second Coming' by W. B. Yeats, continues more ominously, for 'The centre cannot hold.' Most touching of all was the man who, in his hallucination, visited a garden and heard the voice of the Virgin 'coming as if from a star', and describing how the Angel Gabriel bent down and blew the breath of birth and life into Her body. The vision always ended with his feeling the breath of the Virgin herself, filling him with life.

So what can technology do for such conditions? Only drugs and electrical treatments help, but cannot cure. 'Take a pill, take two pills', and you are, as they say, 'back to normal'. Nothing could be farther from the truth.

Elsewhere, the work of curing, relieving and comforting goes on. 'I was reproached,' wrote Shaw, 'during the performances of *The Doctor's Dilemma*, because I made the artist a rascal, the journalist an illiterate incapable, and all the doctors 'angels'. But I did not go beyond the warrant of my own experience.'

14 March 1967 (U)

Confused Thoughts

All this week, my thoughts and feelings have been centred on Anne Owen's programme about schizophrenia. Perhaps because there is a Blake-like inspiration endemic in the elaborate imagery of the condition, we who enjoy the orderliness of so-called 'normality' can never hope to experience its exotic power. We have a sense that the schizophrenic state contains within it an arcane language the meaning of which is forever denied us, a language that perhaps only a Blake, a Coleridge, a De Quincey, or an Edgar Allan Poe had some inkling of. There is at its centre both a beauty and a terror that is denied ordinary mortals, and which, if they only knew, is an unenviable torment of the cruellest kind for the sufferer. 'The schizophrenic,' says the introductory piece in the *Radio Times*, 'lives in a world where thought and feeling are disconnected, where voices speak from nowhere and identity loses its meaning, Even the language sometimes needs to be decoded.'

In any case, which of us really recognises the exact boundary between what we feel and what we are? The poet, Jacques Prévert, wrote of the division of the self:

> Nous sommes sortis tous les deux
>   Moi avec moi.
> (*We went out walking together/ I and myself*)

But are we speaking of illusions or delusions? Is the dreamer in the dream-world really awake? In every case 'the dreamer' is the patient and 'the patient' the dreamer. Nothing and everything seems real. He genuinely believes he can save the world, can work miracles, can will the light to go on, the fire to light itself. These 'primary delusions' can be accompanied by 'secondary delusions' in which extraordinary events are happening around them. But where does delusion stop and hallucination begin? In such a state of consciousness, queer things can happen to you, inexplicable things, unworldly things, and terrifying things. A mental-telepathic wave causes unpleasant bodily sensations and you feel as if your brain is splitting in two. You see nightmarish images, hear 'gangs of persecutors' coming to hound you, and you even hear the voice of God speaking to you in person. All you can do is 'retreat from the world'.

Writing to *The Times,* * William Sargant, of the Department of Psychological Medicine, St. Thomas's Hospital, criticising the content of the television play *In Two Minds*, claimed that 'one in 15 of the population are due to enter psychiatric hospitals in their lifetime.' If this statistic is true then it is also alarming, is it not? But he claims that, whilst there was a widespread use of psychotherapy and social therapy in mental hospitals in the interwar years, from the 1950s, cases of schizophrenia were treated in psychiatric wards of the general teaching hospitals, with additional modern physical treatments to aid social rehabilitation, and with more satisfactory results.

Beyond these confused thoughts, this is a seriously specialised subject fit only for the trained mind, and the layman like myself enters dangerous waters if he attempts to comment only in the most general terms on its complexities.

* 8 March 1967

A closer look at the portrait sketch of Freud on page 177 will reveal the secret of what is on a man's mind!

Music and Myth

10 February 1967 (P)

A Silence Filled with Greek

The artist, Michael Ayrton, has spoken of that 'special dimension of immortality' that the Greek landscape possesses, 'rocks which cradle legends'. He had already experienced this timelessness in Italy, where, for him as for many of us, 1497 and 1947 existed simultaneously as one 'co-existent hallucination'.

On first hearing, I thought of this programme more as a splendid travelogue. There was just a shade of preciousness present in the self-revelation, a tinge of the intensely egocentric that betrayed a certain degree of 'emotion recollected in tranquillity'. There were actor friends, Leo Genn, Rex Warner, Katina Paxinou and Alexis Minotis, to keep the Daedalus image within the bounds of time and space, as well as to carry the spirit of Ayrton towards the sun. On second hearing, I saw that the emphasis was not Greece now, but art, timeless and aspiring.

10 February 1967 (U)

Labyrinthine Lucubrations

In Douglas Cleverdon's excellent production of artist and sculptor Michael Ayrton's *A Silence Filled With Greek*, the listener was asked to travel 'not wide but deep'. Beginning with some eerie electronic music simulating the echoing interior of a labyrinth, we embarked on a journey of discovery, or perhaps self-discovery.

For Ayrton, the Greek landscape had 'a dimension of immortality', where he was content to wander among 'rocks which cradle legends'. According to his wife, Elizabeth, he became 'god-struck', and the god was Apollo, through whose eyes he could observe 'the very marvel of the earth', 'backwards down the flight of Daedalus,' for in those early times, 'the gods lived closer to men than they do now'.

From time to time, one became conscious of a certain preciousness in the self-revelatory style of an intensely egocentric spirit. The gradual unfolding of the mysteries of the Minoan civilisation revealed as much about Ayrton the man as it did about Ayrton the artist. For him, Crete was the very beginning of his obsession with the Daedalus myth.

The discussion was greatly enhanced by the inclusion of Don Burke, Leo Genn, translator and author of books about Greece, Rex Warner, film director Basil Wright, and for good measure, the voices on record of Alexis Minotis and Katina Paxinou.

The inordinately passionate Madame Paxinou spoke of her 'ferocious disgust' of our pronunciation of Ancient Greek in the English style of Erasmus, but then Greeks are very proud of their traditions. Later in the programme, theory seemed not to follow practice when she spoke of her performance of *Elektra* as being 'in a modern tongue which remains Greek, though it is not as Euripides would have understood it'. After all, no-one knows how Ancient Greek was actually spoken.

Myth comes about 'by the weathering of time', being accepted eventually as possessing something universal in the human mind. But myths are not in themselves history. 'If myths are lies, they are no less true to me than fact.'

On a more trivial note, Ayrton considered Greek food 'rather over-rated', Genn expressed a fairly universal impression of 'other aspects of Greek life', which I can only assume to have something to do with bazouki dancing and the ubiquitous stuffed vine-leaves washed down with rubbery-tasting *retsina*. But this is not the Greece we want to hear about. Let us go to Epidaurus.

We can cross the sea to Epidaurus from the island of Aegina. The atmosphere there, as we stand high up, overlooking the ancient amphitheatre, is uncanny. It is as if the rest of the world did not exist — a mysterious place where space and time are one and the same, and all the noise of the world is silenced. Ayrton and his friends took it in turns to break a match in the centre of the arena: it could be heard in every part of the theatre, throughout all the fourteen thousand seats.

It was through Genn that Ayrton met Minotis and Paxinou. 'When

Minotis speaks the role of Oedipus, the rocks reel and cringe from that agony.' This is undoubtedly true. When you have heard Ancient Greek spoken in the traditional way by specially trained Greek actors in an ancient amphitheatre built expressly for the purpose, you have heard the real thing, and you will never forget it. So it was for Ayrton. As if by osmosis, he was able to absorb the very essence of Greek art, sculpture, music and drama. 'I had become identified with Greece.'

Rex Warner claimed that the Greek language meant more to him than any other except English, for it held the key to 'realms of gold'. Since the day he had heard Gilbert Murray reading a few lines of Homer, Warner had experienced that sense of wonder and intimacy that a deep knowledge of the language can afford. Through the sounds and rhythms of the Ancient Greek vocabulary and metre, he could experience 'intimations of immortality'. Warner's contribution brought a real sense of immediacy to the programme at a point where 'one breaks out of a chrysalis and becomes aware of what one is'.

James Joyce

The Greek myths remain a potent force in western culture. The Daedalus myth is primarily a symbol of aspiration and creativity. Ayrton's obsessive preoccupation with this myth has dominated his later work. Like Orpheus, who was slain by Zeus for perfecting his art, the antithesis of the Daedalus myth lies at the heart of its Icarus analogue. Daedalus made wings of wax so that Icarus could fly sunwards into space. The sun melted his wings and he plunged into the sea. It was no wonder that James Joyce made such a powerful metaphor out of Daedalus in the writing of *Ulysses*. The gulf between the attainable and the unattainable can never be bridged. It is every artist's intention, as it was Ayrton's, to try to bridge that gulf, however elusive perfection may be.

I am reminded of W.H. Auden's poem, *Musée des Beaux Arts*, in which he describes his feelings and thoughts in the Parisian art gallery as he contemplates Brueghel's painting of the Icarus myth. We are shown the horrendous event of Icarus literally falling out of the sky, whilst below, for the peasants in the fields, life is going on in its matter-of-fact way:

> .....the sun shone
> As it had to on the white legs disappearing into the green
> Water; and the expensive delicate ship that must have seen
> Something amazing, a boy falling out of the sky,
> Had somewhere to get to and sailed calmly on.

It was not that no-one cared. It was simply that no-one was in a position to do anything about it. So they just went on carrying out their mundane tasks, just as we do when, enjoying our breakfast, we read in the morning newspaper of the death of a celebrity or a horrific genocidal massacre. The ancient myth survives to tell us something very important about our attitude to life.

W H Auden

*

From my notebook: *18 February 1967*

A reader wrote for information on the Daedalus myth.

Homeric Analogues

James Joyce, in his novel, *Ulysses*, introduces the reader to three principal characters: Leopold Bloom, his wife Molly Bloom, and Stephen Dedalus. The plot follows the wanderings of Stephen and Bloom through the streets of Dublin during the course of a single day. Leopold and Stephen are searching for their spiritual counterparts in 'Nighttown' (the centre of the labyrinth). The various episodes roughly follow the pattern of Homer's Odyssey, Stephen representing Telemachus, son of Odysseus, the childless Bloom is Odysseus, and Molly Bloom is Penelope. Joyce had already used Stephen as the hero (or anti-hero) in an earlier work,' Portrait of the Artist as a Young Man'.

In a famous passage, Stephen hears his name called by his school friends:

'Now, at the name of the fabulous artificer, he seemed to hear the noise of dim waves and to see a winged form flying above the waves and slowly climbing the air. What did it mean? Was it a quaint device opening a page of some medieval book of prophesies and symbols, a hawk-like man flying sunward above the sea, a prophecy of the end he had been born to serve and had been following through the mists of childhood and boyhood, a symbol of the artist forging anew in his workshop out of the sluggish matter of the earth a new soaring impalpable imperishable being?'

13 April 1967 (P)

The Voice of the Gods

If we imagine the substratum of everything in the universe as acoustic and vibratory, then we can understand better why men have sought to relate sounds like a roar, a whistle or a song to the ecstatic peaks of religious ritual: 'In the beginning was the Word, and the Word was a sound, and the sound shook the cosmos into life.' This was the beginning of A. L. Lloyd's penetrating account of what Sir Thomas Browne called 'the harmony of the spheres'. This 'holy rasp', says Mr. Lloyd, is an 'ecstasy of air'.

It is impossible to do justice to Lloyd's brilliant essay into the complex world of ethno-musicology. His deep feeling for language, his subtle descriptions of the physical and acoustic processes, made intriguing listening: the two wizards from New Guinea, who sang their sacred song through a bamboo tube, and the guttural *incalzando* of Tibetan priests chanting to the accompaniment of copper trumpets. No doubt, if a contemporary composer reproduced the sound of those exciting ximbombas, bull-roarers, rattles and eagle-wing flutes, he might well be acclaimed as an original.

13 April 1967 (U)

Aa-aa-um-mm-mm!

A. L. Lloyd deals with a profound aspect of the origin of sound in his talk on the Third Programme, 'The Voice of the Gods' — beginning with those 'all-creating' sounds manifest in cosmogonic myths — sounds beyond the reach of meaning, sounds ostensibly natural, like a sigh, a thunder-clap, a howling of the wind, but which belong to the inexplicable and the mystical, sounds having their origins beyond time and space.

In James Joyce's novel, *Ulysses*, he adopts the theory that all human society is subject to three distinct phases: the theocratic (government by priests), the aristocratic ('aristos' — government by the best), and the democratic ('demos' — government by the people). And because the democratizing process inevitably weakens the social structure through the proliferation of choice where everyone has a voice, the resulting state is 'chaos'. The only way to control the situation is through a 'happening' — some cataclysmic event that brings order out of chaos, restores the natural balance. In *Ulysses*, that event comes in a hundred-letter thunder-word that contains the secret of all destruction and creation. The destructive effect of the sound is devastating, with the result that the social order returns full circle to the rigorous theocratic regime. That thunder-word is 'the voice of the gods.' 'In the beginning was the Word, and the Word was a sound, and the sound shook the cosmos into life.'

To understand the process, Dr. Lloyd takes us to Mali (formerly part of the French Sudan) to visit the sorcerers of the Dogon people, who have come together to sing to the spirits. 'The place seems deserted, the silence broken by the distant barking of dogs. The witch-doctors squat in the moonlight, murmuring their ritual song that tells of the creation of man, the appearance of life, the animation of the world.' At this point, we hear unearthly guttural sounds — breathless, tuneless voices that reverberate through the air — strange, uncanny mantras that carry us beyond reality.

Halfway across the world, we meet these sounds again and again —

in the mountains of southern Peru, by the equatorial waters of the Orinoco — this manifestation of the sacred 'voice' set against the tapping sounds of maracas. This is what they call 'the holy rasp'. 'In sacred circumstances,' Dr. Lloyd explains, ' a feeling of radiant strength arises from deep, noisy breathing. By heavy exhalations, the witch-doctor emulates that dreadful wind that first blew into the cavern of nothingness and created the whole acoustic world, the same wind that in Hebrew belief was breathed on the mound of dust that became a man. By means of his intense respiration, the medicine man pretends to swallow the universe and then throw it up again by breathing out. He cultivates what Levi Strauss calls a kind of 'ecstasy of air.'

The subject is elaborate and complex, a brilliant study of our origins, taking us back into the farthest reaches of time before the Word was made flesh, before speech was uttered.

Dr. Lloyd's scholarship is awe-inspiring, so much so that I was constrained to ask for a copy of his script from the programme's producer, Douglas Cleverdon, to allow me to delve more deeply into this absorbing subject.

17 April 1967 (U)

The Xylophone

Douglas Cleverdon brought an equally comprehensive skill to two offerings, both entitled 'The Xylophone', in which Dr. A. M. Jones attempted to relate cultures of Africa and Indonesia through the history and development of this ancient instrument. He provided superb field recordings from many parts of Africa and the Far East. Though the series was recently considered unfavourably by the Nairobi conference on 'Historical Problems of the Pre-Colonial Era', Dr. Jones made the point that musical traditions can serve as a valid source of information, if not actual proof of the ancient communication of races, and developed theories of the pentatonic and heptatonic* scales with skill and insight.

* Five and seven notes respectively

17 April 1967 (U)

A Re-sounding Tinkle!

The most exotic musical sound to be found in Indonesia is the great box resonator called a 'metallophone'. Equally arresting is the sound made by 'two little bells held in the hand and clinked together,' says Dr. A.M. Jones, in the second of his Third Programme talks, 'and with a larger and no less exotic sound you can hear a complete xylophone orchestra.' Dr. Jones gave what turned out to be two far from ponderous talks on 'The Xylophone'.

It seems that, well before the beginning of the Christian era, the inhabitants of Indonesia and Cambodia were braving the stormy seas of the Indian Ocean to trade with Africa, bringing with them new ideas, new words and new musical instruments. The slave trade, which brought about an enforced migration of African slaves to the Americas, accounts for the appearance of a modified form of the xylophone in Guatemala and Ecuador. Even the American Indians made their own versions.

The xylophones, often highly ornamented with inlay and mother-of-pearl, are found from the Niger Basin as far as the Nile and from the Limpopo River on into Zambia. So, as far as Africa is concerned, the instrument is restricted to a clearly defined area.

The rhythms are exciting and syncopated. The hypnotic repetition of musical forms is strikingly contrasted with the high-pitched voices of the singers.

17 April 1967 (U)

Psychedelic Sound

Before I listened to Dr Jones's talk on 'The Xylophone', I would never have thought for one moment that I might be about to hear what might be described as the *sound* of a dream — an indescribably delicate combination of minute vibrations that fuse and interfuse in a multitude of forms and 'colours'. The fine-tuning of the western heptatonic scale and the Eastern equi-heptatonic scale had the strange effect, by ever-sharpening intervals, to lift the tones higher and higher. This, combined with the constantly variable *tempi* (as heard in Bali), made the strangest impression on me, as if in some imagined opium dream.

In Africa the equi-pentatonic scale has two-and-a-quarter tones between, giving a very strange effect. In the island of New Britain, two xylophones are played simultaneously on only two notes. In the islands of Papua, a 'free' xylophone is found on which the keys have no fixed position. In Uganda, two performers play the same instrument, the player placing the notes in between the first player's. In Portuguese East Africa one can hear the remarkable sound of an orchestra of thirty-two xylophones tuned together in consort — "a royal and grand sound" with a bass of almost contrapuntal form weaving in and out below the higher tones.

I had no idea that I was to be led into such a secret world of strange rhythms and exotic sounds that could, I imagine, only be experienced in the pleasure domes of Xanadu, strange echoes of another world than ours. Underlying the music was a complex and subtle system made of gossamer, a magical intermingling of an almost mystical nature.

21 April 1967 (P)

The Anxiety of Art

In the early 1950s, in New York, a group of young composers, including John Cage and Morton Feldman, were experimenting with new forms of musical expression. Introduced by the English composer, Roger Smalley, and questioned by the painter and poet, Andrew Forge, Mr. Feldman put on record some of his views on a new compositional aesthetic in which notation would play a minor part only, and graphical representation (through the dynamics and vertical density of the notes) would become increasingly important, as a way to a kind of musical 'free-thinking'. Three years ago I attended a 'concert' of Stockhausen's music — no performers, an empty stage and an electrician waiting in the wings to switch on and off. Even this, Mr. Feldman considers out-of-date, since the music is 'made, developed and notated'.

So far as the production was concerned, I found the technique perversely arch. Mr. Feldman began by reading extracts from a lecture, in a stilted 'lecturing' tone of voice. Mr. Forge — game for anything— played the role of an initiate willing to be re-educated, only to be told that *avant-gardisme* was in itself 'an exaggerated claim to identity'. Pure sound, said Mr. Feldman, does not know its own history. The composer, to acquire his freedom, yearns to stop seeing himself as a part of an historical process. Sound exists in space: sound is timeless.

Whatever this programme sought to achieve, I had the impression that Mr. Feldman's strivings were entirely gestatory and were going to end up as something quite other than what we or he might expect.

17 April 1967 (P)

The Greek Sound

Mikos Theodorakis

About the same time as discoveries of primitive xylophones in Africa, Archytas was experimenting with a specifically Greek sound, and Pythagoras was studying tonal values on the road to discovering the octave. Now, after a silence of over two thousand years, a new Greek sound has emerged, reflecting the melancholy moods of the old 'rebetika'. There have been few more vital musical-poetical alliances than that of the Greek composer, Theodorakis, and the poet, Yannis Ritsos, who together produced the evocative *Epitaphios*, or 'Lament of the Tomb'.

When I was in Greece in 1961, we dined at a restaurant in Piraeus which advertised a twenty-four-course meal, washed down with a litre of retsina. After course nineteen, we staggered out into a dockside café where we listened to the latest songs by Mikos Theodorakis and Manos Hadjidakis.

I have waited five years for a broadcast on the subject and at last George Angell has compiled an excellent programme with translations by Ian Scott-Kilvert, beautifully read by Hugh Dickson and Olive Gregg, and impeccably produced by George Macbeth. Let us hope for a repeat performance if only for reader Olive Gregg's moving recital of Brendan Behan's 'The Laughing Boy' and Maria Farandouri singing the Theodorakis setting.

Poets and Poetry

May 1966 (U)

Publish and be Damned?

As one who spends much of his time in what is fashionably termed 'creative writing', I was heartened to learn from the Home Service this week that I am by no means alone in the frequently unrewarding pursuit of originality. Before Keats set to writing what was described rather curtly as 'a distressingly large' amount of *juvenilia*, he developed an inordinate hunger for the works of his predecessors. He absorbed, in an abandoned kind of way, most of Shakespeare and Milton. At a very early age he began to read with increasing admiration the works of Wordsworth and Coleridge, especially the *Lyrical Ballads* of 1815. By the time he came to write his 'Sonnet on Chapman's *Homer*' he had found a voice out of 'the realms of gold' (that is, the works of other poets he had read). Shelley thought it was too soon for Keats to publish but nevertheless helped him to bring out his *Poems* in 1817.

John Keats

It is remarkable that Keats was, in a sense, a late-starter, since he did not begin to write seriously meaningful poetry until he was 18 years of age, with only three years to live out the rest of his tragically short life. *Hyperion* shows his difficulty with the Miltonic voice and he failed to complete it, but, with the high romanticism of *Ode to Autumn*, *Ode to Melancholy* and *Endymion*, he reached the Empyrean heights in what he described, in his remarkable letters, as 'the true voice of feeling'.

The political voice in Keats is rare. With echoes of Blake's 'satanic mills', and in true Wordsworthian rhetoric, he can proclaim:

> Hear you not the hum of mighty workings.
> Listen awhile ye nations, and be dumb.

But this is not the Keats we want to hear. We begin to be aware of a new state of mind — 'a fellowship with essence' as he says in his *Hymn to Pan*. There is a true loss of self in all this that raises his soul to a level of maturity unmatched by any other romantic poet, a 'Happy gloom, dark paradise' that leaves him alone with his musings in the 'Cave of Quietude'.

*

28 May 1967 (P)

Golden Corn!

'The Dream of Eugene Aram' was the first poem to bring Thomas Hood fame in the more discerning world of the sophisticated reader. Hood had at last become aware of that fascination for the grotesque and horrific aspects of life, a fascination that had been lurking in the depths of his nature from early childhood. He does not concern himself so much with the murder itself, nor the murderer's unendurable self-devouring remorse that followed the fatal deed. He concentrates on that moment when the doomed man, shortly to face the gallows, is driven to confess the gory details of his crime to an innocent schoolboy in his charge. Bruce Beeby's reading of Hood's masterpiece, in John Betjeman's anthology of popular poetry, caught all the nuances of the grim imagery and built up the nightmarish intensity of the narrative with admirable precision.

What an excellent performance Mr. Beeby gave, too, of Australian poet, 'Banjo' Patterson's 'The Man from Snowy River', the story of a valuable colt that got away and joined the wild bush horses in a mad stampede, finally to be halted by the mysterious stranger from Snowy River:

And he ran them single-handed till their sides were white with foam:
He followed like a bloodhound on their track,
Till they halted cowed and beaten, then he turned their heads for home,
And alone and unassisted brought them back.

Most of Betjeman's selection came into the 'pleasure of pain' category on two levels: first the technical one, for there are few famous first lines that carry the quality through to the last line. After an initial flush of the imagination, the poem descends into a flurry of verbiage that fails to hold the listener's attention. Sir Henry Newbolt's 'Commemoration', with its long and rambling metre, for example, drifts off into a devitalized dissertation, three verses of which Mr. Betjeman wisely chose to omit.

'The boy stood on the burning deck' by Mrs. Felicia Hemans recalled for me a certain unpleasant memory of a hot summer's evening spent in detention with the order to copy out the poem three times and memorise the first three verses! After reciting the first memorable line of this old-fashioned melodrama of 'Casablanca', I was incapable of remembering the rest of the unmemorable.

As for 'The Charge of the Light Brigade', Tennyson read of the incident in the morning newspaper and dashed off the poem in a couple of hours. 'No poet has written so many famous lines between breakfast and lunch,' remarked Mr. Betjeman. Brave is the man who will accept its almost insuperable challenge and read the poem aloud in the strident tones it requires. But brave was Bruce Beeby.

Alfred Lord Tennyson

The best moment in the whole of this programme, presented with such wit and unashamed nostalgia by one of our most popular poets, was Robert Southey's 'The Battle of Blenheim', which I first heard at school recited with great enjoyment by my English master, though I doubt if I realised then its power as a satire on the futility of war.

*

27 April 1967 (U

Speed, Sound and Sentiment

John Gray put together a beguiling and thoroughly entertaining anthology of verse ranging from William McGonagall to Walt Whitman, whose poem 'To a Locomotive' recalled some striking moments of the steam-age:

> Thy black cylindric body, golden brass and silvery steel,
> Thy ponderous side-bars, parallel and connecting rods,
>   gyrating, shuttling at thy side,
> Thy metrical, now swelling pant and roar, now tapering in the
>   distance.....
> Through gale or calm, now swift, now slack, yet steadily
>   careering,
> Type of the modern – emblem of motion and power — pulse of
>   the continent....

The choice of music ranged from Rossini's drawing-room piece, 'Un Petit Train de Plaisir', to Schubert's great C major symphony. And, yes, I had forgotten 'Riding down to Bangor' and 'Lullaby of Broadway', all the delicious nostalgia was there, and in the background always the rushing, rattling, whistling of the trains.

I never found parting such 'sweet' sorrow, and railways stations can sometimes make me feel lonely, but I couldn't help wishing (in spite of Mr. Feldman's anti-historicism) that I could dash off on the Golden Arrow, and thence to some Greek island, a glass of cool retsina, and the tremulous vibrato of the bouzouki.

January 1967 (P)

Choices

The world is one year older. Now we stand at the doorway of the year, or *janua* as the Romans called it, and it is with the remembrance of things past and hopes for the year to come that most broadcasting over the last week has been concerned. 'When all that story's finished, what's the news?' asked W. B. Yeats in his poem, 'The Choice'.

If we are to take Patric Dickinson's word for it, then poetry does not give answers but choices. Shall we, like William Blake, discover 'the lonely traveller's dream under the hill'? Shall we, like Robert Frost, reflect upon 'The Road Not Taken'?

In his sequence of poems, 'Choices', Patric Dickinson explored the possibilities of choice in the work of Yeats and Robert Frost among others. Yeats gloomily prophesies 'the perpetual struggle between good and evil' and wonders how little divides civilisation from chaos. The thought might have prompted (for those who found it still possible to concentrate on higher things after a day of festive self-indulgence) a timely reflection on past events and future eventualities.

I thought Stephen Murray's designedly flat tone of reading brought a singularly ominous note to the programme, revealing with great poignancy the dilemma that faced poets like Yeats and Matthew Arnold. We were finally left to contemplate Robert Frost's ironic lines: 'I never dared be radical when young/ For fear it would make me conservative when old.'

6 January 1967 (P)

The Originality of Arthur Waley

It was a pleasure to turn to Roy Fuller's enthralling commentary on the gifted Arthur Waley*. A deep sense of melancholy pervades his fine translations of those timeless lyrics from the Chinese in 'that incomparable and undervalued style', combining simplicity of language with depth of thought, a supreme comment on a meaning of life which may have eluded us for centuries.

Arthur David Waley (1889-1966), poet and authority on Chinese and Japanese literature. His exemplary and sensitive translations of Chinese poetry were published in 1918.

6 January 1967 (U)

Willow, Willow, Waley O!

My grandmother's willow-pattern plates were among her treasured possessions. Everybody seemed to have them on the kitchen dresser. They were part of the continuing trend in mass production. As a child, I was fascinated by the delicate mandarin figures, the bridge and the willow tree. They were part of a culture I recognised, even at that age, that was markedly different to my own. Some years later, I was given a slim volume of *Lyrics from the Chinese* by Helen Waddell. I remember that same delicacy of expression in the images of those deceptively simple poems that existed in the arrangement of the designs on the plates. That ancient simplicity I also remember in a poem composed in BC 826, almost, it seemed to me, before time itself.

A lover waits under the sheltering leaves of the willows. Night falls but the longed-for belovèd never comes to him. He waits patiently in the darkness. As dawn rises, the morning star shines down on him in his loneliness. One might suppose that such a story is hidden in the willow-pattern design too.

In his programme, 'The Originality of Arthur Waley', the poet Roy Fuller, who, as a young man, greatly admired Waley's translations from the Chinese, told us of his interview with the great man some years ago. Before going to meet him, Fuller began a

Arthur Waley

systematic reading of the translations and realised that the work had been unjustifiably neglected and deserved to be more widely recognised.

Fuller was fascinated by the clarity, the subtle irony, the modesty in the face of praise, all of which went to make up the image of this exceptional poet and man. The metrical techniques, such as the positioning of strong accents on neighbouring syllables and the end-stopped lines, were all akin to the experiments of Gerard Manley Hopkins, Ezra Pound and T. S. Eliot. There was, in any case, a common bond between them as all four frequently dined together in Soho. What we would have given to be allowed to listen in.

One special feature of Waley's work is its deep sense of melancholy, perhaps an intrinsic element of the original Chinese poems themselves. A gentle wistfulness comes through the thin gossamer of the language that appeals to the more subtle sensibilities of the reader. The simplicity of the vocabulary in contrast to the depth of thought is a truly remarkable feature of Arthur Waley's translations. 'Let me live my days on earth again/And be rich when I am young,' and 'What is the use of talking/ When there is no end to talking?'

Roy Fuller's sensitive and perceptive assessment helps us to understand why Waley has to be placed among the greatest translators from the Chinese.

From my notebook: *22 June 1967*

Tea in Bayswater

Success is an elusive god. Basically, in its active form, it requires energy, enthusiasm and opportunity and, in its higher order, integrity, idealism and spirituality. Success may stem from parental encouragement or discouragement. It involves discipline, courage, dedication, humility and any one of a hundred attributes, including an element of luck, that come together in a bewildering variety of juxtapositions, in any place, at any moment, in any given set of circumstances. It may happen once in a lifetime, or never. Man, however, is an aspiring creature, as BBC programmes last week demonstrated.

Edith Sitwell

Dame Edith Sitwell and her *côterie* were the beguiling subjects of Tom Driberg's talk, an account of an extraordinary collection of struggling artists and poets in the nineteen-thirties. In spite of not being well off, Dame Edith entertained, on strong tea and penny buns, many of the subsequently famous, including Arthur Waley, T. S. Eliot, Cecil Beaton, Sir William Walton, Constant Lambert, Roy Campbell and Dylan Thomas.

Most ridiculous and endearing was Pavel Tchelitchew, the young painter, who, on one occasion, hurt his toes on Dame Edith's fender and hopped about, angrily accusing her of being the cause of his discomfort. She described his visits as making her feel like a small child in a perambulator being wheeled round the room by a raging nurse. After the raging was over, she provided a quiet tea with raspberry jam.

'I have a passion for the arts,' she said. 'I have a tenderness for the young.'

19 March 1967 (P)

Betjeman High, Betjeman Low

As one of the half-million unfortunates made redundant by the present economic squeeze, I can sympathise to the letter with John Betjeman's chagrin and cynicism in his poem 'Caprice', in which he is asked out to lunch by his boss in order to be sacked — at the coffee stage! The must of Edwardian England still heavily pervades a small, tantalisingly slim volume of poems, *High and Low*, the latest work of Mr. Betjeman, who seems more and more like a gloomy young Tennyson wandering about his Lincolnshire marshes, reciting in mournful monotones newly inspired poems of despair. It is an altogether lugubrious vision of life. Most characteristic is 'Matlock Bath', a period piece in Mr. Betjeman's best architectural vein, bringing vividly to life the claustrophobic fustian that lingers about the town.

Biblical names such as 'The Heights of Abraham' testify to the strong Nonconformist traditions, while children chant hymn-tunes with an eerie joy:

> *In blest Bethesda's limpid pool*
> *Comes treacling out of Sunday School.....*
> *And attic bedrooms shriek with fright*
> *For dread of Pilgrims of the Night.*

The hyperbole is not complete. He is filled with —

> A sense of doom, a dread to see
> The *Rock of Ages* cleft for me'.

John Betjeman

There is no new image of the poet here, only the old nostalgia, the old regrets, the old macabre dwelling on suffering and death, an ever uglier world in which to eke out our wretched lives. Thank God for Mr. Betjeman's saving grace of wry humour. I might even be tempted to think he could just have been joking all the time.

3 March 1967 (U)

Between Heaven and Hell

A solitary figure sits at a table in a small room littered with crumpled sheets of writing paper. The room is in a small isolated house, close by the waterside. The head of the figure droops over some paper on which are words and phrases scratched out, rejected images that will not fit the vision, test phrases, lists of words, marginal scribbles and half-formulated thoughts that die almost as the pen touches the paper. Light another cigarette! Try again!

On the table, an empty wine bottle and another half-empty. But the picture of dejection that these things might create in the mind of the onlooker do not in any degree match the despair in the heart of the poet. He is comparatively young — in his early thirties — but he hasn't many more years to live. He is obsessed by the shortness of life, its injustice in the context of eternity (or the endless series of lives stretching out into infinity).

Dylan Thomas

So here he is, in the quiet of the Welsh countryside, far away from his favourite London pubs, his drinking cronies and his marital problems — close to the things of the heart and the mind. But his poem will never be finished — at least not in this world — in heaven, perhaps! — the manuscript 'waiting for someone who prints strikingly few copies at impossible prices, on fine soft Cashmere goat's hair'.

This description of a moment in this poet's life, fixed like a frog in amber, is undeniably specious and does not even begin to describe the plight in which he finds himself, but it does make a point: the terrible process of gradual self-destruction in the mind and soul of a deeply romantic, yearning, angry spirit which has still so much genius to give to the world.

It has happened many times before: Keats, Shelley and Byron all burnt themselves out at an early age, wracked by illness and creative (that is, spiritual) exhaustion. Yet, as I stood in that small room all those years ago, those were my thoughts and that is what I saw and deeply felt.

In Country Heaven: an unfinished 'poem-to-be' is Douglas Cleverdon's outstanding tribute to Dylan Thomas, resulting from the remarkable discovery of eight-and-a-half stanzas which came to be printed a short time before in the *Daily Telegraph*. The tone and manner of the poetry is immediately recognisable. It was intended to form part of a 'trilogy' which would include 'In Country Sleep' and 'Over Sir

John's Hill'. 'Each pair of stanzas consists of ten lines, with the length from four to eleven syllables, with the rhymes or assonances in the five lines of the first stanza matching those in the second stanza.

> Always when he, in Country Heaven,
>   (Whom my heart hears),
> Crosses the breast of the praising East, and kneels,
>   Humble in all his planets,
>   And weeps on the abasing hill,
>
> Then in the delight and groves of beasts and birds
>   And the canonised valley
> Where the downfall stars sing grazing still
> And the angels whirr like pheasants
>   Through aisles of leaves.....

It is thus that Dylan Thomas evokes the mood of these elusive verses, discovered when an American scholar sent them to Dylan's fellow-poet and friend, Vernon Watkins — a fragment which Thomas described in a broadcast later published in his book of essays, *Quite Early One Morning*.

This excellent programme marked a further stage in the genesis of 'In Country Heaven', some of which, Thomas tells us, existed only 'in a rough draft in the head, and the rest of it radiantly unworded in ambitious conjecture'.

Basil Jones read the original fragment and then Douglas Cleverdon added into Hugh Griffith's reading Thomas's alternative phrasing and images, thus giving much to our understanding of the creative process. Humphrey Searle recalled that Dylan, towards the end of his life, spoke of the poem as being 'about the shepherds on the moon watching the earth after it had been destroyed in an atomic war.' This was at a time when Thomas was faced with increasing depression about his work and what terrors the future might hold for the world.

'In Country Heaven' has been described as 'an escape from personality'. Its deep melancholy is dark and obsessive. 'I like things that are difficult to write,' said Thomas, and difficult to understand. I like redeeming the contraries with secretive images. I like contrasting my images, saying two things at once in one word, four in two and one in six.' The great merit of Douglas Cleverdon's invaluable production is that it allows us to enter into the inner workings of the poet's moment of inspiration and the arduous process of perfecting and honing that goes in the making of a poem.

Arthur Rubenstein, the concert pianist, was once asked to define genius. His simple reply was: 'Genius is attention to detail.'

3 March 1967 (P)

'In Country Heaven'

Huw Wheldon, as guest of the week in 'Woman's Hour' on St. David's Day, spoke of the reflective moods of the Welsh language and its links with the countryside of Wales, while Richard Burton (as reported in an interview on 'Pick of the Week') emphasized the declamatory character of Welsh, in which he could 'agonize' so beautifully. These two aspects were highlighted in Douglas Cleverdon's outstanding production of 'In Country Heaven', a critical analysis of a poem of eight stanzas by Dylan Thomas, beautifully read by Hugh Griffith. Taking the various extant versions, Mr. Cleverdon hit upon the ingenious method of inserting the variants (read by Basil Jones) into the finished work, thus revealing the processes of creativity through to the final crystallization of the imagery.

Huw Wheldon

The second part of the programme included the 1950 recording of Dylan Thomas reading his masterpiece, 'Over Sir John's Hill', together with 'In Country Sleep' and 'In the White Giant's Thigh'. Thomas's voice was much more self-conscious and theatrical than Christopher Logue's. The rising and falling of the tones was like an oracular incantation, a passionate threnody, akin to the chorus of a Greek tragedy or the lilt of a Celtic saga. In one of those remarkable letters to Pamela Hansford-Johnson, Thomas had once written: 'I want to believe, to believe for ever, that heaven is being, a state of being, and the only hell is the hell of myself. I want to burn hell with its own flames.' 'In Country Heaven' is part of that very process.

*

28 February 1967 (P)

Logue's ABC

The shades of Thomas Hood and Calverley hang gently over the satirical verse of Christopher Logue. Like his forerunners, Mr. Logue has succeeded in remaining outside the main stream of contemporary events. His work has a sharp edge to it, an effective pungency that converts smoothly into a softer mood of satire.

In *Logue's ABC*, a group of twenty-six satirical poems about notable people, Mr. Logue's clear diction was assisted by the sharp plosive and fricative sounds of his verse and the vigour of the Anglo-Saxon vocabulary.

There must always be a certain undramatic inevitability about such an alphabet, relentlessly pursuing its course towards Z, having to deal on the way with the almost insuperable problems of Q and X.

Christopher Logue

Mr. Logue begins with a damp squib about Aeschylus, but saves the situation with a verse on the reputation of Brecht, fashioned with Blake-like simplicity of language clothing a complex image: 'Truth is not the child of Time, But of Necessity.' That has a lyrical ring about it, a wistfulness which characterises later verses about Ni Chen, Quietus (a pathetic utterance on the tricks of fate), and Lao Tse (an eloquent comment on political apathy). There is, on the other hand, an irresistible irony in the poems about Oscar Wilde and Swinburne, De Sade and Marat, and the plagiarism of Yeats. Sometimes, as in the fiery squib about Leonardo da Vinci, Mr. Logue creates an elaborate graffito, like a truculent child scribbling a scurrilous rhyme about Nurse on 'some old-fashioned nursery wall-paper'.

28 February 1967 (U)

L for Logue

There is no doubt that Christopher Logue is every man's poet. His performance of 'Logue's ABC' on the Third had a nice incisiveness that could not fail to grab the attention of the listener. His sharp, clear voice and his mockingly 'elocutionary' style were just perfect for the reading of his sequence of occasionally naughty verses, one for each letter of the alphabet. It was impossible not to raise a smile at the strong over-syllabisation and the hysterical clarity of the plosives and fricatives. All this, added to the lightness of the verbal dexterity, the sharpness of the wit, and the wry innuendo, promised to be a thoroughly entertaining hour.

Apparently the verses were lying about in their unfinished state for years. 'I like sequences of things. It means I have an aim in view and can — possibly — get there in the end.'

Logue's inspiration was the multitude of similar ABC's in German, notably Berthold Brecht's. Usually they were written for children and mostly illustrated with little pictures. The style is, on the whole, in the tradition of nursery rhymes and comic squibs, often reminiscent of Lear, Carroll, Hood and Belloc.

When Logue is in a wicked mood, he resembles a scornful Byron penning a vicious squib about Lord Castlereagh. In fact, the verses, for Logue, were more of a protest against the manner of contemporary poetry than anything else.

'I'm fed up to the back teeth with pretentious, long-faced poems about animals who are always treated as pets, with concrete poems from which you couldn't build a snuff box, diarrhoea-whitman-junki-self-pitying-lousy crapulosities. Maybe I'm just sick of contemporary poetry.'

But what a good performer this man is! That tinge of amused smugness and the inner pleasure he feels with it. From Aeschylus to Zoroaster (Zarathustra), we race through a riot of character studies — artists, novelists, philosophers, poets, religious thinkers, scientists, sculptors. There is an abundance of wistfulness, wry humour, and even a perverse touch of the banal. A clever little squib about Hitler's mother, a neat comment on God's view of time, a cameo of James the Second eating Stilton with Milton, a saucy verse about Scott Fitzgerald and Ernest Hemingway and their views on women, snide portraits of 'the Pictish Calvinist' Knox, Oscar Wilde and 'Algy' Swinburne, the Marquis de Sade and Verlaine, all caught up in the maelstrom race to Z. I am allowed to repeat one of these little gems without infringing copyright — because, after all, you might even go out and buy a copy! Let us try R for Russell (i.e. Bertrand):

> Russell — while he was being tried
> For threatening to demonstrate
> Against the bomb, (aged ninety-five) —
> Was challenged by the judge to state
> 'Why you, a nobleman, contrive
> To act like a degenerate.'
> Whereon that FRS replied:
> 'My lord, to help you stay alive.
> However, now we've met, it seems
> The ends don't justify the means.'

6 May 1966 (P)

Anti-Poetry

No-one with an Augustan turn of mind, and certainly no-one with romantic leanings, could condone the rebellious impropriety of Philip Larkin's line: 'Get stewed! Books are a load of crap.' Yet it is pure anti-poeticism, a far cry from Eliot's demands for 'the common word, exact without vulgarity'.

The more challenging example of rejection in the lines: 'Our Father, Which art in heaven/ Stay there and we'll stay here on earth,' would seem a blasphemy if we did not understand the sincerity of the anti-poetic canon.

In Professor Cohen's view, the anti-poet 'cries for immortality, but faces the blinding light of nothingness.' Following conversations with the Chilean poet, Nicanor Parra, J. M. Cohen assembled a heterogenous collection of anti-poets to keep Parra company, including Villon, Prévert, Larkin, and the American Beat poets. There was Vladimir Mayakovsky, jumping up on the table and strenuously reminding his fellow-poets that Villon was not only a poet but a robber, and railing them with the reprimand: "Darlings, what wedded you to words?"

Parra is an illuminating example of the anti-poetic in his spare language and flat imagery. He is the poet who rejects life, believes in nothing, yet seeks to express this rejection in accurate and appropriate terms, throwing off metaphysical, classical and romantic canons to set free his particular form of individualism. Professor Cohen, with his special talent for rooting out the off-beat in literature, pursued his thesis admirably. Anti-poetry is politically anarchistic and, within the Leninist framework, Mayakovsky's kind of individualism could only end as it did, with suicide.

From my notebook: *29 May 1966* (U)

Further Notes on J. M. Cohen's 'Anti-Poetry'

1. Anti-poetry is politically anarchist. Results from disillusionment.
2. Style: spare language, flat imagery, no embellishment, ironic, defeatist.
   E.g. 'I looked for the locked door'.
3. Attitude of poet: rejects life, poetry, believes in nothing.
4. Dislikes: the Metaphysical, the Classical, the Romantic, the supernatural. No rainbows. 'The heavens are falling to bits'.
5. Likes: mainly material things. cf. Villon's bowls and kettles.
6. Likes women. Though Parra's relationship with them is unsatisfactory. Parra is more comfortable with inanimate things.

1. Jacques Prévert: his is the world of the senses. Has no mystery.
2. Gregory Corso 'cries for immortality but faces the blinding light of nothingness.'
3. With Lawrence Ferlinghetti, 'the individual is only temporarily master of his upside-down world.' His awesome imagery: 'figs burst', the 'sun is white', 'I'll never come back'.
4. Vladimir Mayakovsky: 'Gentlemen poets! Have you not tired of pages, palaces, etc.' His brand of individualism is identified always with Lenin's communism. But the Revolution left him at the mercy of the bureaucrat and the tax inspector. His eventual suicide was inevitable.
5. Thomas Hood has his moments of the antipoetical when he resists the punning.--- viz. his sonnet on the City fire, and one on Vauxhall Gardens beginning; 'The cold transparent ham is on the fork.'
6. The Imagists could be spare in their language yet could avoid the prosaic, unlike the Neo-Imagists who prefer the greys of the poetical palette.
7. With Nathaniel Tarne, some lines are elliptical and the reader is momentarily stopped in his path by the obscurity:

                A clerk with autumnal teeth
                Has had his life on his tongue.

8. His metaphysics are intrusive but one is always beguiled into believing that his imagery is actually beautiful.
9. Cohen's Neruda is a poet of great objectivity; he calls Neruda's poems 'hymns to the dialectic of nature'.
' There is a lushness akin to Blake,' and a Blake-like expression of 'joy' that is quite touching. Sometimes it is difficult to imagine how it was that Neruda led Parra towards the anti-poetical.
10. There is something admirable in Allan Ginsberg's' pleasure to be found in the perfection of this world.' He has no faith in the next. 'I want to go into the supermarket and buy what I want with my looks.'

None of this will ever make an article unless I can pare it down, find the quintessential centre of this erratic bunch of poets. Reshaping what I have already written will carry me over my word-limit and drag me beyond the deadline. And I have only half-an hour to finish it!

29 May 1966 (P)

Master of Nothing

'What is it like, this nothingness, master?' asks the Buddha in Brecht's poem. Is it 'a pleasant nothingness' or 'a mere nothing'?

Such reflections augured well for J. M. Cohen's second programme on 'Anti-Poetry', in which he explored the positive qualities of the anti-poets.

As Mr. Cohen explained, we have in the poetry of Nicanor Parra 'the pure experience of a man lost'. Parra himself endorses this, 'seeing that we are no more than beings, as God is no more than God', but his inanimate world is sparked off from the animate world of Pablo Neruda, who in spite of his rhetorical weaknesses, his political consciousness and his belief in himself as a new poet emerging from a new country, brings a Blake-like mysticism to his lush tropical world, which is highly romantic. His poems, as Mr Cohen describes them, are 'hymns to the dialectic of nature'. Beth Boyd joined the team of readers, all of whom read with due deference to the demands of the text.

*

23 May 1967 (U)

Read on from Here!

Poetry recitals require a special sense of balance, of voice against voice, humourous with serious, dramatic with reflective, to be found invariably in the programmes arranged by John Carroll for the Apollo Society.

Philip Hope-Wallace presented a series of recorded readings of poetry and prose. The first of these included John Betjeman reading his poem 'Early Electric' with that extraordinary throw-away technique of his, and with just an occasional concession to some sort of rudimentary intonation. Yet he always holds the listener under his spell.

Emlyn Williams's reading from *The Tale of Two Cities* was eminently memorable for its cadence, its tone, and the consummate involvement of reader with subject.

The performances by Louis MacNeice and W. H. Auden were particularly fine, with no intrusion between poet and listener, and with the poem in each case meticulously communicated.

*

23 May 1967 (U)

'The Poet Speaks'

Schumann's title to the last of his *Kinderscenen* is expressed by a simple tune that might be equally be called 'The Piano Speaks' for there is a kind of 'voice' that specifically asks the listener to make an aesthetic leap from one medium to another before he even hears any sound whatsoever. The literary emphasis in the title suggests that we are about to hear a poem, and as the pianist begins the first bars the listener is asked to enter into a dialogue with the composer. 'The medium is the message', as Marshall McLuhan would say. So Philip Hope Wallace's programme, 'Read On From Here', delved very neatly into the relationship between the reader's voice and the vocal interpretation of the text.

By now, we all know what to expect when the announcer introduces T. S. Eliot reading *The Waste Land* or John Betjeman reading *A Subaltern's Love-Song*. The very sombre *timbre* of their voices is inextricably conjoined with the texture and 'tone' of the poem, so much so that the listener is quite unable to imagine anyone else daring to emulate the masters themselves. Yet there is some benefit to be gained from such attempts. For example, it was almost uncanny to hear Betjeman reading from Housman's *Shropshire Lad,* and Alec Guinness's 'strangely haunting and persuasive' reading of Auden's 'Hearing of harvest rotting in the valleys'.

T. S. Eliot

We understand why it is quite a different experience, uncanny as it may be, to hear the voices of Robert Browning and Alfred Lord Tennyson speaking to posterity out of a distant past. It is equally impressive to hear the frail, piping voice of W.B. Yeats reading *The Lake Isle of Innisfree*. So it came as a revelation to hear actor, Ian Holm, reading Edward Fitzgerald's *Rubaiyat of Omar Khayyam* in tones that were completely void of the customary sentimentality, giving the poem much greater 'pungency and poetic appeal'.

Suddenly, the phrase, 'The Poet Speaks' becomes more meaningful. Now, too, we can appreciate the poem in a different light when it is read by other voices: Alec Guinness reading the lilting, tricksy, tripping verse of Edith Sitwell, for example, though would we not rather hear that formidable lady reciting it through her megaphone to a Festival Hall audience, with the full orchestral backing of Sir William Walton's suite,

Façade, the brilliant musical interpretation of the poems?

In a sense, T. S. Eliot continues the tradition of the bards of ancient times when illiterate audiences could enthuse over deeds of old through the power of the poet's voice. Today's audiences, living life in the fast lane, have less patience for poetry. The 'pop' song has taken over where public poetry has lost its 'voice'. Now, we have poetry (more like broken lines of prose) read over a pint of beer in our local pub.

17 June 1967 (U)

The Reading of Poetry

Everyone who knows Peter Orr's recordings of modern poets, *The Poet Speaks*, will have been interested to hear him on the Third. Though I do not particularly share his scorn for phoneticians and critics, participating as I do in both these activities, I can sympathize with his distress at the failure of many actors, poets, and readers alike who attempt to speak aloud the printed page in minutely interpreted gradations of sound. Mr. Orr, who draws his thesis from Francis Berry's work, *Poetry and the Physical Voice*, goes far beyond the basic principle that 'all poetry is primarily sound'.

As a practising poet, I do not agree that art makes itself felt entirely through the senses. That would be an over-simplification. To me, poetry and music are similar in one respect only, that the process of arranging a series of crotchets, quavers and minims in varying patterns and densities is very close indeed to arranging a series of vowels and consonantal 'clusters' in a meaningful sequence. But that is as far as the analogy goes. In musical terms, it would appear from Francis Berry's example that his system of notation is at fault, not the theory which he propounds. All in all, these were good talks. Peter Orr has at last said something which should have been said long ago, and has said it with a deep and subtle understanding of poetry and its language as a communicable experience.

25 & 27 June 1967 (U)

Sense, Sound and Sensibility

'Words', said Alexander Pope, are 'an echo to the sense'. Perhaps one could go further than that in a later age and make a claim for words being 'an echo to the sensibility.' Peter Orr has made a major contribution to our understanding of the sound of poetry through his elaborate analysis of the voices of the poets and the readers who recite their poetry.

He begins his theory by challenging our conventional ideas of what poetry is all about. We recognise the sense that lies at its heart but we have to admit that it is the sound of poetry that beguiles us. 'Sound,' says Mr. Orr, 'pleases only because there is the sense that goes with it.' He draws a parallel with music, where the score gives an indication of how the notes are to be played. However, one surely has to be cautious about the comparison, for poetry, whatever else it may be, is not precisely music. In George Bernard Shaw's *Pygmalion*, Professor Higgins tries to show Eliza, his Cockney Covent Garden flower-seller, what intonation is through the slurring of notes on his violin. Conversely, Orr, looking at the problem from a musical angle, cites Schönberg's use of 'speech-song', or 'Sprechgesang'.

But does the *sound* of poetry really matter? It seems that Francis Berry, lecturer at Sheffield University, in his seminal work, *Poetry and the Physical Voice*, has the view that 'all poetry is primarily sound and secondarily meaning'. That is to some extent true, for every one who speaks a text aloud, whether it be a poem, a speech, or a lecture, will unconsciously synthesise the wide variety of sounds and intonations that go to make up their unmistakably individual voice, so that any two readings can never sound the same. As Valéry said; 'l'oreille parle', 'the ear speaks' — an idea that is not satisfactorily translated from the French.

In any case, as is well recognised in the creative process, what the poet writes is 'the result of artistic intention' and 'not a happy accident.' But how the poet speaks is no accident. He is born with a physical voice all his own. In the dull intoning of Allan Ginsberg and the flat tones of

F. T. Prince, there is altogether another value that some listeners might find a barrier to understanding. Certainly poetry may sometimes look like prose, and prose may sometimes have the qualities of poetry. Both may have pitch and cadence and rhythm and reflect the voice of the writer. There is no mistaking what has been called the 'wonderfully crusty, grumpy, growling' tones of John Heath Stubbs reading his poem, *To Edmund Blunden on his 60th Birthday*, but were they so to him, I ask? We are often surprised when we hear ourselves speak on a tape recording. 'That's not me!' you say. 'I don't speak like that.'

A final plea comes from George Rylands, who demands a degree of 'depersonalisation' in the reader, which may be why Patric Dickinson has a real distrust of actors reading poetry.

Nowadays there is a fashion for 'jazzing' and leather jackets. At all costs keep the listeners awake!

2 June 1967 (P)

Sound Poetry

If I fully subscribed to the teachings of Marshall McLuhan I could accept his dictum that 'the medium is the message' and then be in a position to approach more rationally the problems presented in George Macbeth's stimulating programme on 'Sound Poetry'. He began with a mildly mocking tribute to the Scots language by Pete Brown, called 'The Blue Moor':

> Trenglooor muryurrr dyuumm
> remglmmm myoor dirrym
> gmumyooorrmmmmmm gfumm
> Yehoooomm!

Whatever one makes of that is a matter for individual interpretation. It seemed to me that Kevin Crossley-Holland and Edward Lucie-Smith were extremely guarded in their views, but then who would not be? The poem, if it can be called a poem, represents a challenge to everything that has gone before, and certainly would confound those who attempted to define poetry as anything more than, as Sir Philip Sidney defined it: 'a speaking picture.'

Perhaps we may stretch a point and consider 'The Blue Moor' to be a kind of speaking picture. It certainly has its own intrinsic humour. Can one see, perhaps, in these captivating lines, the portrait of a blustering ginger-whiskered ghilly in kilt and tam-o'-shanter proclaiming the beauty of the highlands?

Alternatively, in a less literal way, the poem may possibly, out of its bizarre abstraction, conjure up images of 'otherness' of a kind, as a mantra may.

Another unusual experience was to hear Bob Cobbing recite an extract from 'An ABC of Sound', his complex set of permutations set with an echo, like a Tibetan monk chanting in some exotic eastern temple. If, as Archibald MacLeish has written, 'a poem should not mean but be', then this is perfection itself. It has to be heard, not read, to be fully appreciated. With sound poetry, the printed page is an anachronism.

Pop Songs and Pop Stars

15 February 1967 (U)

Scrambled Egg-head!

There is no doubt that audience surveys are here to stay, but frankly I take no notice of them as I have never been one of the mythical thousand people interviewed, and nor has anyone else I have ever met, unless my friends and acquaintances have been harbouring dark secrets. A year ago somebody decided it would be a good idea if some research was done into how many people listened in to the Light Programme's 'Music Through Midnight'. It appeared that — surprise! surprise! — the results included a number of 'serious-thinking people' like undergraduates, party-goers, night drivers and, according to Francis Crozier in this week's *Radio Times*, 'the occasional burglar over his pre-*coup* cup of tea'. And I was shocked to read Crozier's revelation that 'quite a number of schoolboys have been discovered hiding their transistors under the bedclothes'. Now that would certainly not have happened in my day, but then I was at school in the early 1940's when Matron would never have allowed such goings on! And even more disgraceful, these little boys are sneakily writing letters to the BBC on the subject under the very nose of the house prefect.

Although this insidious development shows a blatant disregard for the traditional proprieties on the part of the very young, as far as I can see, Mr. Crozier does come down on the side of the modern 'Lotharios' who write in for 'their' tune to be played to accompany their nocturnal canoodlings. In our less permissive society, we had to learn to be much more devious and furtive. I do remember one of the chaps in our dorm had a forbidden copy of *No Orchids for Miss Blandish*, whose undoubted charms had to be enjoyed after lights out, between the sheets in the light of a fading torch. How much better off the young are, he writes, than the medieval lover who had to hire a lute-player to twang away 'on moonlit banks'.

According to a report in the *Evening Standard* this week, the Top Ten disc charts had Harry Secombe in the No. 2 spot on the *New Musical Express* list, though the author of the article, Ramsden Greig, wryly comments that Harry 'would be regarded as a square if he were not so round!' But listen up, folks! With Engelbert Humperdinck at No. 1, poor Petula Clark has fallen to No. 8 and the Beatles (with *Penny Lane*) have plummeted to No. 10.

Of course, you are thinking what a knowledgeable chap I am! I can see that, for complete eggheads like me, 'Pop Music' has considerable potential as a subject for serious study. In a crazy 'pop fantasy' future, one might even go the whole hog and take a PhD in 'Pop Linguistics', 'The Love Lyrics of Elvis', or 'Why We Need Alan Keith's 'Hundred Best Tunes'.'

So this week, at the request of the Editor, I have been 'educating' myself. I have been listening to 'Pick of the Pops' (Alan Freeman), 'Start the Day Right' (Jimmy Hanley), 'Easy Beat' (David Symonds), 'Pop Over Europe' (Catherine Boyle), 'Pete's Party'(Pete Murray), 'Dee Time' (Simon Dee), 'Record Roundabout' (Jack Jackson), 'Saturday Club' (Brian Matthew) and Uncle Tim Brinton and all! After which I feel completely scrambled!

On Saturday, as I was about to put out the light, I heard the dulcet tones of Matt Munro sending me a desperate message:

> Where in the world will I find love
> There's no future round the bend.

Well, for an old square like me, this week has certainly sent me 'round the bend', but you know — I think I might surprise my friends when they ask me what I've been listening to and astound them with my knowledge of the fantasy world of pop!

30 March 1967 (P)

Pop Goes a Person

The 'Monkees' are coming to town! Thousands of teenagers, and a sprinkling of 'oldies', no doubt, will race down to the Empire Pool, Wembley, to support a new phenomenon in the world of Pop, or, as

Eddie Rogers put it in 'Pop Goes a Person': 'a robot monster created by big business.'

The BBC is devoting an increasing amount of air-time to pop music. So what is it all about? This week, I've ploughed through 'Monday, Monday', 'Pop Inn', 'Parade of the Pops', 'Pop North', 'Saturday Club', 'Easy Beat' and 'Pick of the Pops', to pass only a few of the hours spent listlessly glued to my radio. To break through the thin layers of the spoken word I had to open one box of tricks after another, like one of those Chinese puzzles, until, reaching the last, I found nothing inside.

28 March 1967 (U)

How It All Popped Up!

Well! Nicholas Barrett, in his *Radio Times* preview of the state of pop to come, took what he describes as 'a look behind the tinsel' of the Pop world. He reminded me of things you and I had long since forgotten. For example: do you remember how Tommy Steele 'burst in on the 'Popular Music' scene and turned it into the 'Pop Music' scene?' Can you hear all the 'shouting, stamping and screaming' as he belted out the raucous strains of 'Rock with the Caveman?'

Steele was followed smartly by 'baybay' Adam Faith, and a weedy teenager called Harry Webb, who stayed the course by changing his name to Cliff Richard and became top 'Singer of the Year' for 1961. Out of a motley crowd of 'groups' from the provinces, Liverpool produced 'The Beatles' with their 'Mersey Sound' ('She loves me, yeah, yeah!') and the Home Counties gave a noisy birth to 'The Rolling Stones', with their nasty remarks about people living in suburban homes. As 'image' became all important, 'The Beatles' retreated behind moustaches and were seriously 'spoofed' by that mimicky little gang, 'The Monkees'.

In their programme, 'Pop Goes a Person', Nicholas Barrett and

Sandra Harris put together a plausible case for Pop and asked if pop groups are personalities any more, or have they been 'swallowed up by big business'? According to one contributor, Eddie Rogers, it was not 'art for art's sake' but 'Money, for God's sake!' 'Nobody seems to want to buy songs now,' he complained. 'They want to buy sounds.' In his view, pop was just a form of escapism for the kids.

So along come 'The Move' where gimmickry takes over and the 'sound' includes chopping up television sets and breaking up old cars, against background images of Hitler and Mao Tse Tung. 'For all the hysteria and screams,' said Michael Cleave, Pop Music critic of the *Evening Standard*, 'people can get steamed up only for a limited time.' As for dying their hair a Stuart tartan, it no longer impresses.

The trouble is there is a tendency to cross-dress: the engineers have become the real artists and the song-writers have lost out to the singers, most of whom can't sing anyway. Worst of all, the public is fickle. The 70 million discs sold in 1964 fell drastically to 50 million in 1967. According to another contributor, David Cardwell, we shall eventually 'press a button and get a computerised record.' As simple as that! And the pop industry as we know it will go pop!

28 March 1967 (P)

Permanent Group Mum

Honor Wyatt spoke amusingly in 'Woman's Hour' about her 'resident' pop group, including their 'shifting group of friends', which she harbours in her house. She sympathized with their long struggle for individuality and the dreams to get onto 'Top of the Pops' and 'Juke Box Jury'. 'It isn't enough to have a strong beat and a strong sound', a thought echoed by Manfred Mann in 'Pop Goes a Person'. So anyway, Mum just slips a pie in the oven when there is a shortage of 'bread' (money). As for their 'gear', 'they may look unusual but they're never dull.

28 March 1967 (P)

Pop Goes a Hymn Tune

Peter Firth made an excursion into the question of pop-music in church in 'Home This Afternoon'. He gallantly pursued a difficult topic by pointing out that every age has its own terms of reference: once it was flowers, fields, and sheep, so now why not cities, factories, and aeroplanes? Hymns should reflect our needs in a modern world.

Unfortunately, where church music is concerned, my aesthetic is fixed and inviolable. The extract from the post-communion hymn, complete with syncopated rhumba rhythm, launched me straight into one of the more hellish pages of Evelyn Waugh's *The Loved One*. I'm not particularly keen to bring Rodgers and Hammerstein into the church, even though the church has found its way into Rodgers and Hammerstein — or a convent, at least. It is the sound of music that matters!

28 March 1967 (P)

'Pop Inn' and 'Pop North'

Anyone who thinks that pop-singing is a piece of cake would have learnt from Manfred Mann's account of the hard grind that went into his latest single – a total of twenty-two hours and 3,000 play-backs, and no one in the group liked it except their agent. Little-known Gerry Dorsey also appeared on 'Pop Inn' (engagingly presented by Keith Fordyce). The extraordinary overnight revolutions that help to change the image of a singer transformed plain Mr. Dorsey into glossy Engelbert Humperdinck and made him a star.

On the whole I grew tired of the terrible puns, the rough word-play and the poor jokes that the presenters put across with such relish, but it is part of the uninhibited fun of the thing, with all its music-hall patter and facetious verbal exchanges. Even if I did want to switch off in the end, just for the sweetness of the silence ('There's a kind of hush all over the world'), I enjoyed many other moments. 'Pop North', for example was well presented by Ray Moore, with a rather  pleasing self-deprecating style. There was none of the smart pseudo-American pace. Mostly, the language of presentation during the week was pretty grim: 'It's thrill-of-the-bill time, folks!' and so on.

During the programme, a honeymoon couple were asked about their favourite number: Sandie Shaw singing 'Puppet on a String'. Apparently its 'bright and breezy' mood and its soft-soapy words reflected their state of marital euphoria to a T:

> Love is just like a merry-go-round
> With all the fun of the fair;
> One day I'm feeling down on the ground,
> Then I'm up in the air.

The whole place went wild when Engelbert Humperdinck came on. How had he coped with success? 'Nicely hectic.' Had he bought a new Rolls Royce and an aeroplane? 'No! I've got myself a new bicycle — a three-wheeler!' Then he brought the house down with —

> Please release me, let me go
> For I don't love you anymore.

Fortunately, two Glaswegian girls asked to hear Vince Hill singing 'Edelweiss' from *The Sound of Music* and I relaxed at last into my own dreams, where happily the world is not round but square!

1 April 1967 (P)

Where's It At, Man?

Chris Denning, described in the *Radio Times* as 'one of the brightest young jocks [sic]', included in his new programme a hot-line call from San Francisco in which Jonathan King introduced us to the pop scene with a new disc, 'The Happening' by the Supremes ('I found my dream. Ooooh! then it happened') and described the occasion as an 'exclusive British air-play of the disc.' It was then that I finally lost touch with the English language. It travels much faster than [the] Light! Mr. Denning also managed a scoop of his own by interviewing a young singer who sings standing on his head: 'It comes out better when I'm upside down.'

A searching look into the world of pop and the people behind it was very well presented by Nicholas Barrett in 'Pop goes a Person'. David Cardwell visualized a computerized industry in which we shall press a button and get a disc made to our own special recipe. Then, I suppose, we can stand on our heads to listen to it. The amazing thing is, after all these hours of pop, I've discovered you really can hear it better when you're upside down!

28 May 1966 (P)

The Fan Cult

It started with a great deal of screaming. Teenagers will always find idols to scream at. From Shakespeare to Garrick, from Kean to Irving, from Valentino to Elvis, fans have followed their idols and waited for hours at countless stage doors. Fans have been around for centuries. Even the poet, Robert Browning, had his adoring lady-members of the Browning Society, who hung on his every syllable.

Rod Argent of 'The Zombies', with clubs in Sweden, Canada, Japan, Poland and America, described what it was like when 40,000 screaming fans voiced their feelings. 'Hysteria makes you feel great,' said Rod. But it can be faked. In the United States, professional fainters and screamers are employed to rouse the fans. This, said Rod, can sometimes lead to a kick in the face. Well, it's kind of you to let me know, Rod, but if you don't mind I think I'll switch over and enjoy a tranquil hour with 'A Hundred Best Tunes', introduced in soporific tones by Alan Keith.

May 1966 (UP)

Square on Pop!

We are told that Disc Jockey (Dee Jay, in pop parlance), Alan Freeman, is 'a man who has an image and is determined to keep it'. I can well believe it when lethargic old me is caught up in his 'relentless verve and neurotic pace' as he reviews EP and LP tracks on the latest releases with fellow Dee Jay, Pete Brady, on 'Newly Pressed'. So it's no relief to turn to the equally breathless presentation of David Symonds on 'Easy Beat'. But praise be, Mr. Symonds has laryngitis this week and is unable to appear.

Oh, but wait a minute! He *is* to appear after all! His usual energetic microphone manner is thankfully tempered by raw tonsils and strained vocal cords. Consequently his normally jaunty commentaries are reduced to a minimum and the listener can concentrate on the songs.

This week, the programme featured 'Charts of the Past' and looked at the BBC 'Top Ten Tunes' of five years ago. We hear Cat Stevens, Manfred Mann, Cliff Richard, Danny Street, and a host of others. The American influence comes through straightaway with the introductory gambits for the kids: "This is your Day of Rest with Sunday zest, folks!" and: "Hi, kids! This is your action-happening programme with everything that's going on with the hit sound."

After that came Frank Ifield, bemoaning the unlikely fact that 'You came along from nowhere' and, in spite of all the 'wonderful dreams, wonderful schemes', what 'If you should go back to your nowhere?' Then Cat Stevens comes along with a song about 'a man going away and coming back with a bang'. "We see everybody shooting everybody else and it's all fun." How does the song go?

> I bin demoralised too many times.
> Now no more.
> I'm gonna get me a gun.'

Well! Quite a few listeners wrote in their objections to *that*! Come to think of it, a gun would come in quite handy for a desperate man like me. 'Shoot the Dee-Jay!" I cry. But no! I'd rather end it all and shoot myself!

Wait! Don't be too hasty! You could just miss a treat.

Now it's the hour, come round on its merry way again, for 'Pop North' with Ray Moore and his 'tip-top pop-time line-up'! Sandra Stevens turns up with — no, please! — Sandie Shaw's 'Puppet on a String' (for the fifth time this week!). Danny Street follows with 'It's all over. Didn't even cry', and The Settlers with:

> I gotta keep travellin' on
> I'm just a good-for-nothin' travellin' man
> Say buddy, can you spare me a dime?

ending with Ray Moore's oddly restrained rendering of the Flanders and Swann classic song about the ostrich:

> Peek-a-boo! I can't see you.
> Isn't it simply grand?

which actually brought a smile to my sagging cheeks, suddenly removed, largely by surprise, when Dave, Dee, Dozy, Beaky, Mick and Tich came on to ecstatic screams, and jokily announced; 'Mick got scragged by some females yesterday' which admission was presumably intended as a lead in to 'Touch me, touch me'. It all ended with the Mal Craig Three singing the futile lyric:

> Tell me you'll love me for a million years
> Then you can tell me goodbye.

I can't help feeling — from an outsider's point of view, you understand — that all this adds up to very little and that there seems to be a need for something deeper, something less ephemeral than the soggy philosophy of life soaked up by 'the kids' from these songs. Sooner or later, the fizz is bound to go out of the pop!

May 1966(U)

The Wind of Change

Can it be that a decade has passed since the Angry Young Men were so young and angry? Now, they are middle-aged and emasculated. Can it be so very long ago since the young invented 'flower-power' and all that 'love and permissiveness' thing, and young protesters linking arms with CND marchers? Nowadays, as Tony Aspler writes in the *Radio Times,* young people are looking for new outlets: 'Psychedelic light shows, wild clothes fashions, LSD, underground films, 'acid-rock' songs, street happenings — these are all manifestations of Underground activity.'

In 'Anarchy in the City', Aspler delves into the roots of the movement and sets out some of the reasons why this remarkable revolution is taking place. It is, he explains, 'a revolution without leaders, without a manifesto.' The Beat Generation had its roots in the novels of American writers like Jack Kerouac and the films of James Dean; the new generation looks to the poetry of Allan Ginsberg and the novels of William Burroughs. Essentially, a hedonistic philosophy is at the heart of it all — the freedom to take drugs and stay out all night without let or hindrance. The relentless pursuit of more and more rights inevitably leads to more and more rules and regulations, resulting in less and less freedom. What answers will the 1970s bring? 'Anarchy in the City' gave us some idea of the way our world is heading.

Poverty and Population

6 May 1967 (U)

Born Free!

'Man is born free and everywhere he is in chains.' So wrote Jean-Jacques Rousseau. Well, times have not changed, it seems, from those pre-revolutionary days. In 'Home for the Day', introduced by Marjorie Anderson and produced by Janet Ryder-Smith, Patrick Montgomery, of the Anti-Slavery Society, stunned listeners with the news that slaves exist today in over thirty countries. We, in our comparatively comfortable 'welfare state', may not be inclined to cast our minds over the harsh realities that exist elsewhere in our troubled world. There is nothing like comfort to help us lose touch with reality. Mr. Montgomery reminds us that chattel-slavery, debt-bondage, serfdom and servile forms of marriage (tens of millions around the globe) are sufficient testimony to the appalling lack of will on the part of the so-called civilised nations to eradicate slavery once and for all.

Did we not learn at school of the deprivations suffered by the cottars under the feudal system — a primitive 'cot' and precious little 'cottage' to survive on. Yet that simple man had more to life than countless millions of people in many places in the world today. There are still whole communities — indeed, whole tribes existing on little else than bread and water, and all too often something rather less than that. And still the killing and disease and death go on.

Most of our information comes through soldiers and missionaries who have had the dubious advantage of witnessing unimaginable cruelties and have given on the spot accounts of what they have seen. The situation is more serious than we think. Some countries have never taken part in a census of slavery, so we cannot know the real extent of the problem.

The truth of the matter is, as this programme reveals, there are still countless human beings living on or below a subsistence diet, slaves sleeping in chains, surrounded by guard dogs and men with guns and whips.

Did we not believe that slavery went out with Wilberforce? One hundred and forty-three years have gone by and still, says Mr. Montgomery, 'political expediency speaks louder than moral principle'.

Ironically, there are no anti-slavery societies in countries where slavery still continues to be practised.

*

9 & 12 July 1967 (U)

Population Explosion!

Thomas Malthus

In 1798, the year when Thomas Malthus published his *Essay on Population*, the view in some concerned circles was that the population of England would be seriously diminished within a generation or two. The same belief that the nation was becoming extinct was still current in the 1920s and 30s. On the other hand, with the post-war official encouragement to parents to bring larger families into the world, by 1966 Sir Joseph Hutchinson, in his presidential address to the British Association, warned that there was a very real danger of over-population in relation to our amenities and natural resources.

David Eversley, Reader in Population Studies at Sussex University, admirably explored the territory with skill and insight. He took issue with the Conservation Society's policy for the safe-guarding of open spaces and beautiful stretches of the countryside, supported, it seems, by a motley collection of fellow-travellers, advocates of soil conservation, vociferous anti-vivisectionists and adherents of the Family Planning Association. All were united in believing that the only answer lay in a reduction of human fertility.

Following the Blitz in 1940, an enforced migration of slum-dwellers to housing estates on the periphery of the city brought about a significant environmental adjustment accompanied by its own social change, and even discontent.

I remember, sometime in 1938, a developer bought a large stretch of land next to our family farm in Essex. The estate was complete and ready for occupation just at a time when hostilities between Germany and the rest of Europe were becoming a real threat. Following the declaration of war on 3rd September and the bombing of London's East End, radical emergency moves had to be made to accommodate the homeless. Where else than in a brand new estate of houses not twelve of so miles away from the devastated area?

Whole families were transported, lock, stock and barrel, to the countryside. They exchanged the antiquated washing, sanitary and cooking facilities of their back-to-back houses for a gleaming up-to-date bathroom and 'mod-con' kitchen. Did they like it? Not for a long time. Some people never! They missed the street-friendliness, the door-step culture, the drink in the local pub and cosy chats in the corner shop. Now those East-enders were surrounded by fields of vegetables, crops there for the taking, and there was a good deal of getting used to mixing with the local country-folk.

In general, there was a resistence in the countryside to this invasion of unruly town-dwellers. The Forestry Commission feared fires, gamekeepers barred people from thousands of acres of land, the Defence Ministry commandeered three-quarters of a million acres. So why, I ask, would town-dwellers want to live with over-crowding in preference to the countryside — in a cosy cottage perhaps, miles from the nearest shops, post-office, doctor, school, and petrol-station, when they could enjoy standing-room only on buses and underground, traffic jams and waiting in queues? Because, says David Eversley, human beings, unlike the proverbial rats, have the intelligence and ability to adapt themselves to their surroundings.

In the days of Malthus, three million people worked on the land to provide food for ten million. In 1960, half a million provide food for fifty million because the productivity of labour has increased fifteen fold. What matters is the efficiency of the population, not the size. So perhaps the trend is to live in town and go to the office in the country!

30 December 1966 (U)

Champions of the Poor

For the novelist and playwright it is generally considered easier to create evil characters than good ones. A good character that wouldn't hurt a fly, like Mrs Moore and her wasp in Forster's *Passage to India*, is not half as interesting as the conniving Iago, the depraved Fagin or the tormented Heathcliff. In the real world, however, in spite of what we hear in the daily news, 'good' people are more common than we think.

One of the truly 'good' people I have met in my life I came across by accident in the violent *melée* that followed a St. Patrick's Day anniversary parade outside the Post Office in Dublin's O'Connell Street, the place of the brutal 'Easter Rising' of 1916, so vividly recalled by W.B. Yeats:

> We know their dream enough
> To know they dream and are dead:
> And what if excess of love
> Bewildered them till they died?
> I write it out in a verse —
> MacDonagh and MacBride
> And Connolly [1] and Pearse
> Now and in time to be,
> Wherever green is worn,
> Are changed, changed utterly:
> A terrible beauty is born.

It was 17th March 1947. And there I was, an unsuspecting first year undergraduate at Trinity College, trying to keep a low profile. I had somehow drifted towards the centre of the crowd to hear the speeches better, angry anti-British speeches, scathing attacks on the British Government and British Prime-Minister, Clement Attlee.

Things looked dangerous. What seemed like a shot rang out close by, a loud report of some kind and a scream that froze one's very bones. Immediately there followed a frenzy of pushing and punching as the riot intensified.

Suddenly, a strong hand took hold of me. A uniformed woman-officer took hold of my arm and marched me off through the crowds. I had never been arrested before. I had not committed any offence, as far as I could see. I was culpable only perhaps in being British.

Later, sitting comfortably by a blazing coal fire in a small ground-floor office off Dawson Street, I was greatly relieved to find that, far from being arrested, I had become a 'guest' of the Dublin branch of the NSPC! And my captor was Nan Wogan, one of the Society's officers. I came to know Nan very well, making almost weekly calls at her office for a strong brew of Irish tea and a chat — the pot was permanently brewing on the hob in the back kitchen.

Sometimes I would accompany Nan on her 'missions' into the poorest districts of the city. The destitution I witnessed there defies description and would have matched anything that Dickens wrote of in his depictions of deprived parts of London's East End. Nan's whole life was spent caring for the poverty-stricken slum-dwellers who, in their hopelessness and spiritual inertia, had no means of improving their own condition. In many senses, Nan was their saviour, their rock.

Our friendship lasted throughout my four years at Trinity. After that I never saw her again. [2] She once admitted that she was surprised to have come across one 'daisent Englishman' in the world at least! Nan was what I call a truly 'good' person, giving her whole life to the service of others.

On the 'Home Service' today, C. R. Hewitt discussed the life and struggle of a truly good man, the remarkable champion of the poor, George Lansbury. Why have we never heard of him? Because, of course, he was 'good'. Who of us has heard of his good deeds? One would like to think that, in the whole history of the working-class movement, his name would be remembered, but clearly it is alive only in the memories of those who knew him personally (and there can't be more than a handful of those) or knew of his work among the poor.

George Lansbury was, Harold Laski once said, a 'moral genius'. He combined Christian values with his zeal to alleviate poverty and deprivation among the people of his home district of Poplar in East London. Thanks to Mr. Hewitt, we learn that George Lansbury founded the 'Poplar Guardians'. He conducted a long battle with the judges of the High Court 'on the legality of Poplar's refusal to levy London County Council rates' for maintaining the Metropolitan Police Force. He campaigned for improved local water supply to fight disease, and made a compassionate plea for more humane mental hospitals. His example and that of Nan Wogan surely extends the parameters of goodness to which a truly 'good' person could aspire.

[1] *James Connolly (1870-1916) Irish patriot, leader of the rebels, wounded in the Post Office insurrection. He was allowed to recover from his wounds enough to be subjected to the death penalty.*
[2] *I heard on my last visit to Dublin in 1999 that Nan Wogan was still alive at the age of ninety-four and living in a convent in Tara.*

9 & 11 July 1967 (P)

Over-crowded Britain?

The shadow of Malthus loomed over David Eversley's series of talks, 'Is Britain Being Threatened by Over-Population?', in which he expertly dispelled any doubt in the minds of those listeners who felt guilty about having 'two children and a motor-car' — apparently anti-social luxuries in the neo-Malthusian wave.

'Do you dislike tall flats, fast cars, the wage freeze, reduced travel allowances, battery-fed hens, and do you think your taxes are used to pay family allowances for shiftless paupers? Do you worry about famine in Bihar, or the atrocious overcrowding in Hong Kong? The Conservative Association, Mr. Eversley informs us, is concerned with these problems.

We in England, however, are not over-populated apparently. All the noise, the traffic congestion, the tensions of speed, are caused by the grossly uneven distribution of population arising from the great drive south. It is disquieting to think that, in the time of Malthus, less than half of the total population of 16,500,000 lived in the south-east. Now, out of 55,000,000, 30,000,000 live south of the line from Exeter to the Humber. Small wonder that one of the newer modern diseases, graphically described by Dr. Claire Weekes in an interview on 'Woman's Hour' last week, is agoraphobia — a nervous illness in which a person loses the confidence to leave the safety of his own home. No wonder the letter-box at Broadcasting House letter-box is stuffed with hundreds of listeners' letters daily, most of them worried house-bound wives writing to 'Woman's Hour'.

29 June 1967 (U)

Underfed and Overcrowded

Rupert Brooke's poignant lines from his famous sonnet, 'The Soldier' are cleverly adapted to suit the theme of Richard Keen's programme 'Corner of a Foreign Land', about immigrants in Bedford. It seems they all flock there for the chance of work the town can offer. One tenth of the population is foreign and there seems to be little tension with the local populace. However, if it escalated, it does seem to me that our indigenous culture might gradually be eroded, which for an Englishman of my age, embedded in an established European tradition, might see as a serious threat.

Rupert Brooke's soldier, buried in alien territory, away from his beloved homeland, has become an icon for the pacifist. It is not easy, in the words of Robert Burns, 'to see oursels as ithers see us' and difficult to imagine that a foreigner should deign to accept our hospitality and then to criticise our national life-style. Rupert Brookes' 'corner of a foreign land, That is forever England', is now woefully out of date. In the Bedford case, we see 'a corner of a foreign land that is for ever Poland, Italy, India, Pakistan, Jamaica, Trinidad, or Barbados.'

Apparently it all began with the Polish war veterans, who, not being able to return home for political reasons, stayed on and found employment in the brickworks. Then Italians arrived, driven out by the depression in Southern Italy. The universal wish for improved living conditions, higher wages, better education and social welfare benefits brought in waves of West Indians and immigrants from Asia and Africa, with resultant over-crowded 'temporary' accommodation. The question is, how do we effectively absorb them all into the system when they have an instinctive desire to remain in their own ethnic groups and have little desire to be assimilated?

*

31 December 1966 (U)

Hit the Road, Jack!

Bill Hartley introduced the last edition of the year of 'Motoring and the Motorist' in which he contended that there were more experts talking

about accidents than there were accidents. This may well be true but some discussion of a dire situation is essential, as Stephen Swingler MP, Joint Parliamentary Secretary for the Ministry of Transport, confirmed.

The pleasant, chatty, even jovial New Year's atmosphere belied the seriousness of the subject. We need to face the facts. There are 10,000,000 vehicles on the roads — a total of 15,000,000 licences.

With more vehicles than ever expected on the roads in 1967, how will the casualty rate compare with the last twelve months? Some 8000 people are killed on our highways and byways every year and a staggering 300,000 are disabled by accidents.

Motorways are to be extended by another 87 miles and there will be a hundred miles more added to the trunk roads, not to mention a number of new by-passes. The £12,000,000 Tyne Tunnel Scheme will be completed next year.

There is considerable doubt that the White Paper to be published in the Spring will suggest any solutions to alleviate the motorist's dilemma. One suggestion is to carry out more spot-checks on the condition of vehicles, but as yet there seem to be no hard solutions being put forward.

In London, the Blackwall Tunnel will be opened with, broader roads and gentler bends, and new fly-overs at Bow Bridge and Edgware Road, it is hoped, will ease congestion. Area traffic will be overseen through computers and through traffic signals.

What, then, about the roadworks that continue to clog the system? As we all sit. stationary on a new fly-over, amidst the lines of traffic cones, how can we look with equanimity on the impassive faces of the road-workers silently drinking their mugs of tea?

30 December 1966 (U)

Cap in Hand with a Begging Bowl

The spirit of Scrooge is abroad in the streets of London. In the 'Today' programme, Jack de Manio included a discussion on the present spate of unemployment among young executives. The coming year looks like being a grim one, due to mergers, automation, the suppression of posts and the great economic squeeze that is forecast. Professional and executive classes, including senior grades, are suffering serious redundancy, with all the humiliation and deprivation that condition brings about — its strain on family life, the realisation of being dependent on the State.

Over a period of three months there have been 20,000 applications for 2,000 jobs. A great deal of moral courage and faith in the system, failing and ailing as it is, has had to be mustered by those suffering redundancy, many even going up to town as usual, briefcase in hand, to avoid telling their families.

*

14 July 1967 (P)

House-Hunting Safari

On 'Woman's Hour' this week, it seemed to me that the other face of agoraphobia could have been the claustrophobia which prompted James Norbury to go on a house-hunting safari outside London, far from what Keats called 'the city's din'. After looking at the advertisements, Mr. Norbury discovered that there were more liars in the world than he, in his innocence, had imagined. The 'cottage in charming rural surroundings' turned out to be next to a large council estate and was riddled with dry rot and rising damp. Mr Norbury, the knitting expert, has decided not to 'cast off' just yet.

25 June 1967 (U)

Storming the Barricades!

Let us dwell for a moment on a formidable race of Amazons, not that fearsome band of female warriors in ancient Greece, but a new breed of women who began, little by little, to make their mark on their own times. In our increasingly enlightened age, women have at last succeeded in breaking through the male-dominated social and political barriers to find fame and fortune — and sometimes notoriety!

Kenneth Harris interviewed the intrepid Baroness Burton of Coventry on the 'Home Service' (produced by Jocelyn Ferguson and Tony Gould this week) in a compelling programme of reminiscences. Glossing over her early years as an accomplished athlete (World Sprint Champion 1920, Yorkshire Hockey First Eleven 1924-32) and ignoring her later distinguished career in industry and business management, she chose to concentrate on the years 1938 to 1942 when she turned from sportswoman to politician through her burning passion about unemployment.

Women did not appear in the Olympic Games until 1928 so by the time Elaine Burton was of age she had plenty of encouragement and training. She remembered running in her first championship when, as she passed a large fat bandsman he shouted: "Go it, littl'un!" Her father taught her to run in spiked running shoes, so she was well-primed for the 800 metres in the Olympics.

Elaine Frances Burton became a teacher in the local Council School in the Rhonda Valley, where the children came barefoot to get a pair of boots, and where, in a place of real poverty, they sang 'Bread of Heaven....Feed me now and evermore,' amidst all the hunger and deprivation. Her problem, as with most visionaries, was lack of money to achieve the vision. She watched homes being systematically broken up by the Means Test. Young people would rush across the street to avoid the 'Means Test man', who came intent on cutting the dole money.

Geronwy Rhys spoke of the unemployment of the entire population of Merthyr Tydfil, turning South Wales into 'a world of stone.' All people could do was to 'go to bed to save energy.' This was the 'honest, awesome' Miss Rhys, who founded the Professional Women's Register.

Following the much-publicised visit of Edward VIII to South Wales, Baroness Burton turned to politics. She took what proved to be an unrewarding job for twelve months at £3 a week, helping a children's organisation, but there was no scope for her high ideals to flourish. The only relief was the cinema. Her favourite actress was Greta Garbo and her favourite film, *Queen Christina,* with its magical snow scenes and its depiction of happiness, of love, of the passing of time. She admired its pristine and ethereal qualities, and above all 'its mystery'. In short everything that real life denied her.

Soon she was offered a job with the National Fitness Council as a swimming organiser, but the Council was dissolved at the outbreak of war. For fifteen weeks she was unemployed and applied to seventy-five places of work, just at the time when Ernest Bevin was saying how badly women were needed by the Nation. Not surprisingly, such an invitation did not escape the notice of a number of determined women. Eleanor Rathbone, in fighting form on the twenty-first anniversary of the Suffrage Act, gave as good a piece of advice as any for the would-be campaigner: 'Those who want to get things done cannot be afraid of reputation.'

Along came the indomitable Violet Bonham-Carter, 'the best woman who never got into Parliament', and Lilian Baker, the dedicated member of the Prison Commission, the adored Gracie Fields, whom 'success never spoiled', and that remarkable 'First Lady', Eleanor Roosevelt, who, with her consummate command of words, inspired her fellow-campaigners with words akin to poetry: 'Each age is a dream that is dying, or one that is coming to birth.'

Two 'aliens' were permitted to enter the chosen circle in the persons of Ed Morrow, and J.B. Priestley (married to the archaeologist and writer, Jacquetta Hawkes), both, like Robert Browning, heavily involved in and beloved of 'the glorious company of women'.

Ed Morrow had the task of telling the American people about the plight of Britain under the Nazi threat, in particular broadcasting graphic descriptions of the Blitz — the searchlights sweeping the London sky, people streaming into the Underground to the sound of sirens wailing, double-decker buses with scant lighting on the top deck, the terror of the ever-present possibility of a direct-hit, and, next morning, people turning up for work as if nothing had happened.

Our Baroness remembered the time when she was working at the John Lewis store in Oxford Street. One morning she came out of Oxford Circus Underground Station to find everywhere flattened after a particularly devastating night-time air-raid. Not a shop remained intact. J. B. Priestley recalled the grim scene and saw the world as 'one indivisible whole of suffering and despair', concluding that 'we are better people than we imagined ourselves to be.' But no one could doubt the bravery and courage of women at war, and afterwards, as prime movers in the rebuilding of the nation.

30 December 1967 (P)

On the Bread Line

Freddy Grisewood

'Any Questions?' visited Eastcombe in Gloucestershire this week. How I look forward to the comfortable voice of that veteran broadcaster, Freddy Grisewood! The first question concerned poverty and family allowances. Lord Waldegrave admitted that one in six children in Britain suffers from malnutrition. While Rosamond John wanted to see family allowances put up, musicologist Anthony Hopkins deplored the fact that there was no guarantee that the money was spent on the children. Malcolm Muggeridge thought that the whole population explosion was humbug — there are not too many people but too little help. 'History books,' he said, 'will judge that very savagely.'

11 May 1967 (P)

Trouble in Hong Kong

Anthony Schooling highlighted the grave population problems in Hong Kong, describing the striking contrasts of wealth and poverty that span the island. Tall skyscrapers housing the banks and insurance companies tower opulently over a water-front jammed with ancient-looking Chinese junks. Up the hill, 'a gigantic dump' of huts, shacks, and hovels provides a home for thousands awaiting transfer to one of the resettlement blocks. Every house holds six times the number of people it was built for, some so overburdened with people that they collapse into the streets with a roar of rubble and dust.

Derek Davies, editor of the *Far East Economic Review*, described Hong Kong as a vibrant, lively place, a jungle, a free-for-all, with no government interference, no import duties and minimal taxation. For the poor, however, there are no sickness benefits and no unemployment allowances. In spite of this, the Hong Kong Chinese are optimistic people.

30 December 1966 (U)

A Cheap Home for Life

While the wheels of industry inexorably turn and technological advancement speeds us ever faster towards utopia (supposedly sometime about 1984!), other spheres of welfare are not always receiving sufficient attention, as David Dimbleby pointed out in his inquiry into local authority housing. In spite of the rather pedestrian treatment of this relentless topic — and setting aside its lack of succinctness and pungency — the message at the core was quite as poignant as Jeremy Sandford's recent play on a similar theme. *Cathy Come Home*.

I also received a certain degree of shock from Keith Hindell's programme on 'Primary Schools in Poor Areas' in which Stuart

McClure perceptively commented on the relationship between poverty and educational achievement. It is all part of what Dan Smith, in his recent talks on regional economic planning, called 'the quality of life' — a twentieth-century attitude towards the environment. It is, after all, a question of the regional machinery being made to serve the national strategy. We do want attractive surroundings to live it. This is precisely where economic planning is falling short of the nation's needs.

11 May 1967 (P)

Wherever Next?

The other day, when I was looking at a wall-map of the world, someone asked me which country I would like to live in if I ever had to leave England. I gazed at the large unpopulated expanses of snow, salt water, sand, and jungle. I could not think of anywhere. I saw so much political upheaval in so many of the more desirable places that I began to feel an attack of agoraphobia coming on.

From my notebook: *11 May 1967*

Shangri-La!

A reader has written inviting me to try British Columbia! He assures me it is the best place in the world for a quiet life!

Revolution and Revolt

22 September 1966 (P)

Russia in 1916

Riots. revolts and revolutions were the subject of Sir Paul Duke's reminiscences of Russia in 1916. Riots in the streets, revolt in the regiments, confusion at court, and the Empress (deluded by the hypnotic Rasputin) hardening the heart of the Tsar against his revised liberal policies, all of which brought an end to the old régime.

Sir Paul described these events, and those which followed, with that compelling style which makes this kind of personal reflection such good listening. His voice was tremulous, but occasionally loaded with the military explosiveness of the old soldier. The account of his days in the press department of the Anglo-Russian Mission, of the progress of the war in Europe, the shortages and disasters at the front, provided a dramatic backcloth to the more momentous events surrounding the fall of Kerensky's* provisional government and the return of Lenin, Trotsky and Stalin from exile. Now Russia will be celebrating the fiftieth anniversary of the Revolution. Yet, in Sir Paul's rivetting account of the assassination of Rasputin and the downfall of the Tsar there was surely a tinge of nostalgia for those bad old days.

Oleg Kerensky's grandfather, who lived in exile in Southport

22 September 1966 (P)

The BBC Sound Archives

The interview with Sir Paul Dukes was an excellent example of the high standard of production that comes out of the BBC Sound Archives. With on-the-spot recordings sent back by war correspondents during the war, a library was built up to supply producers with illustrative material for talks, current affairs and other feature programmes. Then, about ten years ago, a small production unit was set up with a view to exploiting the resources available. Whereas many broadcasting systems in other countries, for example, Germany and France, keep Current Recording libraries (mostly pre-recorded material), usually retained for a certain time and then destroyed, the BBC went in for the preservation of selected recordings at a very early stage, with the result that the Sound Archives now possess the best and most highly-organized collection in the world.

12 September 1966 (U)

More About Rasputin

Grigori Rasputin

Sir Paul Dukes' memories of his life in St. Petersburg, just fifty years ago, at the time of the assassination of Rasputin, were as vividly recounted as if they had happened only yesterday. He emphasised that, rather than being an uprising of the people, the Russian Revolution was principally Marxist in origin.

The mad monk, Rasputin (it means 'Dirty Dog'), was illiterate, uneducated, impatient, explosive, wily, physically strong, a womaniser and, being exceptionally tall, overpowering in his manner and presence. Through his undoubted hypnotic power over the Czarina (desperate to save the life of her dying son), he was one of the principal causes of civic frustration and anger, as much among the ruling aristocracy as among the rank and file of the new Marxist agitators.

Prince Usupov's assassination plan had to be capable of destroying a man not only strong in body and constitution, but of tremendous strength of mind.

First, the priest had to be lured to his place of execution by a trick. Then he had to be poisoned by massive doses of cyanide of potassium, which, though he suffered some serious effects from it, he resisted with all his might. This superhuman will to survive did not end there. He was riddled with bullets and yet still struggled to live on. He was dragged out into the snow to die. His stinking body was bundled into a sack and thrown into the icy river.

Sir Paul's description of this spectacular death and its tragic consequences made impressive listening. We immediately recognised in him both that authoritative understanding of things Russian, and a man whose life-experience was deeply felt and thought-provoking.

2 February 1967 (P)

China in Turmoil

The importance which the BBC attached to the Chinese question prompted them to postpone two programmes and cancel another in order to present an extensive ninety-minute survey, ably introduced and chaired by James Mossman and John Tusa.

Richard Harris of *The Times* saw Mao as 'the visionary saviour of China', attempting to infuse a messianic spirit into the Chinese brand of communism.

After all that, the programme left me with misgivings, especially that experts could differ so widely about what is actually going on inside China at present, and how far the strength of Mao is, to borrow his own metaphor, a paper tiger.

*

25 December 1966 (U)

Culture and Revolution

Who has ever heard of Wu Hang? No? Doesn't ring a bell? Oh! Well, never mind! In case you didn't know, history has marked him down as the opponent of the Cultural Revolution in August 1966. He was courageous enough to stand up and be counted when everyone else was lying low for fear of reprisals. The uprising did not go well in Shanghai, though Nanking openly defied it. Even the President of China himself opposed it, and in the midst of it all, was the not-inconsiderable figure of power and 'persuasion', Chou en Lai.

In parts of this vast country formal studies in schools were closed and pupils returned home, whilst men roamed about the City Streets pasting up posters with large black lettering denouncing the revisionist policies. Anti-Russian propaganda became a regular feature on the national radio, vilifying their powerful neighbour as 'Soviet revisionist swine'. Women openly cut off their plaits and buns to publicly demonstrate their support, in defiance of a traditional practice associated by many with the old feudal times. The streets and the buses were crowded. Everywhere, in every direction, the Red Guards were in evidence.

Richard Harris, in his article in *The Times*, writes of Mao Tse Tung as 'the visionary saviour of China.', and for that reason, many were 'filled with a crazed enjoyment of what was happening'. According to Harris, Mao was extremely skilled in breaking up his opposition and rendering them powerless. In his communes, the State even owned the clothes of its workers. He wanted to 'purify' China, to clean out its intellectuals, the very people who wanted to see progress in their country.

Mao Tse Tung

An interesting part of the discussion centred on the Russian attitude to the movement. Would they be glad to see the Chinese political and economic power collapse into a state of chaos? Would there be problems about imperial advancement? Would the *status quo* be preferable if the existing 'friendship' were to be maintained? Would these two super-powers find a *rapprochement* to suit both sides if the Cultural Revolution achieved its aims? After all, the Russians had been 'gunning for Mao' since as far back as 1959. Suspicion about long-term motives was growing. How much mischief could China do abroad?

Robert Guillard of *Le Monde* claimed Mao had asked too much of the Chinese people and described him as 'a man of tremendous calibre'. He thought that a real world tragedy would arise if China should collapse into disorder.

One of the keenest observers of these events was Japan. The 'verbal warfare' that was carried on between the two powers was frequently based on inaccuracies in translation. The Japanese reporters were telephoning back to Tokyo on indistinct lines. The extent of the real battle, rather than being revealed, was concealed. Tao Chu, the Chinese head of propaganda, was reported to have been dragged through the streets. This was found to be untrue. The only source of information, apart from normal diplomatic observations, was the selected and biased reporting permitted by the New China News Agency. It was important to remember that Japanese reports, however inaccurate, provided an important window for the rest of the world as to what was going on in China.

So the Cultural Revolution was not after all a 'power struggle' — rather 'a disagreement over the way the economy was being run'. Others have thought otherwise, believing it to be precisely a 'struggle of succession', and therefore 'power'. Thus, in Mao's declining years, there was a constant struggle over policies, very similar to what happened before the death of Stalin in Russia.

But where, asked the panel, was China going today — was it in a state of progression or retrogression? The China of today is politically 'primitive', a system in which intellectual freedom cannot survive. Professor Stessinger, a member of the panel, emphasised that Maoists had to be seen as pragmatists, 'consolidating' the gains of the Revolution. According to the Professor, these people believed that 'being orthodox' was ideologically more important than being 'technically proficient'.

Gradually over the years, fewer working hours became an essential part of the new economy, a small degree of ownership of private property was allowed. Presumably, a peasant might once more be permitted to own his own clothes!

But what is the picture as seen through the eyes of Peking radio? We hear the singing of the revolutionary song of the week, we are entertained to the thoughts of Chairman Mao from *The Little Red Book*, we can hear fifteen-minute songs composed on Mao's literary works. The people are constantly battered by repetition from Peking throughout nineteen major stations.

Whilst the radio is a means of controlling the minds of the people, public disgrace also plays its part. Three officials from a municipal government were openly accused of nepotism — they had acquired houses for members of their families and friends. Other offenders of party law were forced to wear dunce's caps or were thrust into the backs of lorries and taken away, never to be seen again. There was no resistence — only absolute submission to the will of the State.

What is clear from all this wide-ranging discussion is that, in spite of all the subterfuge and social indignities, the majority of the Chinese people are loyal to Mao and submit to the 'purification' activities of the Red Guard. Occasional hysterical anti-Soviet demonstrations occur; Chinese students in Moscow are beaten up. Russian diplomats decide things are getting too hot in Peking and move out. Mao's 'paper tigers' retreat. The Chinese dragon still breathes fire and an old Chinese myth is perpetuated.

*

July 1967(UP)

All Greece and No Fat Living!

'In the Public Eye' maintained its high standard of interviews on the 'Home Service' when Judith Listowel and John Tusa talked with Francis Noel-Baker, an authority on Greek affairs. His great-grandfather was Byron's wife's cousin, if that is at all a useful statement. It could perhaps suggest that Mr. Noel-Baker had inside family knowledge of Greek life in those troubled times when Greece laboured under the Turkish yoke. Byron's copious letters can fill us in on the detail but the broad picture of the Greek post-revolutionary struggle was brought to life in a vivid and personal way through Mr. Noel-Baker's first-hand experience of the country.

In the turbulent times when military *coups* are quite the fashion, crowned heads are metaphorically toppled and replaced either by generals with an iron grip on the people or presidents who are no more than puppets. Mr. Noel-Baker may have mixed feelings about such matters as he is a little to the left of centre in the Labour Party, but whatever extremes he may sanction he must surely have regretted the loss of that old Greece beloved of tourists with its spectacular romantic ruins, its abundance of vineyards and olive groves, its elaborate history of gods and goddesses, and its overpowering lust for life.

Now, Greece struggles along under the despotic rule of a military *junta* headed by Colonel Papadopoulos. According to Noel-Baker, the Colonel is neither a fascist nor a Nasserite. That may well be so, but the reality of the matter is that the country and its fun-loving people are repressed by a military dictatorship, with the consequent inefficiency in its parliamentary institutions and blatant corruption in the Civil Service. Noel-Baker made a special point of speaking with the Prime-Minister, urging him not to permit any executions. There should be no retribution.

True, the present *régime* ostensibly promises to hand back the reins of government to civilian authority, but it has to be admitted that the *coup* itself was 'an astonishingly efficient operation' in spite of the resulting near-chaos. Apparently, observers were pretty convinced that the American CIA were mixed up in the event somehow. Andreas, the son of Professor Papandreou, did, however, make an appeal to the anti-monarchist factions and co-operated with the Greek communists to great effect, though he was careful not to take sides — an achievement Macchiavelli himself would have been proud of! The people could not make up their minds and frequently changed sides. There was the ever-present threat of executions, despite Noel-Baker's protestations.

As to the King, whose position was 'delicate', to say the least, he wanted no *coup* and attempted to respect the intentions of the Provisional Government. Since the death of King Paul, the Queen Mother had played no part in public affairs. According to Noel-Baker, who secured an interview with King Constantine, there was a genuine wish to return as quickly as possible to parliamentary government. At present it is difficult to see where this is all leading, so the discussion, perforce, could do no more than highlight the problem.

13 July 1967 (U)

The Great Dictator!

Colonel Abdul-Nasser

Chris Cuthbertson's production of 'Profile of the Month' chose to examine the life of Gamal Abdul Nasser, President of Egypt, in a rivetting talk by Michael Adams. We were taken through 'a frantic succession of triumphs and disasters' on what could only be described as 'a tempestuous career.'

Egypt was ruled by a degenerate and corrupt régime under foreign domination. The fact that Nasser could keep a secret in a country widely given over to gossip made him a skilful and effective conspirator. He could play on the widespread resentment to a system based on wealth and privilege. Once in power, he took care to manage a smooth change-over by securing a pledge of loyalty in the hour of disaster. As Michael Adams suggests, had Nasser been another Hitler, he would undoubtedly have risked assassination or a judicial execution 'unless the discredited leader were able to slink away to oblivion in some villa on the Riviera'.

The revolution of 1952 overthrew the Egyptian monarchy at a time when military *coup d'états* were part of the Middle east political fabric. In many ways Nasser was 'the prototype of Arab military leaders.' His technique was swift and effective. He began by swooping on the all-important radio station and a few key government offices. He then introduced land-reforms and effectively broke up the old feudal estates.

He had succeeded in triumphing over the 'holy alliance' of Britain, France and Israel, but the creation of a Jewish state on Arab soil, resulting in a confrontation with Israel, might have been less troublesome if Syria had not adopted an extreme position and provoked reprisals. Nasser moved his forces into Sinai and declared a blockade of the Gulf of Aqaba. The risk he took was incalculable, given the Russian, British and American pressures. He played a double game in not aligning himself with either the Eastern or the Western bloc, and was now in a position to resist any further foreign domination.

There is no doubt, his Israeli opponent, General Dayan, underestimated Nasser, thinking him 'a paper tiger'. But, once in power, he brought economic growth, more industrialisation, women's emancipation, and promoted birth control. Adams attended a Press Conference in Cairo at which Nasser was asked: 'Are you a dictator?' to which he replied: 'Well, if I am, the people seem to like it!'

*

13 July 1967 (P)

What's in a Name?

Last week, at the end of the Middle East debate in the Commons, the Foreign Secretary issued a firm reprimand to all those Conservative members who had neglected to refer to President Nasser in the proper manner. The most polite called him 'Colonel Nasser' and the most impolite have referred to him as 'Dictator Nasser'. 'The fact remains', said George Brown MP, 'that he is President of his country.' General Dayan recently called him 'a paper tiger', using Mao's Chinese simile.

Judging from Michael Adams's 'Profile of the Month' in 'Study Session', Gamel Abdel Nasser does not exactly fit any of these appellations. He is no longer a colonel, still lives in the suburban villa he occupied as a young army officer, and is little changed by political power. To Egypt, he has brought economic growth, industrialization, women's emancipation, and land reclamation.

Michael Adams, who was in Cairo soon after that unparalleled act of fealty, when in the midst of national disaster, the Egyptian people refused to allow the President to resign, gave a lucid account of the pattern of life of a man who has risen from small beginnings as the son of a post-office employee to become President of his country, a man who has altered the path of Egyptian and Arab history, and who has succeeded in giving Egypt a sense of nationhood.

13 July 1967 (U)

Myth and Nationalism

President Nasser's 'political awakening' referred to in a recent article, and his relationship with the Egyptian people at large, might suggest, according to Professor Barbu, Professor of Sociology at the University of Sussex, that the construction of a political leader's 'glorified image of himself' is more than likely to be a pre-requisite for the creation of 'a myth about his power and abilities'. This individual image, when it appears as a collective image, becomes the social and political myth on which nationalism is founded.

Nationalism, says Professor Barbu, 'is rooted in an idealised group consciousness.... It postulates the nation-state and the unity of the ethnic group as ultimate norms in the life of the individual'. Usually, even invariably, such a process arises out of conflict, as in Egypt and after more cataclysmic events such as the French and Russian revolutions. The same hypothesis could be applied to almost any post-revolutionary state that had undergone 'deep structural conflict.'

I am not entirely convinced by the ethnic argument, but it is certain, as the Professor says, that 'modernisation' is undoubtedly the prime cause of social conflict and in many cases political upheaval. He puts it all down to three inevitable processes: industrialisation, urbanisation and democratisation.

Admittedly, comparisons are odious. Egypt did not experience 'la grande peur', as in France, 'when peasants, frightened and, at the same time, excited by rumours of revolution, poured out their aggression against authority, and the land-lords in particular.' Clearly, there was a need for a new form of social integration or, as Barbu says, of a sense of 'belonging.' There are no longer peasants, bourgeois and aristocrats. There is simply the broad social category of 'Frenchmen'. The old traditions and social order — 'divine right' for example — now gave way to a recognition of talent and merit.

But it does seem to me that, like the 'ethnic' argument, the 'meritocracy ' idea has its dangers and weaknesses too. The 'myth' begins to creak at the seams because 'nationalism is a kind of regression to an emotional and irrational form of solidarity'. In the Germany of the 1930s, and in many countries throughout the world since, the mythic vision has proved to be part of the grand design of things that repeats itself endlessly.

From the dawn of history, leaders, good and bad, from Alexander the Great to Nasser, from Napoleon to Stalin, from Cromwell and Nelson to Jefferson and Churchill, have sought to identify themselves with that mythic process.

Scandal and Intrigue

9 March 1967 (P)

A Secret Shared by All Europe

An illicit love-affair between a young Russian writer and a brilliant Spanish prima donna provided a subject for excited gossip throughout the salons of mid-nineteenth-century Europe. That the singer was also married gave rise to considerable speculation. The fascinating Pauline Viardot-Garcia, friend of Chopin and de Musset, utterly enchanted the youthful Turgenev when she visited St. Petersburg in 1843. For forty years he never ceased to love her, and never once compromised her by any passionate outburst, though their love was 'A Secret Shared by All Europe'.

Turgenev

April FitzLyon's talk, which included extracts from the Turgenev letters (read by Gary Watson), gave a lucid account of the vicissitudes of the affair, veiled only by a thin film of incredulity, stemming largely from lack of evidence, for the whereabouts of Mme. Viardot's letters remains a mystery. Twice, Turgenev engineered a meeting in subversive circumstances, first by contriving to meet Louis Viardot on the grounds that they shared sporting interests, and then when he entered Moscow from exile on a forged identity card, risking everything to see her. In 1847, he followed the Viardots to France, where he visited them regularly at their country house at Courtavenel, once when Gounod was staying there, a house from which grew the shape and tensions of *A Month in the Country*.

Though Turgenev was inspired to work hard, his writing was of secondary importance to him; only his letters revealed the turmoil of his loneliness, more endearing now, never breaking into impropriety. 'I tried to write some poetry for you, but it all broke into fragments...I could only look, dream, remember.' The ethics of sending his eight-year-old daughter (by a Russian peasant girl) to Mme. Viardot might well be questioned, fraught as they are with overtones. His subsequent removal to an apartment in the Viardot household made a very curious *ménage à trois*, a relationship which Turgenev's Russian admirers regarded as shameful and humiliating.

*

9 March 1967 (P)

Sex and Mr Gladstone

Victorian England was in the throes of controversy concerning the private life of Mr. Gladstone. On his way home from Parliament, he was frequently observed to accost prostitutes, chat with them and invite them into his home. He was also known to have visited a brothel and to have persuaded one of the inmates to go home with him. In spite of this, his enemies failed to discover any signs of impropriety.

Mr. Gladstone's preoccupation with 'fallen women' was legendary among the scandalmongers. His great ally was W. T. Stead, who had written a series of sensational articles in the *Pall Mall Gazette* exposing the iniquitous sale of young girls into prostitution, articles filled with salacious details which could gratify the hunters of pornography. Furthermore, Gladstone had found it convenient to support the cause of Charles Bradlaugh, the atheist, whose association with the estranged wife* of the Rev. Frank Besant was again the subject of unpleasant gossip. The sensational Dilke affair, with all its content of insinuation and intrigue showed the Prime minister in a highly equivocal light.

In brief, these facts form the background to one of the strangest trials in legal history, in which Gladstone's son succeeded in protecting the family name from disgrace and, once and for all, vindicated the private aspirations of his illustrious father. 'Sex and Mr. Gladstone' was a dramatisation of the proceedings.

Arthur Swinson's script regrettably lacked that bite that the listener might have hoped to find in such sensational material, the pattern of which resembled closely the initial phases of the conflicts between the Marquess of Queensberry and Oscar Wilde. Captain Peter Wright (vividly played by William Fox) was brilliantly cross-examined by the most feared of advocates, Norman Birkett (less impressive in William Harrison's interpretation, I imagine, than in real life). Gladstone's association with the actress and star of the music halls, Lily Langtry, and Parnell's mistress, Kitty O'Shea, invited accusations of hypocrisy in a man who in public life was the personification of the Christian ethic. Lord Milner's remark that 'Mr Gladstone was governed by his seraglio' set off a series of derogatory statements which led the stalwart Captain Wright to ably defend the reputation of the long-deceased Mr Gladstone, which had languished for so long in the murky labyrinth of suspected immorality.

William Gladstone

As it happened, the evidence was circumstantial and nebulous. Gladstone's reputation as an upright Victorian gentleman remained untainted. Unfortunately, Stanley Williamson's production failed, at least for me, to build the tension up to the final admission by Captain Wright that his remarks had, after all, been 'intemperate'. There was no sense of the climactic. The final verdict did not absolve Gladstone from accusations of dissembling and hypocrisy, but proved him to have been beyond doubt a good husband. Even in 1926 the Victorian family ethic was triumphant.

* Annie Besant, President of the Theosophical Society, supporter of the cause of Indian self-government

9 March 1967 (U)

Pros and Cons!

The trial of William Gladstone, Prime Minister of England, was unusually enlivened by Lord Salisbury's remark that he had known more than five of Queen Victoria's Prime Ministers who had committed adultery. In fact, there were nine! Numerous rumours had circulated about Gladstone:

1. Apparently he had unwisely tried to make advances to a lady outside a shop.

2. He had dallied on a regular basis with Lily Langtry, who had a string of wealthy lovers, including the King. She sent a telegram from Monte Carlo strongly denying the affair.

3. He succumbed to the allurements of the godchild of the Tsar, the seductive Olga Novakov, who had been sent over by the Czarina as part of a Russian plot to prevent Britain going to the aid of Turkey.

4. As for the courtesan, Laura Bell, she was described in Court as being 'all things to all men and most things to most women!' Gladstone had hoped, apparently, to discuss 'her religious beliefs with her'!

William Gladstone

5. He had acted as a go-between in the sensational affair between Parnell, the darling of the Irish, and his lover, Kitty O'Shea..

6. He was declared — horror of horrors — to be a governing member of the Milbank Penitentiary for Fallen women.

Is there any more damning evidence? You may be sure that the perspicacious and ruthless prosecution in the person of Norman Birkett QC would find some if there were.

This was, however, a strange case since Gladstone had been dead for nearly thirty years. It was his reputation, nobly defended by his son, Lord Gladstone (formerly Governor-General of South Africa), against the accusations of a Captain Peter Wright, who had written that Mr.

Gladstone appeared 'to speak the language of the highest and strictest principle, and in private to pursue and possess every sort of woman'.

Stanley Williamson, the producer of this gripping radio drama, quotes in the *Radio Times* the legal maxim: 'the dead have no rights and therefore can do no wrongs'. To prove the matter, he drew together a competent cast in William Harrison (Norman Birkett), William Fox (Captain Peter Wright), Garrard Green (Mr Justice Amory), with the assistance of Richard Carey, Peter Schofield, Jim Wiggins, and David Marlowe as narrator.

The verbal duel was played out by two angry opponents with Gladstone's reputation as the winner's trophy. Lord Gladstone accused Wright of being 'a liar, a coward and a fool,' and 'a foul fellow'. Wright angrily retorted that his adversary was 'an arch humbug'. The jury was out for two-and-a-half hours. Finally, the verdict was that the great William Gladstone, one of Queen Victoria's most distinguished Prime Ministers, was found to be not only respected but respectable. Thus this extraordinary episode in legal history, a web of post-Victorian dissembling, humbug and hypocrisy, came to a close and was consigned to the bottom shelf — at least until author, Arthur Swinson, rediscovered it and made from the court proceedings an absorbing radio play.

Shirkers and Workers!

2 May 1967 (P)

Focus on the Lazy British!

Bruce Angrave's *Radio Times* illustration for 'Focus on the Lazy British' showed a corpulent John Bull reclining peacefully in a hammock, dreaming of 'Swinging London' and bingo. George Fischer's programme was introduced by Edgar Lustgarten, who began with Arthur Shadwell's remark, made as far back as 1906, about the English being a nation at play.

Mr. Lustgarten interviewed a number of experts on industrial productivity. Dr. R. B. Buzzard, Research Director of the National Institute of Industrial Psychology, proclaimed that for at least four hundred years the British have been putting out this kind of propaganda about themselves, and foreigners have been gullible enough to take it seriously. Lohter Philips, a German economist living in Britain, had some pointed remarks to make about tea-breaks and knocking-off time on shift work, as well as the tens of thousands of workers who take time off to watch football matches.

It is the intensity of work that is less well developed here than in other countries. Dr. Tim Pearce, of Esso Petroleum, and Mary Goldring, business editor of *The Economist*, had some constructive observations to make on the relationship between time and management and the need for specialist management training. 'We have too many gifted amateurs'. We are now paying the long-term penalty for having started the industrial revolution. Because of that, developing countries can jump ahead one hundred and fifty years in as many months. The worker here still feels he is going to be exploited. He is suspicious of change and authority.

We laugh warmly at Michael Flanders and Donald Swann singing of their domestic disasters in that hilarious number, 'The Gasman Cometh', though it is uneasy laughter. It is just that other nations don't talk

Donald Swann

about their faults as much as we do. As Ogden Nash says in his poem, 'England Expects', we are too busy being 'reticently thrilled and tinglish'

*

2 May 1967 (U)

Pride, Prejudice and the British Working Man

The English masochism of lying down and allowing ourselves to be torn to shreds by foreign wolves is legendary. The truth is, we are not disturbed by criticism as much as we might think. We even allow ourselves to laugh at foreigners' jokes about our sex-life, but then, who doesn't love his hot water bottle? As for foreign influences on our daily lives, we accept only the most expedient. We adopted Saxon Law, Scotch whisky and Indian tea. We rejected written constitutions, central-heating and shish-kebab. Our divorce laws, property laws and adoption procedures show us to be maddeningly intolerant. According to many critics of our society, we are snob-ridden, inefficient and resistant to change, our weather is appalling and our food is even worse. But wait a minute! This is the sixties, not the thirties, nor even the forties.

I can just remember that amiable old performer, Robb Wilton, reducing audiences to uncontrolled laughter by opening his comical reminiscences of the British working man with the words: 'The day war broke out...'

Any seasoned traveller would know that pride and prejudice are international. But show me a country more tolerant of foreign foibles than England, more welcoming to foreign settlers (at least those who ever get through the Home Office nets), and more indifferent to attacks in the foreign press.

Tolerance is central to our particular brand of humour. The trouble is we enjoy a good laugh, even if the jokes are on us. We rarely laugh at other people because that requires a healthy superiority complex (or do I mean inferiority?). Anyway, our Anglo-Saxon blood wouldn't allow it. Few countries expose their faults to the world so blatantly as we do and laugh at them so much.

Roy Castle introduced extracts from one or two of Robb Wilton's sketches, including a clever satire on the British working man:

'I began as a fireman. Now, I'm a chief. (*Pause*) Now I've got nothing at all to do with fires. (*Laughter*) I've simply got to ring the bell and the men spring onto the engine. (Pause and titters) That's if they're there, of course. (*Laughter*) Mind you, I know where to put my finger on them. (*Laughter*) I've only just come out myself! (Laughter and applause).

*

April 1967 (U)

When is a Worker not a Worker?

An interesting word of caution was aired on the Third Programme last week about the meaning of the term 'worker'. Apparently we have a stereotype in mind whenever the word crops up in discussion. Here is a man who clocks on every morning, goes through the same activity for the prescribed eight hours, five days a week, and then clocks off at five. He divides his spare time between a session or two a week down at the local pub with his mates, and occasionally, when things flare up with the bosses, joins in a protest march just to show his muscle. However, Professor Paul O'Higgins asks in his talk whether it is not time to reconsider the meaning of the word, which until now has been synonymous with older forms like 'servant', 'employee' and 'workman'. But before we start trying to redefine it, we should consider the legal definition.

Well, apparently there is no precise definition. Roughly, says the Professor, 'a worker is someone who has a contract of employment with an employer.' But then, what is 'a contract of employment'? Does it establish the power of the employer to control when and where the 'worker' does his work and how he does that work? If this is so, then it does not apply comfortably to highly skilled people like airline pilots and medical staff. Then there is Lord Denning's 'integration test', in which 'a man is employed as part of the business'. As an example, a full-time surgeon is an integral part of the hospital set-up.

Strictly speaking, anyone who enters into a contract with an employer becomes a 'worker', even if a 'contract for services' is entered into with an independent contractor. In this case, he 'sells not so much his labour as the doing of the job,' but with the difference that 'he is not subject to the control of the employer on how he does the job'. The professor puts his case neatly together by example:

'The taxi-driver who agrees for a price to drive a man from his home to the station is an independent contractor, whereas a chauffeur who is permanently employed by a wealthy man is a worker.' He makes a powerful point by referring to the controversy currently going on in the building industry where the role of the worker and the independent contractor is a burning issue difficult to resolve. What about pension rights and insurance in the work place? What about a 'labour-only' sub-contractor who provides the men to do the job? The size of the problem is enormous: there are currently 49,000 labour-only sub-contractors in the building industry, over one sixth of all building workers.

There are always the Wages Councils Act (1959) to protect minimum wage violations, the Trade Disputes Act (1906) to pronounce breaches of contract and sort out any 'trouble at mill', the 'Industrial Training Act' to finance employment schemes, and the 'Contracts of Employment Act' to sort out conditions of work and redundancy problems. As far as I can see, the Courts are being kept pretty busy. 'Perhaps the solution may lie in legislation extending the protective provisions of labour and social security law to cover workers and independent contractors alike.'

The Professor's answer to his original question: 'When is a worker not a worker?' is, not surprisingly, 'When he is self-employed'! Now, why was it that I expected some incredibly simple answer to this question? And there it was all the time! You see, 'the rules of labour law and social security legislation are designed not only to protect the individual worker, but also to protect the community as a whole'. The trouble is, what happens when workers are replaced by gangs of self-employed persons?

28 May 1966 (U)

What a Waste!

Barney Bamford interviewed Peter Barnes, a sewage disposal operative.

'I am a middle-aged man inclined to portliness,' said Mr. Barnes. 'Of course, sewage is not everybody's cup of tea!'

Sportsmen and Gamblers

September 1967(U)

Moral Ethos and Social Evil

With true British caution, we have resisted until now the establishing of a State Lottery in Britain. How could we even begin to think about such an idea? Just because half Europe has gone in for lotteries does not mean to say we should follow suit. However, it seems that the powers-that-be are determined that we should all have a lottery whether or not we actually want one. It is a fine Orwellian example of the State manipulating the people. 'We know what is good for them. They shall have it.' After all, a lottery could bring in as much as £100,000,000 per annum. Not bad! The annual turnover on gambling could be as much as £10,000,000! So what are we waiting for? Never mind putting temptation in temptation's way.

Neil Hepburn's production brought together two members of Parliament, a representative of the Church and two economists to discuss the matter with Leslie Smith.

L. J. Ludovici thought the lottery would work, his view being supported by Dr. Alex Rubner, who considered gambling as a natural form of consumer expenditure and a valuable source of revenue. By comparison, the Government, he said, spends money on discouraging people from smoking, raises tax on it and still doesn't actually repress the addiction.

But is the lottery socially desirable? Even if it is, many opponents are not convinced that it is *morally* desirable. Sir Cyril Osborne MP suggested that it might bring in a 'something for nothing' attitude and considered it 'economically unsound'. If we take the Government's moral stance on the betting tax (at only 2½%), we find a much more draconian attitude in places like Israel (12½%) and France (22%). 'Sterling' means 'worthwhile, fine, good, dependable' apparently, so why can't we be allowed to enjoy a 'flutter' now and again?

The discussion wandered into a consideration of ethical points. For example, what about the dubious encouragement of 'getting something for nothing' without having to work for it? In a time when people want more and more for less and less, where does 'work' come into the frame? Rather do we need to encourage a 'willingness to work'. 'No-one is entitled to live well unless they work well.' The conclusion on that point was that work justifies our existence.

Norman St. John Stevas MP was of the opinion that we had to 'work' as an important part of the 'moral ethos'. In times of national crisis, work was an essential ingredient in the recovery process. But is gambling a social evil? Probably, since it has a bad effect on the moral consciousness of the individual. And the Government is already deeply involved in an enormous gambling exercise since it gathers a considerable revenue in taxes from football pools and greyhound racing.

Clearly, this matter was not going to be resolved, in spite of presenter Leslie Smith's efforts to lead the discussion towards some sort of conclusion. There were strong views on both sides. All we can say is that, from the experience of other countries from Rhodesia to Russia, state lotteries play an important role in raising revenue, so we had better go off and read Dr. Alex Rubner's book, *The Economics of Gambling,* before we place the next bet, and especially before the Government gambles any more of our future away than it has already!

17 March 1967 (U)

The Lone Navigator

As I write, Sir Francis Chichester is sailing north into the curious doldrums, with their periods of equatorial calm, and that mysterious marine wilderness, the Sargasso Sea. Claude Muncaster, the distinguished artist and veteran sailor, vividly described these hazards in 'Radio Newsreel'.

'It's the greatest challenge of his life to round the Horn on his own. Nobody knows what it means.'

Brian Hawkins compiled a programme, 'The

Sir Francis Chichester

Lone Navigator', from BBC Sound Archives, successfully laying bare the heart of the man, the driving force of the adventurer, the faith and courage of the great navigator.

It is 'a race against ghosts', said John Anderson, a drive to surpass the achievements of the ancient masters of sail.

After it is all over, what then?

'It's the effort that counts, not the success,' said Sir Francis.

But to the crew of *H. M. S. Protector*, who stood aghast at the pitch and roll of *Gypsy Moth IV*, it can only remain, as for us all, a triumphant example of human spirit and endeavour.

17 February 1967 (U)

Honi Soit Qui Mal y Pense!

In 'Any Questions?', chaired by Freddy Grisewood, this week, Anthony Hopkins broached the subject of the sensational refusal by the Lord Mayor of Portsmouth to grant the Freedom of the City to Francis Chichester, he who had become an national icon for his courage and tenacity in challenging oceans and storms to achieve his vision.

After all, had not Sandie Shaw won the European Song Contest? If the freedom of the City could be given for the 'cavorting of a shoeless pop-singer', then is not the courageous achievement of Mr Chichester to be considered by all to be beyond compare?

Rosamond John urged the Lord Mayor to reconsider. Lord Waldegrave thought the whole matter 'too silly for words'.

As might be expected, Malcolm Muggeridge openly claimed to be 'a despiser of honours' and congratulated Mr Chichester 'on his having missed it!'

20 June 1967 (P)

The Stanley Matthews Story

Sir Stanley Matthews

Struggle and disappointment were the distinguishing features of 'The Stanley Matthews Story', a series of revealing extracts from his autobiography, abridged by Derek Parker and read by Denis Goacher (though with just a shade too much adulation and sentimentality).

Sir Stanley Matthews had the advantage of an enthusiastic and understanding father, constantly advising and encouraging in moments of humiliation or triumph. After one game, which drew the attention of the national press, the boy rushed home to hear his father's comments and was greeted philosophically with the remark: 'Son, you'll play a lot better and you'll play a lot worse.'

There were other bitter moments when, for example, young Stanley missed the ball and heard a crowd of 40,000 groan as one man. Again, thanks to his father's encouragement, he regained his old form and played before a record crowd of 149,000 at Hampden Park. His name was on everyone's lips, but he had the humility to remark that 'they'd got things out of perspective by calling me the wizard of this and the wizard of that'. By the time success was within reach, and a cup-winner's medal at Wembley within his grasp, his age was against him. Through sheer determination, he finally won that medal.

6 October 1966 (U)

It's Just Not Cricket, Old Chap!

Sports have rarely been my *forte*, so I never enjoyed the privilege of being a member of the school *élite* and never achieved the dizzy heights of playing with the First Eleven, like my three brilliantly sporty cousins. In fact, I was unusually prone to disasters on the field. In a crucial house game, I was brutally stung by an angry bee and, much to the annoyance of the house captain, was promptly carried off to the sanatorium, where a large egg-shaped bump soon appeared on the top of my head. I was never quite the same again!

In later life, as a young master at a Sussex prep school, whilst fielding in a 'Masters versus School Eleven' match, I reached up to catch the ball, which was hurtling down towards me at a rate of knots, was immediately knocked senseless and carried off the field in disgrace.

I think I hit the ball at most once or twice in any tennis match I ever played and that was a pure fluke! As for squash and ping-pong! Well, need you ask? I could never understand why my fellow players got so frightfully shirty about my name being drawn out of the hat! They didn't seem to appreciate my prowess at long-distance walking, though even that's no advantage when you're running the 'hundred yards'!

Arthur Calder-Marshall

I did win the three-legged race with my mother once, at a fête to raise funds for our local W.I. It was just as well we won because Mother was the local Chairman and was considered to be rather 'the lady of the manor'. She couldn't be seen to lose against the gawky and fleet-of-foot Miss Ridley, who owned the sweet-shop at the end of the cinder-path. She had plenty of regular practice running after the local kids when they scooted off with her liquorice laces.

All I can say is, at least one of the masters didn't shoot me in the foot during a cricket match, as befell little Tangent, son of Lord and Lady Circumference, in Evelyn Waugh's *Decline and Fall*.

Don't take me too seriously though. I am only making a point of humour at my own expense — as is often my way. Self-parody is like a boomerang. It has a habit of flying back and hitting you where it hurts most.

Humour, like time, tends to distort not only reality but truth too. Perhaps I wasn't really tied leg-to-leg to Mother after all, but to my adorable art mistress, the fair Phyllis Hall. Now that would really be a memory to cherish. Much more exciting than winning an egg-and-spoon race any day.

Now Arthur Calder-Marshall, that most urbane of wits, is in my view one of the 'chaps' after my own heart. He didn't shine in the starry galaxy of School's sporting heroes either. Nor did he relish much of the team spirit. He was, to say the least, 'an original'.

Arthur evoked memories of warm summer days when he talked about his time of 'beflannelled misery' on the cricket field at his prep school. I immediately recognised a kindred spirit when he slyly admitted that his favourite position was 'long stop', which had 'a great deal to recommend it,' having 'only one chance in five of being drawn into the picture.' You could, of course, always put in a plea for a downpour.

As for football, 'nothing but the death of the headmaster could stop the game'. The principal disadvantage of football was that there was no 'long stop' position. At least with rugby, you could 'fall on the ball', but of course you ran the risk of 'a loose scrum being formed over your inert body' and you turned up at tea hideously bruised and misshapen.

No! Prep school was all nose-bleeds, hunger, irregular verbs and the looks of scorn in the eyes of onlookers booing on the touchline.

Technology and Pussy Galore!

20 May 1966 (P)

The World and Marshall MacLuhan

It seems to me that writing about anything as abstract as the theories of Marshall MacLuhan might well end up as a piece of pretentious intellectualism. MacLuhan, Director of Toronto's Center for Culture and Technology, is one of the most influential theorists of the mass media. His seminal study of the popular arts, *The Mechanical Bride* (1951), was followed by *Understanding Media* (1964), described as 'a strategy for survival', and purported to present a new vision of 'unified man' by means of an analysis of electronic media.

George Steiner saw Dr. MacLuhan as an iconoclast who thought of the world as an electronic village where everything was interrelated, and foresaw a genetic change in man as essential in such a world if man was to survive. McLuhan, he said, 'fights against our discriminatory logic'.

Andrew Forge, the artist, clung to the established ideas of art as self-expression and the body as a source of pleasure. He rather sadly asked how artists could exist if they could not express themselves lineally. Jonathan Miller admired McLuhan for his original analysis of the devices through which we obtain knowledge, but abhorred his deplorable English, his appalling puns, and his poorly assimilated information. Since Dr. McLuhan considered art would become a form of play, Miller foresaw that the man of the future would be a playful creature, motiveless, existing only in an effortless world. It is clearly all a matter of time!

30 May 1966 (U)

Brave New World

With the all too rapid growth of technology the world is changing at an alarming rate. Our daily lives are assisted by a growing number of labour-saving devices which in no time at all go out of date and are supplanted by other equally ephemeral innovations. As for art, it is only the expression of 'thwarted effort' and is therefore doomed to die. Along with all this will come genetic changes. Would automation reduce human endeavour to a web of pointless 'fragmented tasks'? As power decentralises, there will be, it seems, a gradual tendency to 'drop out' of traditional roles such as father, mother, teacher, politician. There will be a 'sudden dislocation' of society, even of life itself. The teacher will be the pupil and the pupil the teacher, the writer the publisher and the publisher the writer. There will be no clearly defined borderlines.

According to Marshall MacLuhan, human beings are merely receivers, bombarded by countless impulses which not only continue to increase with time but travel towards us at a ever-increasing speed. In the symbolist poems of Baudelaire and Rimbaud and in T.S. Eliot's masterpiece, *The Waste Land*, we discover a new interpretation of the world, where everything is 'simultaneous'. There is no causality and no effect. So, in this 'electric' age, everything will be directed by a new 'mythology of simultaneity' in which all events occur at the same time.

Unlike Eric Mottram, I am suspicious of MacLuhan. I believe he has latched on to certain defined principles that are alien to the human spirit. But then there is no room for the human spirit in MacLuhan's concept of our future. Leonardo da Vinci's 'whole man' is exploded into a multitude of specialisms (see p 36). Apparently, society can only be integrated in these conditions by instantaneous communication. There is no doubt that MacLuhan is sincere, but so were the ancients who thought the world was flat!

As we are more and more entrapped by the media, and since everything is interrelated, the work of art will only be preservable in pre-electronic terms. Art is no longer meant to last, is instantaneous, like the pop song or a television programme. MacLuhan wants to rid the world of its 'ancient snobbery' and give the new media free reign.

Jonathan Miller thought this would 'open doors to chaos.' The planet itself could become an out-dated art-form, 'an old piece of camp.' In his view, 'we are in the amphibious stage,' poised uncomfortably between the old mechanical world and the new electronic age. It is understandable that writers like Rabelais and Joyce are crucial to the MacLuhan canon. He is the supreme iconoclast.

27 & 29 February 1967 (P)

The Old Woman of Redditch

An eighty year-old woman of Redditch has spent her life putting 200,000,000 eyes into (presumably) the same number of fish-hooks. She works at a rate of 2,000 hooks an hour and, on average, produces 65,000 eyes a week. 'What do you like about fish-hooks?' asked the innocent interviewer in 'Midlands Today'. Alas, what answer could any of us give to such a formidable question? Mrs. Annie Mander replied that they occupied her mind. In a sense, it was a primitive technological problem, and one which Gale Pedrick thought interesting enough to include in his popular programme, 'Pick of the Week'.

23 January 1967 (P)

Is Technology Unnatural?

Mrs. Mander's highly individual approach to technology seemed to me to represent a small part of what Dr. Ian Jarvie spoke of in his talk. His argument indicated that extremes of adulation and fear of technological advances were harmful to a clear-sighted appraisal of recent and future developments. That Dr. Jarvie's thesis arose out of a consideration of the artificiality of a topless dancer from San Francisco might at first seem far-fetched. False from painted toe-nails to eyelashes, here was 'the perfect, put-together girl' — inflated bosoms, remodelled facial features, the lot! — so convincing that we fail to tell the real from the artificial. That is technology for you! Where will it all end? ' We don't know,' said Dr. Jarvie guardedly. 'Perhaps it will never end.'

25 January 1967 (P)

A Bond Dishonoured

That technology could possibly be related to sex and sadism might seem obscure to the uninitiated, yet no fastidious author of thrillers and science fiction can now afford to ignore the matter. *Analog* enthusiasts would soon be on his tracks, as well as ballistics experts, like Geoffrey Boothroyd, who wrote to Ian Fleming in May 1956: 'I dislike a man who comes into contact with all sorts of formidable people using a point .25 Beretta. This sort of gun is really a lady's gun, and not really a nice lady at that!...If Mr. Bond gets himself a Centennial Model .38 Smith and Wesson Airweight, he will have a real man-stopper weighing only 13 oz.' As for the sex angle in the novels, he remarks: 'I have no criticism of the women in them, except that I've never met any like them and would doubtless get into trouble if I did.'

Sean Connery as James Bond

This letter points to two important aspects of the Fleming formula. First, the expertise and the accuracy of the technological detail: Bond's car is equipped with oil-spray, smoke-screen device and ejector seat. Secondly, the translation of the technological into the sexual: guns and fast cars represent sexual drive.

Bond was a symbol of the state of mind of the nineteen-fifties and sixties; this at least was one clear-cut notion that came out of a conversation in John Bowen's programme on the spy cult in literature and the cinema. He made a point about the sado-masochistic element in the Fleming formula: Bond has a licence to kill, yet is punished for it in some of the most brutal scenes in literature.

The conflict of wanting to hurt and be hurt is a complex dilemma. The matter was disappointingly dropped from the discussion. At one moment the argument was so fierce that the poor listener had to be content with a concerted shouting and bawling that would have been better suited to a protest meeting. I strongly objected to being denied a discussion of Fleming's technique, which, we were informed, would be beyond our comprehension! To align Fleming with Spenser and *The Faerie Queen*, as one deluded contributor attempted to do, was sheer absurdity, though comparisons with Graham Greene's *Our Man in Havana* and John Le Carré's *The Spy who Came in from the Cold* were more ably dealt with. There were other more felicitous moments, but on the whole this was an ill-organised programme. The James Bond novels, with all their absurd patriotism and far-fetched plots, may well belong to the realms of sub-literature, but if technology and sex must join forces then give me Pussy Galore every time!

*

7 March 1967 (U)
Paradise Lost?

One of the most impressive series of documentary programmes this week has been Gerald Leach's 'Biological Backlash' (see p 181). Its theme is immensely important to our survival, and centres on the conflict that has been developing since the industrial revolution between nature and technology — in other words, the natural world and the man-made world imposed upon it.

The technologists, says Gerald Leach, are single-minded in their search for perfection at the expense of our 'huge and complex natural world', which is frequently damaged 'gravely and irredeemably', with the result that the natural world lashes back at us. He asks the most crucial question of all: 'Are we able to spot the impact, to forecast it?' We will certainly need to if we desire what he calls 'a dignified future.'

A dozen or so distinguished biologists, including three Fellows of the Royal Society, were questioned about these weighty issues and asked to meet the challenge head on with a view to 'designing our future'.

Professor Morris began by drawing attention to the major housing problems experienced by countless communities around the world. Professor C. H. Waddington FRS, of Edinburgh, stressed the need to invent a means of controlling population growth and revolutionising our approach to food-production.

According to Dr. Palmer Newbould, we have been far too

dependent on ancient agricultural methods. We now have chemical engineering, by which we can convert one organic (inedible) substance into another (edible) organic material. But still our crops only achieve one to two per cent efficiency which, with a little change, could become thirty per cent. The introduction of plastic domes could vastly improve high-technology farming by producing three or four crops a year (though no reservation seemed to be made about the resultant decimation of our countryside). Agriculture would, with the advancement of technology, become 'a semi-leisure hobby'. Farmland would be turned into 'playgrounds' and town-dwellers would be raising a few sheep themselves. Surprisingly, all the contributors saw this as 'an exciting vision', though a Utopian one. The countryside could become a place of 'rural tedium' or 'a pastoral paradise'.

7 March 1967 (P)

A Universal Cure-All

Whilst Gerald Leach's first programme in the 'Biological Backlash' series dealt with environmental problems, the second concentrated on the effect of technological advances on the human race.

Coincidentally, in this week's episode of 'The Saint', a professor discovers a health-giving serum, but, needless to say, he is murdered before he has time to develop his wonder drug! Is the human race to be 'murdered' before it has time to learn how to prevent illness, before it is forced to find the means of curing it?

Professor Morris began by emphasising the need for opening up more research into preventive medicine, which, no longer viewed as science fiction and purely speculative, was now discovering a more effective treatment of streptococcus and long-term diseases like renal failure and coronary thrombosis. But things were already beginning to move. There was now an American gadget that could break down the condition of a patient's blood in two minutes flat. Gerald Leach advocated the screening of the whole population. Such a revolutionary decision would transform the nature of the Health Service.

It was generally agreed that our 'biological happiness' could only be achieved if we began to see the body as a 'biochemical machine' which needed to be 'tuned up to optimum level'. At present, all we can do is replace the defective 'sparking plugs and carburettors', but miniature recording equipment on a patient could assess the physical condition.

What impressed me most about these discussions was the fact that realistically, far from finding answers to these riddles, technology is still groping in the dark. We desperately need a more active experimental approach in the area of psychiatric research, for example in the field of aggression and the encouragement of more spontaneous responses. We need to address ourselves to the problems of old age, in an effort to reduce the misery, the loneliness and resultant depression.

Professor Thorpe, the Cambridge pathologist, believed that we had to become 'ecologically-minded' if we were to understand the 'give and take of nature'. We can still learn much from animal behaviour and instincts. The television has done much to highlight this aspect of life. Whereas the rural inhabitant had a pragmatic view of animals, the town-dweller might view the domestic pet as largely a version of a child, a plaything, a companion for walks in the park.

Professor Joseph Hutchinson FRS was concerned about the schism between town and country. There is a growing tension, a loss of empathy. Townspeople had acquired the image going out into the country for a picnic and not once stepping out of their cars. To most townsmen, the maintaining of the countryside was a mystery, even an irrelevance. There is a need for a revised system of ideals and ethical beliefs that have ruled man's life in the past. The Professor admitted that such a change in our biological thinking would be virtually impossible since 'religious conviction is not present in the majority of mankind.'

The conclusion, as far as I could glean from this very complex discussion, was that technology is in itself not enough. We cannot allow 'the continual raping of the earth'. We must always be aware of the danger of the technocrats taking over. 'We tend to act with a mere cleverness and not with a broader wisdom in these matters.' 'The biologist's attitude, is not one we can afford to ignore.'

Travel and Foreign Places

5 May 1967 (P)

Misconceptions

Eskimos live in igloos, Frenchmen are great lovers, Germans are models of efficiency, Hawaiians wear grass skirts. These are only a few of the misconceptions about foreigners that many of us used to have and, as such, almost outnumber those chestnuts beginning: 'There was an Englishman, an Irishman and a Welshman.' But we only have to look around the world to see for ourselves.

12 May 1867 (P)

The Eskimo Solution

Nigel Murphy, in 'It Takes All Sorts', interviewed David Ward about his Eskimo ancestry. It seems, after all, that there is still one place in our troubled world where honesty and love are prime concepts in the Eskimo way of life. Eskimos are, however, in danger of extinction. Mr. Ward grew up in fear of the white man, though his father was of English-Canadian stock. Eskimos, he said, are 'numbered', like migrating animals. His Eskimo mother felt no bitterness at her ill-treatment, clinging only to her belief in ultimate love and truth. 'There is,' said Mr. Ward, 'nothing more important than one's fellow human beings.'

12 May 1967 (U)

There is a 'Greenland' Far Away!

Eskimos are in danger of extinction. The sad fact is that, today, there are less than 20,000 Eskimos inhabiting the Greenland, Alaska and Siberian territories. In a land where the worst crime is theft, it seems to me that it should be nothing short of a miracle in the modern world to find a people who seem to represent the higher qualities of human life. They are honest, are innocent of the meaning of profit, take everything at face value, believe in ultimate truth and love, share everything, and revere their elders. They work when they feel like it or when necessity requires it of them. They seem to be natural Christian Scientists for they have no doctors and know how to heal themselves naturally. They build igloos, tan hides, fish through ice. Their life is rugged and hard but they rarely complain. Physical attraction is low down the list for the qualities of a good wife. Children are very often promised to each other from birth.

Yes, all this is very well. It sounds to be the perfect idyll, but only in the summer months of the Northern Solstice when daylight comes. In spite of the traditional glass of 'happy juice' given to shivering tourists to warm their flagging spirits, living such a large part of one's year in darkness would take a great deal of getting used to!

The story of their exploitation by the white man is grievous, for who else but a white man knows how to profit from honesty and truth? But life in the snows is harsh and what the white man cannot do to destroy the life of the Eskimos, the climate will erode in the end.

11 May 1967 (U)

Paradise Islands?

I sailed away with the delightful Avril Mollison this week, over idyllic 'translucent waters', to a place where seven hundred islands are 'scattered like confetti across the Gulf Stream' and where, 'dropping anchor in some tiny cove', we could bathe at midnight under the 'hibiscus-laden scented air'.

Now Avril didn't know I would be accompanying her on this exotic trip and no doubt would have put a stop to it. In fact, Avril doesn't even know of my existence, and she never will, at least not until she reads this piece, and then she might begin to wonder what she has missed! Then again, I think she might not!

I have always wanted to holiday in the Bahamas, so you can imagine what excitement I felt at the prospect of hearing Avril talking about her recent visit to the islands.

All was not what it seemed however. A radical change was taking place. Self-government was in the process of being introduced and the old charm and hospitality was, to say the least, becoming unfashionable. The whites seemed 'nervy and withdrawn', the coloureds 'hostile and bitter'. The trouble lay largely with the local mafia who gained exemption from the 'no-gambling' rule, with the inevitable result that protection rackets and prostitution prospered. It was all blamed on the 'old white regime', which was generally regarded as 'corrupt'. The island had become, in her words, 'the Coney Island of the Caribbean'.

But just a moment! I think I've got the whole thing wrong! Miss Avril Mollison was actually on a fact-finding tour. There was none of this 'hibiscus-laden air' stuff! This was genuine commentary on a pretty serious situation.

She first set out to interview the new Prime Minister of the interim government, Mr. Lyndon Pindling. He was confident, he said, of succeeding with his new policies on education, welfare and agriculture. The pace and pattern of the new government, he said, would be 'quite different.' But how different?

Different? I mean, what about all this 'midnight bathing' thing? Isn't that what the British want? They don't want to know about 'welfare policies' and stuff like that. They want the sun-drenched beaches and the casinos — not forgetting the good old fish and chips!

Well then? The Prime Minister was right when he said: "What we want to do is to put more money in your pockets.' And.......

Hold on! What did you say? Why are all those Cadillacs parked outside those run-down shacks over there? How can that be?

Maybe I would have felt more at home in the hotel. In fact I'm pretty sure of it because, as the coloured chamber-maid assured the lovely Miss Avril Mollison: 'We have a lotta intelligent-behavin' people here!'

*

8 May 1967 (P)

Utopia Down Under

Dodie Coates emigrated to Australia some years ago, as she told 'Woman's Hour'. Once there, she found she had arrived in a man's world. 'Women are second-class citizens.' They open their own doors, carry their own cases, and light their own cigarettes. The cost of living is three times as high as in London. With some employers, there is still something of the old master-and-convict attitude, and there is a certain snob-value in being able to claim a convict for your family tree.

On the whole, 'the Australians don't hate the British, since they are not good haters.' Maybe we are living in a world of falling standards in the Old Country, but can such a Utopia exist where bus-drivers and taxi-men don't hate their passengers and shop assistants are pleased to serve you?

Yes, apparently. In Sydney!

9 May 1967 (P)

Health and Efficiency

In 'Woman's Hour' (produced by Anne Howells this week) the likeable Marjorie Anderson introduced Kim Korte, who married a German and became a 'Hausfrau in Dusseldorf'.

Mrs. Korte found the Germans fanatically tidy, and, unlike the orderly English, they never queue. They seem to prefer fighting tooth and nail, using everything from a strong elbow to a sharp umbrella to get first place. She was baffled by the 'forbidding-looking mob of battling housewives' at the butcher's shop, and the brawny butcher-women with their cleavers and their bulging muscles.

The talk highlighted the problem of isolation that every foreigner must feel, by definition, when living in a society largely alien to his own. How many of us have been exhausted by the ceaseless etiquette of shaking hands and kissing on both cheeks, customs which seem to distance people from each other rather than draw them closer. I can sympathize with Frau Korte about the efficacy of those feather beds! Her cameo of the boy chimney-sweeps perilously balancing on the high roofs was vividly described.

*

6 May 1967 (U)

Balancing Act

Frau Korte's account of the little German chimney-sweeps was very well worth the telling. It showed something of that strange mixture of the old and the new in post-war Germany.

One day, she noticed with some horror a tiny blackened figure climbing out of an attic window. He perched precariously on the narrow apex of the roof, then began tip-toeing dangerously along a ledge, his arms held out to balance himself. He had a thick coil of weighted rope and brushes twined round his shoulders. Thus from house to house he moved, like an aerial ballet-dancer. Herr Korte simply remarked: "That's a piece of good fortune — seeing a chimney-sweep before midday!"

*

25 December 1966 (P)

Journey to Jerusalem

In a year in which the Queen sent a special exhortation to the women of the Commonwealth, it was fitting to listen to a variety of broadcasts about extraordinary women. 'Journey to Jerusalem' was a reconstruction by Vivian Ogilvie of a journey across the Sinai Desert undertaken by three Victorian ladies* in the winter of 1875. All three were profoundly religious; all three, pilgrims in a strange land. Mrs. Seymour, the redoubtable leader, soon became reconciled to her camel — all 'sweetness and docility' — not quite the bad-tempered creature I bestrode at Beersheba last year!

The ladies were impressed by the grandeur and starkness of the desert, and often the 'weary land' fell far short of the religious mystery of a place such as Mount Sinai — stern, cold and desolate, 'looking as if God had left it.'

**Frances Seymour, Cecilia Davenport, and Kate Whitehead. These indomitable ladies spent four weeks riding on the backs of dromedaries. Their journey from Cairo to Mount Sinai was hard, under a blistering sun, always in the shadow of danger and risk. They followed the trail of the Israelites out of Egypt and through the wilderness of the Promised Land. Then, riding ponies and mules, explored Beersheba and on into the Lebanon. Their letters home describe their moving and often alarming adventures. They were stoned by the inhabitants and ever at the mercy of greedy, untrustworthy Bedouins. Lebanese Arabs stole their bread and four Turks beat up their manservant.*

12 May 1967 (P)

Down, Out, and Broke in Syria

David Makinson talked about his experiences of travelling penniless through the Middle East. He set out, guitar in hand, rucksack on his back, and no money in his pocket. A kindly Arab saved him from near-starvation by giving him a meal of kebab and rice. Faced with the prospect of getting his throat cut by a wily Bedouin, he cadged a free lift on a bus crammed with goats and chickens, all heading for Beirut, where he had to sell a pint of blood at a hospital to buy himself a square meal — a false economy, surely, and subject to the law of diminishing returns!

Mr. Makinson ended up on the Irani-Turkish border, cold — his sleeping bag had been stolen at Dover— and hungry. A soldier shot a stray dog and the starving traveller fed hungrily on its fried flesh. It is a miracle he is alive to tell the tale.

12 May 1967 (U)

Living on the Edge

On his way to Damascus, Makinson ran across an Arab who wanted a European wife. Makinson explained that he had a sister in London. In return for her photograph and 'her address', the Arab parted with the equivalent of ten shillings in anticipation of future pleasures. Makinson was able to add to his hard-earned wealth by selling a further pint of blood on arrival in Jerusalem. There he marvelled at the hustle and bustle of the street markets and found peace in the Garden of Gethsemane.

Baghdad, where he relished the hot tea, he found dirty and run down.

In Kuwait he had to exercise some skill to avoid being propositioned by men in the street. On one occasion he did a deal with a Colombian sailor to buy Scotch whisky and resell it over the border at vast profit, but it proved to be 'a fool's errand.'

He trudged over the barren mountains of Persia, passed through such exotic places as Shiraz and Isfahan. In Teheran, which he did not take to, he enjoyed traditional Persian hospitality but always ended up paying for everything!

He grew tired of being used as an itinerant language teacher.

'How are you, mister? I Mohamed. You teach me English, eh?'

In the end, Makinson sold his watch, his harmonica, his cigarette-lighter.

One night, he suddenly found his head swimming and everything in his room began to slide about. Shouting in the streets signalled violent earth-tremors and two thousand people died within minutes.

Time to move on. In Thessalonika he sold more blood for a fiver. He finally 'kipped down' in a German Approved School. On one floor there were petty thieves and youths who had absconded from home; on another, thugs and hardened criminals.

Time to head for home.

'Bumming about is O.K.,' he said, ' until you run out of money!'

11 May 1967 (P)
Travelling Light

Noel Barber's impressions of Amman were very different—flashy American cars, the boom in washing-machines and radios — a new, young, exuberant, flourishing city, in fact. In the hinterland, still the harsh nomadic life and the black goat's-hair tents and most incongruous of all, the shepherds driving their flocks through a traffic jam of Cadillacs.

Amidst all this widespread unrest, even Avril Mollison's interesting talk, 'Nassau Revisited' and Francis Noel-Baker's disturbing account of 'The Greek Crisis', left me thinking 'I'll just stay where I am for the moment and put up with the relatively minor snags,' in a Britain that may well have dropped the 'Great'. As a London Jewish Rabbi was wont to remark, whenever he was in difficulty: 'Keep calm! Remember you're British!'

26 September 1966

On the Track of Lawrence!

John Dayton, whose firm rebuilt the Hijaz Railway, gave an interesting personal account of his time working on the initial survey. In company with *The Seven Pillars of Wisdom* and *Arabia Deserta*, he revisited the line that T. E. Lawrence had wrecked. Dayton found that Lawrence had blown up all the bridges. Some eighteen trains were discovered abandoned on the line. At a Turkish fort he found the desiccated skeletons of Turkish soldiers. He noted also how accurate Lawrence's information had been.

However, a talk that led the listener tumbling along six hundred miles of rehabilitated track could tend to be just a trifle repetitive.

The line may be carrying pilgrims down to Mecca in a year or two, so there is some sense of destination at least.

30 December 1967 (P)

In the Public Eye

'In the Public Eye' is a stimulating series which explores contentious issues with a very real concern for human rights. Apartheid in international sport was the subject of a gripping interview with South African, Dennis Brutus, who believes that sport should be non-racial.

Considering the cruelties he suffered at the hands of his prison guards, he took a surprisingly 'loyal' stance. He was shot through the intestines, trying to escape in a Johannesburg street, then made to slave in a quarry, pushing barrows loaded with heavy stones. It was not surprising that he sounded dispirited in recounting the experience.

'I don't think any man can do any good in prison, except break stones,' he said. 'Nothing is worse for a human being than to be rendered useless by his own society. I have come out [of South Africa] in order to go back.'

30 December 1967 (P)

Two-and-a-half Square Miles

A topical talking-point was raised by Sonya Callingham in her feature about Gibraltar. This unique island, flanked by foreign frontiers, with the Union Jack flying over its Moorish castle, the Indian bazaars, the 'pump' politics, is, as one Gilbraltarian claimed, 'not exactly English though proud to be British.' I liked the image of 'The Queen's Man' (the Governor) walking about his 'doll's-house kingdom', as one contributor put it.

Lady Anderson, wife of a former Queen's Man, gave a vivid account of the war days when the people of the island refused to be evacuated and 'clung like limpets to the Rock'.

Now there is the uncertainty, the frustration, the cultural claustrophobia which the young especially must endure. 'We're in the thing together...come what may'.

Miss Callingham, whose script maintained the right balance between the historical and the futuristic aspects of the situation, asked what was left that was attractive. 'Home', was the reply. Patrick Harvey's production gave just the right note of urgency and restraint that are part of good documentary features.

13 July 1967 (U)

Social Conflict and National Myth

Before 1952, when President Nasser overthrew the Egyptian monarchy, the Arab peasant had much in common with his counterpart in any of the neighbouring Arab states, but this horizontal integration of Saudi-Arabian Arab with Egyptian Arab ultimately gave way to the vertical integration of Egyptian peasant with Egyptian professional man and bureaucrat. This is what Professor Barbu calls 'the status-awareness of the individual' (see p 261). His contention that the transitional aspect of nationalism is first dependent upon a crisis of social solidarity through the weakening of traditional bonds may well apply to France and Egypt.

In the case of Israel, it is the strengthening of those bonds that has surmounted the crisis in the end, and what he calls 'the mystique' of the nation arises precisely from those ancient traditions. Nationalism is national immaturity, the expression of a collective ego which possesses its own peculiar dangers, as President Nasser astutely realised.

I found Professor Barbu's talk acutely perceptive and especially thought-provoking in the light of recent events in Africa and the Middle East.

6 , 13 & 20 July 1967 (U)

A Seasoned Traveller

Some people are born with drive and dynamism, have a natural *charisma* which makes for fame (if not fortune) and celebrity. Peter Ustinov is one of them. Vastly intelligent, witty, urbane, a brilliant actor, writer, playwright, philosopher, entertainer and teller of tales. It seems unfair that one human being should possess so many enviable talents. He is now also one of the busiest of men, so we were able to benefit from his experience of travelling the world, in a series of conversations with Leigh Crutchley, entitled 'Love of Five Continents'. 'We rolled out the canvas,' said Mr. Crutchley, 'and he painted his sound-picture of the world.'

Peter Ustinov

Ustinov reminded us right from the start that he had not a drop of English blood in him but he was proud of his British passport. He had relations everywhere from the United States to the Soviet Union, even in unstable countries where revolutions have broken out or are about to break out, but as he says, 'you never have to worry because they always try to miss the summer season!

Among great men, he admired Cecil Rhodes, who once told him: 'Remember that you are an Englishman and have therefore won the first prize in the lottery of life.' Leigh Crutchley reminded Ustinov that he had, after all, been born in England. 'Yes,' said Ustinov, 'but I was born in Swiss Cottage!' And in any case, he now lives in France, which accounts for the interviews being held at the BBC studios in Paris.

Through the chuckles and laughter of these entertaining conversations, we get the sense of a man whose benign yet ironic view of the world is one of God-like acceptance of the frailties, wickednesses and cruelties of the human condition, and hopefully helps to bring into play its dwindling virtues of compassion and tolerance. 'The conscience of mankind is a very opulent thing and a very real thing.'

He admires the shrewdness and ingenuity of the Greeks, their *laissez-faire* politics, their loyalty to the memory of Byron 'and other excesses!' As for their old enemy, the Turks, he finds them a 'dour, land-locked people' who detest the sea and lack any humanitarian military tradition.

Albania, turbulent close neighbour of Greece, is still, in Ustinov's view, 'primitive', 'held back by pride,' and still searching for a national identity. He is surprised by the preponderance of Chinese influence in official circles. 'Even the toilet-paper has a dragon on every sheet!'

The Italians have established themselves as the world's best lovers, but, says Ustinov, the truth of the matter is that the Chinese win that game hands down every time. The Scandinavians do a good deal of talking about love and analyse their feelings too much.

He sees Spain more as a world power, for its considerable influence over South America and points to her basic mistrust of the United States of America, after the 'gratuitous Spanish-American War'.

In Mexico, he luxuriates in the cool tiled courtyards of the interior, with its 'soft-spoken people' and 'atmosphere of silence', but he deplores the noise and aggression of Mexico City and the pride and arrogance of its citizens.

As for the United States, he is depressed by many aspects. He sees the country as 'a phoenix rising out of our flames,' perpetually obsessed with guilt over Vietnam. He believes America to be suspicious of the British approach to management, putting 'technical comfort at the expense of strategic ruin'.

Accepting that the Japanese will one day 'produce nuclear weapons the size of a table-lighter', he admired their technical skills in bringing out cheaper and often improved copies of Western goods, and described them as 'the paper-back editions of the world'.

Pursuing his tour of five continents, he turned to Africa, now freed from colonial rule, with new names for countries we had learnt at school as Tangyanika, Swaziland, Zululand, Bechuanaland and so on. Setting aside the vast population of Africa, he saw the real problem with independence as being how to increase production to match the growing birth rate. He looked forward to a 'United States for Africa'.

Ending his tour in Australia, he found a predominantly white country, with the Aborigines still the victims of paternalism. However, Australians need a proportion of foreign population. At all costs these 'New Australians' have to be hard-working. Germans are accepted for that reason. The Asian influx, however, is regarded with caution. The 'indigenous' Europeans, it seems — the older generations at least — like their tennis, cricket and surf-riding too much to consider work as an option. Ustinov prefers to praise their achievements in opera, ballet and broadcasting.

When he speaks in his serious tone, he is Ustinov the idealist, the proselytiser, the man of the world. But whilst we long to know the true thoughts of great men, do we not long for the great thoughts of a truly compassionate, worldly-wise traveller, who gives us a sense of proportion at a time in our history when 'nations so furiously rage together?'

2 February 1967 (U)

East is East and West is West

A clue to Chinese attitudes to the West may well have been detected in Dr. Raymond Pannikar's reflections on the basic differences between western and eastern thinking. For our own good, he said, contact between East and West must be deeper than 'diplomatic smiles and trade relationships'. It must stem from a greater understanding of basic concepts.

Western philosophy teaches the 'myth of first principles'. It starts from the beginning of time, the alpha of our existence, whereas the oriental mind looks to future fulfilment and completeness, the omega of our existence.

The engaging Dr. Pannikar proved a stimulating catalyst in spite of his occasional linguistic lapses and excitable nature. He made me wonder whether, for all our sophistication and expertise, we might be playing at ostriches, our western heads buried in the eastern sands.

*

12 May 1967 (P)

Understanding Other Societies

Mutual understanding is vital if we are to live together in a world so easily given over to strife and conflict. In the first of her programmes on international understanding, Rosemary Jellis brought in Lord Ritchie Calder, a member of the Duke of Edinburgh's Committee for Volunteers Overseas. The Committee is currently introducing anthropologists and sociologists who are attempting to analyse the qualities needed in nations and individuals if we are to live amicably together.

A simple anecdote served to pinpoint the problem. When Lord Ritchie married, his wife engaged a Cockney house-help. 'We're Scots,' she explained. 'Oh, that don't worry me,' said the Londoner magnanimously, 'I worked for a Chinese couple once!'

It is all a question of good working relationships— finding the common ground in a world that has shrunk to a neighbourhood. Of course differences exist, as Kipling pointed out in his poem, 'We and They':

> Father, Mother and Me
> Sister and Auntie say
> All the people like Us are We,
> And everyone else is They.
> And They live over the sea,
> While We live over the way,
> But — would you believe it?
> They look upon We
> As only a sort of They.

Clearly it is the arrogance and the nationalism that must go if we are to get over our problems.

Deanna Boga had some interesting things to say about shade-consciousness in British Honduras, and David Evans emphasized the whole question of cultural loneliness. There will certainly be millions of displaced persons, refugees, immigrants, and foreigners residing in isolated cultural climates all over the world who feel that loneliness deeply.

The pity is, there are not more observers like Lord Ritchie Calder who care enough about survival to cherish the hope that one day mankind will come to its senses and not remain persistently blind to the potentiality of the human spirit and the reality of happiness within our grasp.

War and Peace

16 September 1966 (P)

The Custer Legend

General Custer

If it is a truism that history glorifies war, then the story of Custer's last stand at the Battle of Little Big Horn in 1876 numbers among the most glorious episodes in military history. Yet General George Armstrong Custer of the 7th US Cavalry, reckless, vainglorious, 'dubious hero of the West', romanticized in films and novels, often depicted fighting on horseback, clad in buckskin, sword and pistol in hand, appears to have fallen the victim of his own impetuosity and flamboyance.

Tony Thomas, in this programme, successfully exploded the myth and destroyed a few common schoolboy misconceptions. The 'glorious' war to exterminate the Dakota Indians was, after all, no different from any other war. If anything, the plight of the Indians seems the more poignant in the telling.

The cavalry regiments attracted to their ranks, in much the same way as the French Foreign Legion, the social misfits, the failed businessmen, the clerks who had absconded with the firm's cash and petty criminals too. There was a deal of torture, mutilation and brutality on both sides, but when Custer foolishly and needlessly attacked an Indian village, he was unheroically felled by a stray bullet and defeated. It was really the Indians who lost. They were penned in on the reservations and the wars ended. For the 'Boy General' Custer, the myth of bravery remained, in spite of everything.

27 May 1966 (P)

The Decline of the Western

I came home too late to review Laurence Kitchin's programme, but what I heard of it was interesting. The 'Western' represents half a century of American fantasy on millions of feet of celluloid. It became a 'commercial myth' which dominated the cinema for generations. In its idealised form, the male protagonist was little less than a hero — brave, honest as the day is long — and those days were *very* long in some of the epic westerns! But the wanderings of 'The Covered Wagon' were over. They lost the plot. Fact began to fade into fantasy too far, diluted by social and political comment. Only Howard Hawkes knew how to save it but, even then, he could not in the end effect a miracle cure. The 'Western' has been described as 'moving figures in a landscape' and in that image it is equivalent to poetry.

22 September 1966 (P)

Bader's Battle of Britain

This week's edition of 'South East' reminded us that the Battle of Britain took place twenty-six years ago today. Douglas Bader, hero from those dangerous times, reflected on how the landscape has changed in the intervening years: the airfields had been built over, taking with it the spirit of an era. Now, there was a whole new philosophy of life.

Asked how he felt about losing both his legs, he replied:

'If things happen to you because of your own fault, it is easier to bear. If there is an accident, then bitterness and frustration must be beaten by courage, fortitude and humour. You have to be able to laugh at yourself.'

Douglas Bader

13 September 1966 (P)

War in the Countryside

Those who could bring themselves to listen to Patricia Penn's heart-rending account of the war in Vietnam will not forget the agonized wailings of the chronically burned woman at the Province Hospital in Qui Nhon as she suffered the intolerable pain of having her dressings removed without sedation, while the wounded streamed into the hospital, often walking forty or fifty miles with compound fractures and severe abdominal wounds.

Gruesome vignettes piled one upon the other: the child shot through the jaw by a stray bullet; the field nearby used as a 'vast open latrine' by the families who came to tend their relatives; the small, courageous group of New Zealand doctors and nurses, labouring in heavy heat, with little or no water and hardly any drugs.

All these painful realities Patricia Penn neatly assembled to make one of the most harrowing feature-programmes. And she did not pull her punches. Many of these patients are innocent victims of a war they care little for, many maimed or wounded by American as well as Vietcong bullets and bombs.

13 September 1966 (U)

Vietnam Horror

Patricia Penn reported that there were at one point 108 patients in a ward of 30 beds, patients often lying three to a bed, others making do with litters and hammocks, with one nurse to a ward of sixty, patients lying in their own filth in the mornings, no night treatment, 400 operations a month, horrifying burns (often covering 80% of the body).

On 24 March, a 14-year-old child was brought in with pitifully pigmented skin from wounds inflicted by an anti-personnel mine. In other distressing cases, patients themselves could not bear the odour of their burns and bored holes in the plaster to let the stench out.

In the midst of this bravery, a little boy of twelve miraculously nursed his mother back to health in the oppressive heat. There were no coolies to clean up, the wards had no sewage-disposal arrangements. As the railways had stopped running, essential dextrose and blood supplies could not get through. So low was the morale that anaesthetists were knocking off for lunch in the middle of operations. There was no water to wash surgical instruments. The only recourse was stoicism and a faint glimmer of hope that life must surely have some greater meaning that this appalling suffering could offer up, something better at the end.

13 July 1967 (P)

Into the Firing Line

I first came face to face with the Arab-Israeli conflict in the summer of 1962, when sleeping in a small house in the Ramat Rachel district of Jerusalem, just two hundred yards from the Jordanian border. I was woken by machine-gun fire somewhere nearby. I learned the next day that two Israeli soldiers had been killed in the incident. Three days later, we were allowed to be driven as far as the observation post to look down over Bethlehem and meditate on the birthplace of the Prince of Peace.

In 1963, during my last visit, fourteen civilians were killed in the Hula district close to the Syrian border. I remember the strangely conflicting impressions that assailed me as I wandered along the tranquil shores of Galilee, stepping over trenches, and chatting with armed kibbutzniks. Everywhere there was evidence of a strong, vital and dedicated community, drawn from many parts of the world, and motivated by a singleness of purpose and endeavour which, by virtue of its blinding intensity, and the skill and military expertise of General Dayan, brought the five-day war to such a rapid conclusion.

The implications of Zevedei Barbu's analysis of social conflict and its relationship to national myth seemed to me to go far beyond the confines of the French political history he used as his starting-point.

Indeed, much of his thesis could be satisfactorily applied to the emergence of a new stage in the political development of the Middle East in both Israel and the Arab states. 'Nationalism,' to use the Professor's words, is rooted in 'an idealized group consciousness' and 'the unity of the ethnic group'. For the individual this implies a sense of 'belonging'.

*

3 February 1967 (P)

No Winners, Only Losers

I cannot say I actually enjoyed Elizabeth Young's disturbing talk, 'No Alternative to Politics', for it dealt with the cold facts and complexities of anti-ballistic missile defence. It was fascinating to hear Mrs. Young speak so expertly about a field of knowledge in which I have, in the rush and tear of life, for so long shown a deplorable lack of interest.

What she had to say was immensely cogent and vital, if not downright depressing. I found it cold comfort to be assured that the arms race is not as dangerous as it might seem, for 'in an endless race there can be no winner' — surely a concession to a blind fatalism. A gloomy visionary might well see total annihilation as the winner of that race.

Mrs. Young saw 'Cold War Two' as an alignment of Soviet Russia and the United States of America against China, a situation uncannily close to Marghanita Laski's nightmarish vision in her highly controversial radio play, *The Offshore Island*.

*

18 January 1966 (U)

Bluff and Counter-bluff

History has proved to us that human beings are the most aggressive creatures in the world. Down the ages, we have sought to destroy one another with alarming regularity. In spite of all our so-called moral sense, our human conscience and sense of decency, we continue to kill the thing we love most — life itself. By numerous massacres, insurrections, tribal wars and mass murder, we destroy the very fabric of our society over and over again. Why?

In a compelling 'Horizon' programme, *Sons of Cain*, ethnologist and student of animal behaviour, Konrad Lorenz, sought to show how the sudden outpouring of violence in human behaviour can be seen in the light of the new thinking on the subject. To quote the *Radio Times* introduction: 'To be able to kill a brother — a fellow human being — is not unhuman; on the contrary, it is a very human trait. No animal other than man deliberately sets out to destroy members of its own species.'

On a major scale, the threat of 'the Bomb', of germ warfare and similar horrors, tend to lead us to ask ourselves how civilisation can possibly survive. We need, says Lorenz, to find a way of controlling our animal behaviour, and, as if this is not insulting enough to the animals themselves, it suggests that we are superior in our instincts. Animals, after all, can get aggressive if there is an invasion of territory, or a need to protect their young. Where tooth and claw are all an animal requires, human beings, blessed as they are with intelligence and imagination, have, through their diabolical ingenuity, invented lethal weapons of mass destruction as if they were a gift to ensure the survival of mankind. Yet ask the same human beings to go out and kill a rabbit or wring the neck of a turkey for the Christmas dinner, and the boot is on the other foot.

According to Lorenz, 'there is no hate where there has not been love.' Our diplomacy is a game of bluff and counter-bluff, a smile, a hand-shake, which may well come to a catastrophic conclusion. 'Smiling, damned villain!' as Hamlet cries. Who said that laughing men don't shoot! Personally, I wouldn't care to trust one, laughing or crying, with a gun in his hand.

Another programme, 'On Aggression', brought together John Bowen, Desmond Morris, Curator of Mammals at the London Zoo, and Lord Chalfont, Minister of State responsible for Disarmament.

Lord Chalfont cited the example of all-in wrestling. Here, he said, was brute violence in the raw. And what about the yells and catcalls, and the aggressive expressions on the faces of the spectators? It would take a modern-day Hogarth to do justice to the grotesqueness of the scene. Perhaps the whole thing is a throw-back to the bad old days of cock-fighting, bear-baiting, and public executions when the public came to be entertained with 'last dying speeches'. Is it not, suggested His Lordship, 'a welling-up of our natural biological aggression?'

Desmond Morris made the point that the release of the aggressive drive can come, not only through the cathartic experience of the spectator, but also through enthusiasm for a cause. There is no doubt, however, that overcrowding, in its wider sense, and over-population, excite the aggressive instincts. It is a violent interpretation of the survival of the fittest. So the obscene idea that war is one way of pruning the population is echoed in Anthony Burgess's novel in which people are tricked into war and the dead bodies are turned into canned meat.

Let us therefore consider the habits of rats! An unwholesome deliberation, no doubt, but one which provides us with some useful clues to aggressive instincts and territorial threats. Such a chaotic spread of aggression could only lead to mass-suicide.

After all the pessimistic conclusions of his colleagues on the programme, Lorenz defiantly affirmed, with a blind faith, the survival of the human species. We can only have the satisfaction of knowing that, if we become extinct, we would certainly be replaced by another species of a protozoic kind. Now, isn't that comforting to know!

January 1967

The Peacemaker

Idly tuning in to the 'Home Service' this week I happened to hear the comfortable voice of Lord Chalfont, Minister for Disarmament, who had just returned from 'rubbing off ideas against people in Bonn, Paris and Peking', which is by way of saying that he had persuaded officials in Germany, France and China to try to arrive at some kind of consensus on arms control. Five powerful countries, it seems, have atomic weapons now, so it is even more desirable to the world to scale down the nuclear threat. But as His Lordship pointed out, 'no country is going to sit back and watch other countries build up their stock-piles'. At the same time, so long as China remains outside the Test Ban Treaty, India must be given some kind of security against attack. A 'Non-Proliferation Treaty' should encourage a more peaceable view of the situation. He had serious doubts about a European independent nuclear deterrent in any case.

Lord Chalfont, interviewed by Peter Jenkins, admitted to having been regarded as 'luke-warm' about the European Union, but had now come round to believing that Britain should be part of it all once the major differences of the Common Agricultural Policy, capital movements in sterling, our Anglo-American ties, and Commonwealth issues are solved. Frankly I cannot share His Lordship's faith in the political ties that bind Europe's nations together. But one of the driving forces of my own life has been a passionate belief in our common culture. Europe has given birth to some of the most influential and profound works of literature, of music and painting. Our philosophers from ancient times to the present day have provided us with a pattern of positive thought and a belief in the ultimate power of good over evil.

From my notebook: *29 September 1966* (U)

War and Peace

Quote from Tennyson's *Locksley Hall* for possible use in 'The New Science Fiction' (see p 71): In spite of the bright vision he hoped for, he foresaw a world of terrifying conflict, the horrors of which would, in just seventy years, become reality with the First World War.

For I dipt into the future, far as human eye could see,
Saw the vision of the world, and all the wonder that could be.....
Heard the heavens fill with shouting, and there rained a ghastly dew
From the nations' airy navies grappling in the central blue....

And after the holocaust comes peace and tranquillity, and the welcome return of common sense, of compassion, above all, of reason.

Far along the world wide whisper of the south wind rushing-warm,
With the standards of the people plunging through the thunderstorm,
Till the war-drums throbb'd no longer, and the battle flags were furl'd
In the Parliament of Man, the Federation of the World.

Was this remarkable vision fulfilled by the languid efforts of the League of Nations and, after an uneasy peace and a Second World War, the abortive attempts by the United Nations to eradicate war and all forms of genocide, torture, mass murder and racial hatred that threaten the survival of the human race?

*

16 March 1967 (P)

The Rise and Fall of CND

Few of us can fail to respond to the challenge of renewal and awakening that Easter holds. Whether we concern ourselves with religious speculation on survival after death, or fall willing victims to the vicissitudes of an English spring, it is always the life-giving force that is in the ascendant. Yet Easter is also a time of protest against the established order of things.

The Campaign for Nuclear Disarmament is a movement which has left an ineradicable mark on the face of society, and which has inspired young people to get up and claim a future for themselves from out of the smug stoicism of older generations. The sit-down in Trafalgar Square on 17th September 1961 must surely remain one of those unique events in English history in which protest has followed the pattern of civil disobedience.

Few scenes in English history have, in recent times, equalled those Easter Aldermaston marches. For the tenth anniversary of CND, the

BBC resuscitated a year-old programme on the subject (produced by Anthony Moncrieff) and gave it an up-to-date scrub and polish. It vividly brought to life the principal protagonists in the campaign in a programme compiled by Ivan Yates of *The Observer*. Mr. Moncrieff's production was a fair and balanced assessment which succeeded in raising the threshold of interest in the minds of those who were normally allergic to thinking about foreign policy — perhaps the most prevalent of British failings.

*

16 March 1967 (P)

A Certain Anachronistic Inconsistency

What of Bertrand Russell, the man behind the CND Movement? What of the prophet behind the creed? There is a sublimity about the early struggles of Bertrand Russell that mirrors those of greater men than he.

From his earliest years, he longed for oneness with the larger mass of humanity, a longing opposed only by his inability to identify himself with the supporters of the very causes he most believed in. His militant pacifism, which ultimately led him to uphold the warmongering policies he despised, his odd ideas on love (a selfish caring for others), his ecstasy, which is not love but a romantic wonderment at the universe — all this came over admirably in Richard Keen's excellent discussion of Lord Russell's life and work in which Professor Stuart Hampshire, Baroness Stocks and Norman St. John Stevas MP, with Robert Kee in the chair, discussed the paradoxical nature of this formidable nonagenarian.

Bertrand Russell

Stuart Hampshire, interestingly enough, came to the conclusion that, though Lord Russell's philosophy is primarily a search for answers, his solutions are not always convincing. All the speakers affirmed his technical brilliance, his intellectual honesty, his intensity of vision, the beauty and precision of his language, and above all, his compassion for his fellow man.

'Three passions, simple but overwhelmingly strong, have governed my life: the longing for love, the search for knowledge, and unbearable pity for the suffering of mankind. These passions, like great winds, have blown me hither and thither over a deep ocean of anguish....'

In spite of this, or perhaps because of it, Russell has never been taken at his full stature, nor consulted as an oracle, but has remained somewhat apart from the policies of governments and international relations, and outside the more consistent position of a thinker like Harold Laski.

Robert Kee's questions led perfectly into a stimulating discussion which, for once, in this expository kind of programme, reached to the heart of the man and his work.

There are two Bertrand Russells: one, the iconoclast throwing stones at old idols; the other, an old man who cares very much about a world he will never live to see, a future he has revealed to the young with all his unquenchable enthusiasm. It has been remarked of Charles Lamb that he possessed a 'wisdom of the heart'. Bertrand Russell also possesses that wisdom to the very highest degree, and, alas, with all the limitations that the condition implies.

28 December 1966 (P)

An Old Soldier's New Year Thoughts

Like Milton's blinded Samson Agonistes, the nations of the world have been treading out 'dark steps'. War in Vietnam, rioting in Hong Kong, insurrection in Greece, guerilla warfare on the borders of Israel and Aden, and serious disputes between Gibraltar and Spain— all symptoms of a disease which is dangerously infectious. 'Why do the nations so furiously rage together?' Twenty-two years after the Second World War, man does not seem to have learnt his lesson. Political restlessness continues to feed hungrily on the resources of law, order and common sense.

There may be many of us who would agree with the *Radio Times* description of 1966 as a 'none-too-lamented year'. Field-Marshall Montgomery reminded us that 1967 marks the twenty-fifth anniversary of the Battle of El Alamein. In May, he told us, he would be visiting the battlefield again. With the sound of those clear, clipped syllables, back came the memory of that sharp, keen intelligence so familiar to wartime radio listeners of the nineteen-forties.

Field-Marshall Montgomery

His hopes for 1967? Well, he had had a lifetime of fighting. Now he was heartily sick of it.

'At last we may have some peace,' he said. 'That's what I want.' That's what we all want.

29 May 1966 (P)

Spring in Washington

Alastair Cooke, in his 'Letter from America' this week, chose the theme of Spring and its effect on the political climate of America. There is a touch of Joseph Addison about the personal beginning:

'I was at dinner the other night with Senator C. and Senator S. and their lady-wives, as Lord Halifax used to say.' Senator C. was an isolationist 'hawk'. Senator S. was a liberal 'dove'. There was plenty of talk, most of it excellent and impassioned, about Vietnam. Senator S. believed American forces should retreat to certain coastal areas and dig in. But President Johnson had already made it clear that this would be 'retreating to a target', and added that staying in Dunkerque did not win the Second World war.

One is reminded of Milton's words in the *Areopagitica*: 'Such bickerings to recount, met often in these our writers [read 'warmongers']. What more worth is it than to chronicle the wars of kites and crows flocking and fighting in the air?'

Judging by the amiable pleasantries that passed between the two Senators on so vital a topic, Mr. Cooke assumed that Spring was largely responsible for such *bonhomie*.

True to character, Mr. Cooke warned us that, while England slept, Churchill was telling us of Germany's rise to power and that Hitler meant what he said. And it may well be that Mao Tse Tung means what he says when he points to 'wars of liberation', the modern euphemism for 'aggression'.

As with all his talks, Mr. Cooke invariably comes to a neat conclusion. Out of the 'ranting dogmatism of winter', when Britain once argued about Suez, and America now argues about Vietnam, American politicians have come out into the sun, doves and hawks, and President Johnson proclaims the message on the sun-drenched lawns of the White House: 'We shall survive and overcome!'

This, concludes Mr. Cooke, is a response to Spring and the renewal of life!

27 July 1967 (U)

Last Words!

Now that my time as critic for 'The Spoken Word' has come to an end, I have been looking back over the past year and a half — 25,000 words and a minimum of several hundred hours of listening — to rediscover a whole tapestry of human activity in the work of many writers, producers, presenters, technicians, editors and broadcasters. The exploratory aspect stands out most of all — the sheer intellectual and creative energy that goes into the making of programmes of such infinite variety. After today, released from my bondage, I am free to listen in at my ease and for my personal pleasure.

This evening, I found much enjoyment in listening again to those genial conversationalists, Sir Compton Mackenzie and Peter Ustinov. These two masterly *raconteurs* revealed all that is best in BBC Radio.

27 July 1967 (U)
My Very Last Words!

Established authors usually say writing is a case of 'more perspiration than inspiration'. And plenty of exasperation, too, I would say! In the midst of Hamlet's deliberations on the perplexing problems of this life and the beyond, Polonius asked him what he was reading. What else could he reply but 'Words, words, words!'

Any critic worth his salt has an undeniable obligation to be fair to his authors. I believe it was Cardinal Newman who was reprimanded for not regarding truth 'a necessary virtue'. I hope at least I have been true to the originals and that I have, after all, accurately recorded the thoughts and words of my chosen authors, even if it was all to my own advantage in resurrecting their contributions to broadcasting.

It has not been easy. Words have a way of running away with you, often in the wrong direction. It is possible to end up with quite a different article to the one intended, which accounts for the inclusion of some of my alternative drafts. It is perverse that, following a frustrating period of 'writer's block', words can come in a wild rush. It is wise to resist the onslaught. 'Never use two words where one will do.' Such was the valuable advice given by W. B. Yeats to young writers. I am sure I have committed such offences many times over in the pages of this book in praise of BBC broadcasting. Nevertheless, an author must always keep to the rule of 'Cut, cut, and cut again!' as far as conscience, obstinacy, taste and personal whim will allow. Deadlines and word counts are an effective deterrent to any tendency to prolixity.

It is also one of my habits to introduce incidents and experiences from my own life to prove a point, an indulgence which has its dangers, especially where 'truth' is concerned.

These 'necessary virtues' I acquired in the days of my youth, when I sat admiringly at the literary feet (metaphorically, you understand) of those masters of words, Logan Pearsall Smith and Cyril Connolly, who inadvertently taught me so much about writing — and even more about myself. Only they can carry the blame for my literary lapses.

Words do not always come easily to us if we are under pressure. There have been times when, at the midnight hour, I have prayed for inspiration to get me out of a linguistic fix, as Lady Lurewell did in Farquhar's *The Constant Couple*:

'Grant me some wild expressions, Heavens!.... Words, words, or I shall burst.'

Enough said! No more deadlines!

I shall go on exploring our language at my leisure. I am reminded once more of Mayakovsky's revolutionary challenge to his fellow poets when, leaping up on the table in a frenzy, he cried:

'Darlings, what wedded you to words?'

Well! I know what wedded *me* to words. The love of words.

The End of the Line

From my notebook: *10 July 1967*

On the Grapevine!

Following on from the programme about President Nasser recently, the BBC, with appropriate impartiality, will present a profile of General Dayan next month. However, it seems I shall not be reviewing it. A whisper in the silent corridors of Broadcasting House tells me that 'The Spoken Word' column is to be dropped.

There will, no doubt, be more news of this event in due course.

From my notebook: *17 July 1967*

Coup de Grâce!

So! The time has come for the axe to fall. Yesterday I went into the BBC's Langham Place office as usual to deliver my copy for the week. The new editor, Karl Miller, broke the news to me that changes were being planned for *The Listener* and, as a result, I would have no column to write for.

Feeling like Ariel freed by Prospero, I flew across to the BBC canteen to say my farewells to some of the producers and broadcasters I had come to know during my time as critic.

As I was writing notes for my last piece, a cheery face loomed up out of the crowd.

'May I introduce myself? I'm 'The Singing Farmer'. Would you be interested in reviewing my show?'

'I'll certainly listen to it. Send me a note of the date and time.' He could not know I was already writing my final sentence!

April 2006
Looking Back: Decline and Fall

With the coming of television in the 1950s, *The Listener*, under the editorship of Alan Thomas, assumed the title: *The Listener and BBC Television Review*. These were turbulent moments in the management's fight to survive in a world of rapidly changing values. By 1958, when the next editor, the distinguished historian, Maurice Ashley, was appointed, the threat of increased television reporting and the appearance of Sunday colour supplements was beginning to bring in a new kind of readership. Looking back, it seems to me now, even as I began writing my weekly articles for 'The Spoken Word', the feature was already in its death throes.

In the edition of 3 August 1967, the new editor, Karl Miller, set out plans for his new style. The next morning, *The Guardian* reported that many readers must have felt heartsick when they picked up their morning papers and saw how *The Listener* had been transformed. They complained that only three 'Third Programme' talks were printed in the latest issue and only one of them reached two pages long. The gloom felt by *The Guardian* was deepened by the new proposals.

'We'll have more about, and from, television, which means there will be fewer published scripts.....we shall be carrying fewer transcripts and fewer reprinted talks.'

With a clever, almost Marxian, misquotation of the MacLuhan canon, says *The Guardian*, the new Editor justifies his views by stating that 'the media are the message.' In short, he was seen to have 'misconceived the function his newspaper can best serve.'

Only a few of the literary establishment remained and almost overnight a new galaxy of 'stars' began to shine in the pages of succeeding editions. The list for the remaining months of 1967 alone included, among some hundreds of contributors, John Arlott, Alan Bennett, Brigid Brophy, Anthony Burgess, Alastair Cooke, D. J. Enright, Seamus Heaney, Ted Hughes, Frank Kermode, Francis King, Jonathan Miller, George Melly, James Mossman, Malcolm Muggeridge, Iris Murdoch, Conor Cruise O'Brien, Enoch Powell, A. J. P. Taylor and Alan Whicker.

From the high-sounding aims and hopes of its inception, T*he Listener* became the victim of a plethora of policies supposedly formed to follow the vicissitudes of the times. In 1981, Richard Gott, features editor of *The Guardian*, was expected to take over as editor but, following a sensational interference by MI5, his appointment was blocked because of his 'ultra-Leftist' sympathies. By way of compromise, Russell Twisk was brought in to take his place. This was one instance among a number when *The Listener* was to defy the BBC hierarchy and fight for the independence of its critics, which became the established norm under the literary editorship of J. R. Ackerley and later his successor, Oleg Kerensky.

From a position of equality with its two distinguished rivals, *The Spectator* and *The New Statesman* (superior to them in fact in its political impartiality) in 1986, following the Peacock Committee Report, *The Listener* was removed from the safety of its subsidised position to the inevitably precarious position as part of 'BBC Enterprises Limited'. Thus its former literary standards were at the mercy of the market place. As it was said at the time, *The Listener* had moved from 'the contemplative to the contemporary.' Hardly had a year elapsed than it was placed under an umbrella organisation, a joint partnership of BBC commercial activities with their rival Independent Television.

Seeing that the exemplary eclecticism of the original periodical, with its largely intellectual and artistic content, was considered to have no real focus, the extraordinary decision to convert it into a more humorous guise was decidedly ill-judged. Alan Coren from *Punch* was brought in to save the day, but even such a talented editor could not succeed in winning back an already alienated readership. Peter Fiddick was to succeed Coren, but market forces were eventually to have their way.

Trouble came in 1990 when ITV withdrew its joint support. Within the space of a few months, a proportion of once loyal and devoted readers began to transfer their allegiance to other journals and newspapers.

The Listener had trodden a distinguished path from its first issue on 16th January 1929 and, after the discontinuance of 'The Spoken Word' column in July 1967, carried on in its new form for twenty-five years more, finally giving up the ghost in 1991. In retrospect, Karl Miller was probably right to do away with that final page of independent lightweight reporting and commentary. My departure was a convenience for both of us.

Looking through my bound volumes of *The Listener*, I can only marvel at the quantity and quality of writing, on all manner of subjects, by so many distinguished contributors. All the more tragic therefore was it to witness the slow decline in sales (though not I feel in quality) over the succeeding years.

I still treasure my old dog-eared working copies of 'that extraordinary nine-pennyworth' and am pleased to have been given the opportunity to play even a very small part in its distinguished history.

Diary of Events for the 1960s

Diary of Events for the 1960s

(Page numbers in brackets refer to related topics discussed in this volume)

1960   Betting and Gaming Act (276)
Brezhnev appointed President of Russia (304)
Ideological dispute between Russia and China (254-256)
Military *coup* in Turkey
UAR National Assembly inaugurated
Civil War in former Belgian Congo
Sharpville Massacre: 67 Africans killed
Creation of African republics following Pan-African troubles
Political unrest in Ethiopia. *Coup d'état* fails.
John Kennedy elected first Roman Catholic President USA.
Gary Power, US pilot, shot down in Urals and imprisoned.
Marriage of Princess Margaret to Anthony Armstrong-Jones
Cuba aligned with Communist *bloc*
Former Head of Gestapo, Eichmann, arrested in Argentina.
A. J. Ayer's *Logical Positivism* published.
John Betjeman's *Summoned by Bells* published.
Robert Bolt's play, *A Man for All Seasons* (about Thomas More)
Harold Pinter's play, *The Caretaker*
Terence Rattigan's play, *Ross* (about Lawrence of Arabia)
Penguin Books published unexpurgated edition of D. H. Lawrence's novel *Lady Chatterley's Lover*
Teilhard de Chardin, French philosopher, published *Le Milieu Divin* (The Divine Mean i.e. ratio) (166-167)
Sculptor Michael Ayrton's bronze, *Icarus III* (186-188)
BBC White City Television Centre opened
Stiletto heels fashionable (109)
Benjamin Britten's opera, *Midsummer Night's Dream*
Lawrence Olivier stars in John Osborne's *The Entertainer*
New £1 note issued
US Polaris submarines stationed in Holy Loch
USS *Enterprise*, first atomic-powered aircraft carrier
US launching of communications satellite *Echo I*

Galaxy 6000 light years away photographed in US
Russian satellite, *Sputnik V*, launched with two dogs aboard

1961 Census gives population of Britain as 51,295,000 (237, 241)
Betting Levy Act (276). Consumer Protection Act. Factory Act
Britain applied for membership to join Common Market
Influx of West Indians and Asians into Britain
Dag Hammarskjöld, Secretary-General of United Nations
Berlin Wall built
State of Emergency in France
Census in India; population of 438,000.000
Coup d'état in Syria
Iraq's claim over Kuwait
South Africa became a republic
New English Bible; *New Testament*
Asa Briggs: *Birth of Broadcasting,* History of BBC Vol I (252, 326-328)
Ivy Compton Burnett novel: *The Mighty and Their Fall* (57)
The Letters of Sigmund Freud 1873 - 1939 (176-178)
Iris Murdoch, *A Severed Head*
Ogden Nash, *Collected Verses* (110, 146)
Muriel Spark, *The Prime on Miss Jean Brodie*
Lionel Bart's musical, *Oliver*
University of Sussex founded (Brighton)
University of Essex founded (Colchester)
End of BBC's *Children's Hour*
New Towns Commission set up
Italian film, *La Dolce Vita*
Yuri Gagarin, first USSR man in space
Alan Shepherd, first USA man in space
End of Bradshaw's *Railway Time Table* (founded 1839)
Mini-cabs in London
Excavations at Pompei

1962 Joint Committee for reform of House of Lords
Commonwealth Immigrants Act

William Vassall arrested for spying for Russia
European Economic Community: 2nd stage of integration
Geneva Disarmament Conference on nuclear weapons (314-315)
Assassination attempt on life of General De Gaulle
US established military command in Vietnam (310)
More independence for former British Protectorates
Russian missile base in Cuba
Edward Albee's play, *Who's Afraid of Virginia Woolf?*
A. L. Rowse, *Raleigh and the Throckmortons* (150,150n)
Anthony Sampson's *An Anatomy of Britain*
Arnold Wesker's play, *Chips with Everything*
Benjamin Britten, *War Requiem*
Chichester Theatre opened
Coventry Cathedral consecrated
Dr. No, James Bond film with Sean Connery (287)
Western, *How the West Was Won* (308)
Centigrade scale adopted by Meteorological Office
Franco-British agreement over construction of *Concorde*
US launched communications satellite, *Telstar*
US launched British satellite *Ariel* to study cosmic radiation

1963
Harold Wilson elected Leader of Labour Party
John Profumo, Secretary for War, resigned over sensational sex scandal
Contracts of Employment Act (272-273)
Great Train Robbery
Philby discovered to be 'Third Man' in Burgess-McLean spying affair
Anglicans and Methodists propose eventual union
Nuclear Test Ban treaty signed between US, Russia and Britain (312, 314)
Kenya and Nigeria became independent
President Kennedy assassinated at Dallas
Honest to God, by Bishop of Woolwich, John Robinson (cf 84-86)
A. L. Rowse, *William Shakespeare*

Victor Pasmore's *Abstract in White, Ochre and Black* (229, 231n)
Newsom Report on Secondary Education
Robbins Report on Higher Education (40, 45)
University of York founded
Le Corbusier's Carpenter Centre for the Visual Arts
    completed
Beatle's 'Pop' Group achieve international fame (109, 226)
Beeching Report of British Railways closing half the stations and
    one third of track
Buchanan Report *Traffic in Towns* (243)
Construction of Victoria Underground Line
Channel Tunnel construction recommended (243-244)
First woman in space, Valentina Tereshkova
Flood disaster in northern Italy kills 2000 people
Cyclone in East Pakistan kills 10,000
Hurricane in Caribbean kills 6000

1964
General Election with majority of 4, Harold Wilson Prime
    Minister
Hire Purchase Act
Libraries and Museums Act
'Mods' and 'Rockers' riots at seaside resorts
Greek and Turkish communities in Cyprus in conflict
Malta became independent
Pope Paul's pilgrimage to the Holy Land
King Saud deposed in favour of Prince Feisal in Saudi
    Arabia
Indonesia invaded Malaysia
War in South Vietnam. Government troops versus
    Vietcong (310-311)
Harold Pinter play, *The Homecoming*
C. P. Snow's novel, *Corridors of Power*
The Oxford Book of Nineteenth Century Verse
Universities of East Anglia, Lancaster, Stirling and
    Strathclyde founded
BBC2 opened as second TV channel

	Windmill Theatre closed

Windmill Theatre closed
Dr. Strangelove, film with Peter Sellers
China exploded first nuclear bomb
Zorba the Greek, film with Lila Kedrova
Topless dresses worn in London (109)

1965
Edward Heath Leader of Conservative Party
Race Relations Act
Gerald Brooke, British lecturer, imprisoned in Moscow
Spain renewed claim on Gibraltar
Terrorism in Aden by National Liberation Front
US bombed North Vietnam
Unilateral Declaration of Independence, Rhodesia
Negro riots in Los Angeles
Norman Mailer's novel, *An American Dream*
Frank Marcus's play, *The Killing of Sister George*
Sylvia Plath, *Ariel* poems
Boots' Circulating Library closed
Plans for comprehensive schools (162)
Post Office Tower opened
John Le Carré's *The Spy Who Came in from the Cold* as film with Richard Burton (288)
Natural gas discovered in North Sea
Cigarette advertising banned on commercial TV on Britain
Capital Gains Tax introduced

1966
General Election. Labour Party returned.
Cultural Revolution in China. Purge of Revisionists by Red Guards (254-255)
Billy Graham, American evangelist, opened Greater London Crusade
The Times newspaper taken over by Lord Thompson. News on front page for first time
International Treaty on peaceful uses of outer space
City University founded
Brunel University founded

Loughborough University founded
Bradford University founded
Surrey University founded
Opening of Parliament televised for first time
Harold Wilson voted 'Man of the Year' (81-82)
Jackie Kennedy voted 'Woman of the Year' (81-82)
Florence floods (34-36)
Drastic economy measures
Aberfan mining disaster: 116 children and 28 adults killed
Severn Bridge completed
Widespread mergers and takeovers in British business

1967
Abortion Act, permitting termination of pregnancy
Criminal Justice Act
Road Safety Act, introducing breath tests (243)
Sexual Offences Act, legalising homosexual acts between consenting adults (178)
Defence White Paper: drastic cuts in armed forces
Jeremy Thorpe, new Leader of Liberal Party
Gibraltar decides to stay British after referendum (300)
Communist riots in Hong Kong (249)
Military *Coup d'état* in Greece. King Constantine II flees to Rome (257-258)
Press censorship in Greece under Papandopoulos (258)
Start of Six-Day War between Arab States of Egypt, Jordan and Syria (259-61)
Israel occupied Gaza strip and west Bank of River Jordan
Civil war in Nigeria. Biafra defeated
'Che' Guevara, Latin-American revolutionary, killed in Bolivia
Francis Chichester sailed alone around the world in *Gypsy Moth IV*. Knighted by the Queen at Greenwich (277-278)
Liverpool Roman Catholic Cathedral consecrated (86, 89)
Plowden Report: *Children and Their Primary Schools* (171)
Queen Elizabeth Hall opened on the South Bank, London
Royal College of Art granted Royal Charter

BBC Radio programmes re-organised as Radio 1, 2, 3, and 4, with new Radio One exclusively for 'Pop' music (222-233)
BBC TV serial, *The Forsyte Saga*
Julie Andrews in film, *Thoroughly Modern Millie*
First British colour TV broadcast
Donald Campbell killed on Coniston Water in *Bluebird*
Devaluation of pound sterling
Foot and mouth disease in Britain
Hydrogen Bomb exploded in China

1968   Clean Air Act
Commonwealth Immigration Act; restriction of Kenyan Asians
Race Relations Act
Trade Descriptions Act
Civil rights disturbances, Northern Ireland
Welsh Home Rule cause bomb outrages.
Argentina claimed Falkland Islands
Sorbonne students in anti-government riots
Basque Nationalists curbed in Spain
Martin Luther King assassinated, Memphis, Tennessee
W. H. Auden, *Collected Longer Poems* (188-189)
C. Day Lewis appointed Poet Laureate
End of censorship in the English theatre by the Lord Chamberlain (121)
France exploded hydrogen bomb
Senator Robert Kennedy shot by an assassin in Los Angeles
Richard Nixon elected President USA
Post Office two-tier system for first and second posts
End of steam locomotion on British railways

1969   Representation of the People Act lowering voting age to 18
Divorce Reform Act
Permanent abolition of death penalty
Investiture of Prince Charles as Prince of Wales
White Paper, *In Place of Strife*, on reform of trade unions

336

Bomb outrages in Wales by national extremists
More civil disturbances in Ireland by IRA
De Gaulle resigns in favour of Pompidou
Border clashes between Chinese and Russian troops
Mrs Golda Meir, Prime Minister of Israel
Open University founded for teaching through television
BBC series *Civilisation*, by Kenneth Clarke
Fifty pence piece, first new British decimal coin circulated
Supersonic airliner, *Concorde*, maiden flight from
    Toulouse
First 'test tube' baby
Maiden voyage of Cunard Liner, *Queen Elizabeth II*
Asian flu outbreak in Britain
Neil Armstrong, in spacecraft *Apollo II,* first man to set foot on the
    moon

Acknowledgements

The Bramber Press wishes to thank the following copyright holders:
Motion Picture and Television Photo Archive for permission to include the cover photograph of Jackie Kennedy (© Mark Shaw Photo Researchers).
The Flanders & Swann Estates (Donald Swann Archive) for the photograph of Donald Swann (page 270)
The National Portrait Gallery, London, for permission to use the following images:

J G Ballard	72
Arnold Bennett	64
Arthur Calder-Marshall	280
King Charles II	154
Alastair Cooke	158
Charles Dickens	cover & 50
T S Eliot	217
William Gladstone	266, 267
Kenneth Horne	123
John Keats	198
Christopher Logue © Roger Mayne	211
Edgar Lustgarten	102
Compton Mackenzie	68
Nijinsky	118
Sir Hubert Parry	111
Amyas Paulet	150
Queen Elizabeth I	cover
Queen Victoria	157
Dante Gabriel Rossetti	33
Bertrand Russell	317
Vita Sackville-West	132
George Bernard Shaw	cover & 117
Alfred Lord Tennyson	200
Peter Ustinov © Trevor Leighton	302
Francis Walsingham	151
H G Wells	53
Huw Wheldon © Estate of Bob Collins	209
Colin Wilson	70
Harold Wilson	81

Note on the Vignettes

The miniature pen-and-ink sketches that embellished the pages of the *Radio Times* during the period when I was writing for *The Listener*, are worthy of mention. Most of these delightful and ingenious vignettes were published anonymously and, though my searches have proved fruitless, it is sad to think that we no longer know some of the names of such original and inventive artists. The names of the artists we do know of are as follows, although our attempts to track them down in the *Radio Times* archives have proved unsuccessful:

Bruce Angrave .... title page, 33, 223, 226, 229, 231, 233, 242

Basil 23

Biro 251

Dinarde 16

Dunkley 29, 275

Dursley 55

Eric Fraser 3

reinganum 53, 11, 17, 28, 33, 42, 158, 283

Toynbee 27

Monica Walker 18

Index of Persons

Aberconway, Dowager Lady, friend of H. G. Wells 53
Aberconway, Lord 132
Ackerley, J. R., Literary Editor of *The Listener*, novelist 327
Adams, Michael, broadcaster 259-260
Addison, Joseph, 18th century essayist 319
Adrian, Max, actor 116
Aeschylus, Athenian tragic poet 117
Agis, Maurice, artist.. 30
Alain, French medieval philosopher 87
Albee, Edward, American playwright 332
Amies, Hardy, Royal couturier 162
Anderson, John, contributor 278
Anderson, Lady, wife of Governor of Gibraltar 300
Anderson, Marjorie 236, 295
Andrews, Julie, singer and film-star 335
Angell, George, broadcaster 196
Angrave, Bruce, illustrator............................... 109, 270
Angus, Marion, poet 153
Argent, Rod, member of 'Zombies' pop group 230
Argyle, J. M. writer 40
Arlott, John, cricket commentator 326
Armstrong, Neil, astronaut 337
Armstrong-Jones, Anthony, interior designer 330
Arnold, Matthew, author 134
Ashley, Maurice, historian, Editor of *The Listener 1958-67* 326
Aspler, Tony, broadcaster 109, 233
Auden, W. H., poet 20, 188-189, 216-7, 334
Ayer, A. J. ,philosopher, broadcaster 330
Ayrton, Michael, artist and art historian 186-188, 330

Babington, conspirator 150, 151
Baden-Powell, Lord 62
Bader, Douglas, pilot, wartime hero 309
Baker, Josephine, singer, Folies Bergère .... Cover, 122, 123
Baker, Lilian, member of Prison Commission 247
Ballantyne R.M. novelist, author of *The Blue Lagoon* 68

Ballard, J. G., science-fiction writer 21, 72-73
Bamford, Barney, interviewer 274
Barber, Noel, BBC correspondent 299
Barbu, Professor Zevedei, Professor of Sociology, Sussex . . . 261, 301, 311
Barnes, Peter. Sewage disposal operator 274
Barrès, Maurice, French novelist 34, 36
Barrett, Nicholas, presenter 226
Barry, Sir James, playwright 46
Bart, Lionel, composer 331
Batchelor, Denzil, broadcaster 59
Baudelaire, Charles, French symbolist poet 32, 33n, 285
Beardmore, George, contributor 62
Beardsley, Aubrey, illustrator 162
Beatles, The, pop group 109, 226
Beat Poets, American 213
Beaton, Cecil, fashion designer 205
Beckett, Samuel, playwright 21, 71, 91
Beeby, Bruce, reader 199, 200
Beeching, Dr., pruner of British railway network 333
Behan, Brendan, Irish playwright 196
Belloc, Hilaire, poet and author 212
Beney, F. W., Queen's counsel 96
Bennett, Alan 326
Bennett, Arnold, novelist 21, 62-65
Berry, Francis, author of *Poetry and the Physical Voice* 218, 219
Besant, Annie, theosophist 266n
Besant, Rev. Frank, preacher (see *Annie Besant*) 265
Betjeman, John, poet 21, 77, 199-200, 205-206, 216-217
Birkett, Norman, advocate in Oscar Wilde trial 266-267
Birmingham, Bishop of 112, 182
Blake, William, poet 111, 169, 170, 183, 202, 211, 215
Blériot, Louis, aviator 46
Bliss, Sir Arthur, composer 54
Bloom, Archbishop, Russian Orthodox Church, London 163
Bluebell Girls, English dance troupe, Paris 122
Boga, Diana, broadcaster 306

Bolt, Robert, playwright 330
Bonaparte, Napoleon, French Emperor 67, 113, 114, 262
Bonham-Carter, Violet 247
Boothroyd, Geoffrey, ballistics expert 287
Boros, Ladislaus, philosopher 162
Botticelli, Sandro, Florentine painter 36
Boult, Sir Adrian, orchestral conductor 112
Bowen, John, writer and broadcaster 287, 313
Boyd, Beth, actress 148, 149, 216
Bradlaugh, Charles, free-thinker 265
Braganza, Catherine of, Queen of England 153
Brannigan, Owen, opera singer 78
Bray, Barbara, author and broadcaster 37, 88, 89, 168
Brazil, Robert, broadcaster 24-25
Brecht, Berthold, German playwright 211, 212, 215
Breughel, Flemish painter 189
Brezhnev, President of USSR 330
Briggs, Asa, Professor, historian and broadcaster 330
Britten, Benjamin, composer 330,332
Brophy, Brigid. novelist 326
Brontë sisters, novelists 68
Brooke, Gerald, lecturer in Russian, Central London Polytechnic 334
Brooke, Rupert, poet 242, 243
Brown, George, British Foreign Secretary 260
Brown, Pete, sound poet 220
Browne, Sir Thomas, author of *Urn Burial* 190
Browning, Robert, poet 21, 43, 77, 78, 217, 230, 247
Brutus, Dennis, South African sportsman 300
Buddha, The 215
Bunyan. John 36
Burckhardt, Jacob, art historian 28, 29
Burden, Hugh, actor 59
Burgess, Anthony, novelist and critic 326
Burghley, Lord, chief minister to Queen Elizabeth I 151
Burke, Don, broadcaster 187
Burke, Peter, author, broadcaster 141-143

Burnett, Alastair, newscaster 157
Burney, Fanny, diarist and author of *Evelina* 156
Burroughs, William, American novelist 233
Burton, Baroness 112, 246-247
Burton, Richard, actor 209
Buzzard, Dr. R.B., National Institute of Industrial Psychology 270
Byron, Lord, poet 147, 208, 212, 257, 303

Cage, John, American composer 195
Calder, Lord Richie 145
Callas, Maria, Greek opera-singer 21, 120, 121
Callingham, Sonya, writer and broadcaster 300, 301
Calverley, Charle Stuart, lawyer and parodist 210
Donald Campbell, water-speed ace 335
Campbell, Roy, poet 205
Camus, Albert, French novelist, author of *L'Étranger* 70, 88
Canterbury, Archbishop of 90
Čapek, Karel, Czech writer and humorist 104, 106
Carder, Matthew, artist 30
Cardwell, David, broadcaster 227, 280
Carroll, John, creator of *Apollo Society* poetry recitals 216
Carroll, Lewis, author of *Alice in Wonderland* 69
Casals, Pablo, Spanish cellist 112
Castle, Roy 272
Castlemaine, Lady, mistress of Charles II 154
Castlereagh, Lord 212
Cézanne, Paul, French Impressionist painter 33
Chadwick, Professor Owen, Master of Selwyn College 77.78
Chalfont, Lord, Minister of State for Disarmament 313-315
Chandos, John, broadcaster 59
Chardin, Teilhard de, philosopher 165, 166-7, 329
Charles, Prince 336
Charles II, King of England, Scotland and Ireland 153-155
Chaudhuri, Nirad, broadcaster 106, 109
Cheatham, Anne, presenter 90
Cheung, Mao Tse, President of Chinese Republic *see* Mao Tse Cheung ....

Chesterton, Gilbert, author and poet 85
Chevalier, Maurice, French music hall singer 122
Chichester, Sir Francis, world-class yachtsman 277, 278,335
Chopin, Frédéric, composer 264
Chu, Tao, Chinese Head of Propaganda 256
Chu en Lai, Chinese politician 255
Churchill, Sir Winston 164, 262
Clark, Petula, popular singer 227
Cleave, Michael, *Evening Standard* critic 227
Cleverdon, Douglas, producer 21, 93, 186, 192-3, 208-210
Coates, Dodie, broadcaster, traveller 295
Cobbett, William, author of *Rural Rides* 69
Cobbing, Bob, sound poet 221
Cohen, Harriet, concert-pianist 62
Cohen, Professor J. M., literary critic 21, 214-215
Cohn, Professor Norman 142
Coleridge, Samuel Taylor, poet 71, 183, 193
Collier, Patience, actress 87, 169
Comfort, Dr. Alex, broadcaster 182
Compton Burnett, Ivy 57, 331
Connery, Sean, film star 287
Connolly, Cyril, author, editor *Humanity* magazine 170,324
Connolly, James, Irish patriot 239, 241
Constantine, King of Greece 258, 335
Constantine, Leary, cricketer 165
Cook, Captain James, navigator 39
Cooke, Alastair, journalist and broadcaster 32, 157-158, 319-320, 326
Corelli, Marie (see Mary Mackay), English novelist 52
Coren, Alan, Editor of *The Listener* 1988-89, author and journalist 327
Corso, Gregory, American poet 214
Crosby, Theo, architect 30
Crichton, William, Jesuit conspirator 150
Cross, Roy, interviewer 40
Crossland, Anthony, Minister of State 161
Crossley-Holland, Kevin, poet and critic 20, 221
Cuénot, Charles, biographer of Chardin 166, 167

Cullen, Dr. S.M. , lecturer in zoologist, Oxford University 46, 47
Custer, General George Armstrong 308
Cuthbertson, Chris, producer 259

Dante, Alighieri, Florentine poet, *La Divina Commedia* 28.35
Danvers-Walker, Bob, broadcaster 134, 138
Darwin, Charles, naturalist, author of *The Origin of the Species* ... 142,166
Davies, Derek, editor , *Far East Economic Review* 249
da Vinci, Leonardo, Florentine artist 30, 210, 285
Dayan, General, Israeli leader 260, 311 322
Day Lewis, C, Poet Laureate 336
Dayton, John, contractor for Hijaz Railway 299
Dean, Basil, contributor 62
Dean, James, iconic filmidol 233
Dearmer, Percy, editor, *Songs of Praise* 84-85
De'Ath, Wilfrid, producer 70
Dee, Simon, disc jockey and pop music presenter 225
De Gaulle, General Charles, President of France 331, 336
Delius, Frederick, English composer 42, 112
de Kadt, Emanuel, contributor 86
Delderfield, R.F. novelist and playright 67-68
De Manio, Jack, popular current affairs broadcaster 244
de Musset, Alfred, French novelist 264
Denning, Chris, disc jockey 230
Denning, Maurice, broadcaster 98
De Quincey, Thomas, *Confessions of an English Opium Eater* 183
de Sade, Marquis, French writer 211,213
de Vere Stacpoole, H, author of *The Blue Lagoon* 124
de Wolff, Francis, actor 124
Diaghilev, Russian ballet impresario 119
Dickens, Charles, novelist 50-51, 240
Dickinson, Patric, poet and critic 202, 220
Dickson, Hugh, reader 196
Diderot, Denis, French philosopher and critic 31
Dilke, Sir Charles, Liberal statesman 265
Dimbleby, David, broadcaster 104, 249

Dolly Sisters, music hall act 123
Donatello, Italian sculptor 35
Dors, Diana, actress and singer 41
Dorsey, Gerry, alias Engelbert Humperdinck, pop singer 228
Douglas, Bill, BBC weather-man 138
Doyle, Brian, contributor to *The Boy's Own Paper* 60
Doyle, Conan, as contributor to *The Boy's Own Paper* 61
Drabble, Margaret, novelist, author of *The Millstone* 70
Drake, Sir Francis, adventurer and circumnaviagator 148
Driberg, Tom MP, author and politician 205
Duffy, Maureen, novelist 70
Dukes, Sir Paul, ambassador to USSR 21, 22, 163, 164, 252-253
Duncan Frank, reader 84
Duncan, Isadora, dancer 117
Durden-Smith, Neil, presenter 97, 98
Durrell, Gerald, zoologist 38
Durrell, Mrs, wife of Gerald Durrell 38
Duval, Paul, founder of *Folies Bergères* 122
Dyson, Andrew, Chaplain of Ripon Hall, Oxford 166

Eaton, Wallas, actor 28, 35
Edinburgh, Duke of 305
Eichmann, Adolph, Head of the Gestapo 330
'El Ingles', See Hitchcock 40, 44
Eliot, T. S., poet 57, 204, 205, 217, 285
Elizabeth the First, See Queen Elizabeth the First of England . 148, 149-151
Elliott, Francis, Professor of biochemistry 166
Elwes, Polly, presenter 51
Enright, D. J, Professor, poet, literary critic. 326
Erasmus, Desiderius, Dutch humanist and philosopher 187
Eskimos, The 21, 292, 293
Esslin, Martin, producer 71
Ettlinger, Professor Leopold, art historian 26, 27, 28
Evans, David 306
Evans, Norman, interviewer 108
Evans, Dr. Willard E. authority on the calendar 160

Eversley, David, Reader in Population Studies 104, 237, 238, 241, 322

Farandouri, Maria, Greek singer 196
Farquhar, George, Restoration dramatist 324
Feeny, Patrick, broadcaster 180
Feldman, Marty, comedian, script-writer 124
Feldman, Morton, American composer 195, 201
Ferlinghetti, Laurence, American poet 214
Fiddick, Peter, last editor of *The Listener* 325
Fielding, Professor K.J. 50, 51
Fields, Gracie, popular 2nd World War singer 112
Firth, Peter, broadcaster 228
Firtgerald, edward, poet, author of the *Rubaiyat of Omar Khayyam* ... 217
Fitzgerald, Scott, American novelist 212
FitzLyon, April, producer 264
Flanders, Michael, entertainer 232, 270
Fleming, Ian, novelist, inventor of 'James Bond' 287
Fletcher, Ian, broadcaster 33
Flotsam and Jetsam (B. C. Hilliam and partner) radio entertainers 161
Fordyce, Keith, presenter 228
Forge, Andrew, artist and writer 29-31, 195, 284
Forster, E. M., novelist 64, 239
Fortuin, H. B., producer 119
Foster, Birket, artist and illustrator 135
Fothergill, P. G. , Senior Lecturer in Botany, Newcastle 166
Fox, William, actor 266, 268
Frobisher, Sir Martin, explorer, Drake's Vice-Admiral 148
Francis, Derek, actor 124
Fraser Hayes Four, vocal group 123
Freud, Anna, writer 176
Freud, Sigmund, psychoanalyst 21, 125, 141-142, 178-179, 331
Frost, Robert, American poet 202
Fry , Roger, painter and art critic 32
Fuller, Roy, poet and critic 202-204

Galatapoulos, Stelios, biographer of Maria Callas 121

Galbraith, Professor, economist 21, 143-144, 323
Galsworthy, John, author of *The Fordyte Saga* 69
Garaudy, Roger, Director, Centre for Marxist Studies, Paris 166
Garrick, David, actor 230
Gascoigne, Bamber, quiz-master, 'University Challenge' 81
Gatenby, dictionary compiler. *See Hornby* 107
Gemell, Alan, panellist and broadcaster 82
Genn, Leo, actor, writer of travel 81, 82
George III, King of England 155-156
Geroult, Denys, producer 186,187,188
Gibbs, Suzanne, producer 46
Gilbert, Anthony, constructionist painter 30
Gimson, A. C., author of *The Pronunciation of English* 107
Ginsberg, Allan, American poet 215, 219, 233
Giotto, Florentine artist 27, 29, 34
Gladstone, Lord, Governor-General, South Africa 267
Gladstone, William, Prime-Minister 265-266
Glover, Brian, contributor to *The Boy's Own Paper* 62
Glover, C. Gordon, broadcaster 40, 134, 138
Goacher, Derek, reader 279
Goethe, Johann Wolfgang, German poet 32
Golding, William, novelist 59, 73
Goldring, Mary, business editor of *The Economist* 270
Gombrich, E.H., art historian 27, 28, 29, 324
Goodall, Hedley, reader 46
Gott, Richard, Features Editor, *The Guardian*, Editor of *The Listener* .. 327
Gounod, Charles, French composer 264
Graham, Billy, American evangelist 334
Grainger, Percy, composer 134
Gray, John, broadcaster 201
Green, Garrard, actor and reader 268
Green, Hughie, TV presenter 77
Greene, Graham, novelist 288
Gregarin, Yuri, Russian astronaut, ... 331
Gregg, Olive, reader 196
Greig, Ramsden, critic 224

Griffith, Hugh, Welsh actor 209, 210
Grisewood, Freddy, question-master, 'Any Questions?'81, 133, 145, 248, 278
Guevara, 'Che', Latin-American revolutionary 335
Guillard, Robert, French journalist, *Le Monde* 255
Guinness, Alec, actor 77, 217
Guise, Duc de, Claude de Lorraine 153
Guttnacher, Dr., German medical adviser on George III's insanity 156
Gwynne, Nell, actress mistress of Charles II 154

Hadjidakis, Manos, Greek composer 196
Haile Selassie, Emperor of Ethiopia 21, 158
Hall, Phyllis, painter, teacher of art, Brentwood School 24, 26
Hammarskjöld, dag, Secretary-General, United Nations 331
Hampshire, Stuart, Professor 317
Handley, Tommy, ITMA comedian 79
Hang, Wu, Chinese rebel 254
Hankin, Douglas, actor 152
Hansford-Johnson, Pamela, author 109, 210
Hardy, Thomas, novelist 70
Hare, Robertson, comic actor 125
Harris, Ellen, Reuters correspondent 164
Harris, Kenneth, broadcaster 112, 264
Harris, Richard, of *The Times* 254, 255
Hart, Charles, script-writer 125
Hart, Rosemary, producer 60
Harrison, William, actor 266, 268
Hartley, Bill, presenter 243
Harvey, Patrick, producer 301
Hassan II, King of Morocco 158
Hawkes, Howard, American film director 309
Hawkes, Jacquetta, archaeologist and writer 247
Hawkins, Sir John, admiral 148
Hawkins, Brian, broadcaster 277
Hayes, Patricia, comedy actress 161
Heaney, Seamus, poet 326
Heath, Edward, Leader, Conservative Party 334

Hemans, Mrs. Felicia, poet 200
Hemingway, Ernest, American novelist 212
Hepburn, Neil, producer 276
Hepburn, Professor R. W., Professor of Philosophy, Edinburgh 169-172
Herbart, Johann Friedrich, psychologist 32
Herbert, George, metaphysical poet 88, 168
Heshel, Thena, presenter 180
Hewitt, C. R. broadcaster 240
Hill, Vince, vocalist 229
Hindell, Keith, presenter 104, 240
Hitchcock, Charles Vincent, bullfighter (See 'El Ingles') 40, 44
Hitler. Adolph, Chancellor, Third Reich 47, 212, 227
Hogarth, William, caricaturist 313
Hogben, Lancelot, author and linguist 54
Holm, Ian, actor 217
Holst, Gustav, English composer 112
Hood, Thomas, poet 199, 210, 212, 214, 323
Hook, Brian, lecturer in Chinese Studies ....
Hope-Wallace, Philip, theatre critic 216, 217
Hopkins, Anthony, musicologist 133, 145, 146, 248
Hopkins, Gerard Manley, poet 204
Hornby, *Advanced Learner's Dictionary of Current English* 107
Horrabin, Frank, writer 52
Housman, A. E., poet 217
Howells, Anne, producer 295
Howerd, Frankie, comedian 125, 126
Howlett, Noel, broadcaster 148, 149
Hoyland, Francis, art critic 36
Huddlestone, Father, priest 155
Hughes, Ted, poet 326
Hughes, Pennethorne, presenter 136, 137
Humperdinck, Engelbert, pop singer (see Dorsey) 225, 228, 229
Hunter, Dr. Richard, psychiatrist 155
Hurndall, Richard, narrator 153
Hutchinson, Professor Sir Joseph, FRS 237
Huxley, Aldous, novelist, author of *Brave New World* 73

Huxley, Sir Julian, writer 53, 57, 112
Huxley, Thomas, Victorian philosopher 169

Ifield, Frank, vocalist 231
Indians, Dakota 308
Innes, Hammond, novelist 217
Irvine, St. Irvine, Irish critic 51, 64, 65, 66
Irving, Sir Henry, actor 106

'Jack the Ripper', serial murderer 97
James, Colin, producer 84
James, Henry, novelist 54
James VI, King of Scotland 152
James II, King of England 155
Jarvie, Dr. Ian, writer 286
Jellis, Rosamary, presenter 305
Jefferson, Thomas, American President 262
Jenkins, Florence Foster, wealthy American amateur singer 80
Jenkins, Peter, interviewer 315
John, Rosamond, Schools Care Service 133, 145, 248, 278
Johnson, Adrian, producer 86
Johnson, Lyndon, President of USA 319
Johnson, Alastair Scott 124
Jones, Dr. A. M., historian and broadcaster 193, 194
Jones, Basil, poetry-reader 209, 210
Jones, Professor Daniel, author *The Phonetics of English* 107
Joseph, Sir Keith, adviser to Prime-Minister Thatcher 144
Joyce, James, Irish novelist 176, 188, 189, 191
Jung, Carl Gustave, Swiss psychiatrist 21, 176, 177, 178

Kean, Charles, actor 230
Keats, John, poet 33, 198-199, 218, 230, 245
Kee, Robert, journalist and broadcaster 317
Keen, Richard, producer 242, 317
Kedrova, Lila, Greek film actress 333
Keith, Alan, 'Your Hundred Best Tunes' presenter 225, 231

Kennedy, Jackie, wife of US President .... Cover, 82, 359
Kennedy, John F., President of the United States 330, 332
Kennedy, Robert, senator, United States Senate 336
Kennedy-Bell, W. D., director, St. Martin's Singers 84
Kenny, Anthony, producer 162
Kenyon, Professor J. F., historian 153, 155
Kerensky, Alexander, Head of Russian government, 1917 252
Kerensky, Oleg, Literary Editor *The Listener*, ballet critic, *Daily Mail* 20, 327
Kermode, Frank, Professor of Modern English, University of London . 326
Keun, Madame Odette, friend of H. G. Wells 53
Kierkegaard, Søren Aabye, Danish theologian 165
King, Francis, novelist and short-story writer 326
King, Dr. Horace, Speaker of the House of Commons 93, 112
King, Jonathan, disc jockey 230
King, Martin Luther, preacher and black evangelist 336
Kipling, Rudyard, novelist and poet 305
Kitchin, Laurence, broadcaster 308
Korte, Mrs. Kim, 'hausfrau' 295-296
Kosygin, Alexei Nikolaevich, Head, Soviet Union 158
Knapperbusch, Franz, German orchestral conductor 49
Knox, John, Scottish Calvinist theologian 212

Lamb, Charles, essayist and poet 318
Lambert, Constant, composer and orchestral conductor 205
Langtry, Lily, actress 266, 267
Lao Tse, Chinese poet and philosopher 211
Lansbury, George, philanthropist 240
Larkin, Philip, poet 20, 213
Laski, Harold, political theorist and writer 54, 240, 318
Laski, Marghanita, writer 312
Lawrence, D. H., novelist 330
Lawrence, T. E., author of *The Seven Pillars of Wisdom* 70, 299
Leach, Gerald, broadcaster 181, 288-289
Leach, Dr. Penelope, medical practitioner, social psychologist 177
le Carré, John, novelist 288, 334
le Corbusier, French *avant-garde* architect 30, 332

Lear, Edward, poet and artist 212
Lee, Archie P., producer 69, 104
Lee, Dr. W. R. editor, *English Language Teaching* 107
Leffaux, Charles, producer 117
Leicester, Earl of Leicester, Elizabethan courtier 148, 149
Lenin, Vladimir Oulianov, Russian revolutionary 111, 213, 214, 252
Lew, Dyan Dr. Myer, member of Chief Rabbinate 90-92, 93, 172-173
Lewis, Naomi, writer and broadcaster 51
Lloyd, A.L. writer, presenter 190, 191-192
Logue, Christopher, poet 21, 210-215
Lord Chamberlain, The 121
Lorenz, Konrad, naturalist, historian 313-314
Lotbinière, S. J. 46
Lovejoy, Arthur, American historian 142
Lucie-Smith, Edward, critic 221
Ludovici, L. J., broadcaster 276
Lustgarten, Edgar, broadcaster 102, 108, 180, 270
Luther, Martin, religious philosopher 141
Lynton, Norbert, art critic 28, 29n

Macalpine, Dr. Ida, psychiatrist 155
Macbeth, George, producer 72, 196, 220
Macciavelli, Niccolò, author of 'The Prince' 258
Macdonald, Gregory, contributor 86
MacGowran, Jack, actor 71
Mackay, Charles, editor of *The Illustrated London News* 51
Mackay, Mary (see Marie Corelli) 51, 52
Mackenzie, Sir Compton, novelist, *raconteur* 21, 53, 54, 68-69, 104, 324, 363
MacLeish, Archibald, critic 221
MacLuhan, Marshall, economist 21, 284-285, 326
MacNeice, Louis, poet and BBC producer 216
Mailer, Norman, American novelist 334
Makinson, David, back-packer 297, 298
Malthus, Thomas Robert, authority on population 237, 241, 323
Mander, Mrs. Annie, of Redditch 286
Mann, Manfred, pop singer 227, 228, 231

Mao Tse Tung, Chairman Chinese Communist Party 163, 227, 255, 320
Marat, Jean-Paul, French demagogue 211
March, David, actor 152
Marcus, Frank, playwright 334
Margaret, Princess 330
Marsden, Betty, comedienne 123
Marshall, Arthur, humourist writer and broadcaster 280
Martin, Kingsley, journalist and broadcaster 54-55
Marx, Karl, author of *The Communist Manifesto* . . . 88, 142, 166-7253, 323
Mary, Queen of Scots 69, 149-153
Masaccio,Tommaso Giovanni, Florentine painter 35
Matthew, Brian, presenter 'Saturday Club' 225
Matthews, Sir Stanley, footballer 21, 112, 279
Maugham, Somerset, playwright and novelist 66, 76, 176
Mayakovsky, Vladimir, poet, leader of Russian futurism 213, 214, 324
McGonagall, William, Scottish poet 201
Meir, Mrs Golda, Prime Minister of Israel 336
Melly, George, jazz singer 326
Mencken, Henry Louis, American critic 82, 82n
Merrill, Judith, broadcaster 72
Meynell, Sir Francis 54
Mikes, George, humorist 104, 106, 109
Millais, Sir John Everett, painter 33
Miller, Jonathan, writer and theatrical producer 284,285, 326
Miller, Karl, Editor of *The Listener* 326, 327
Miller, Max, music-hall comedian 127
Milner, Lord 266
Milton, John, poet 198, 212, 318, 319
Minotis, Alexis, Greek actor 187, 188
Mistinguette, French singer 123
Mitchell, Julian, author 70
Mollison, Avril, writer and traveller 293
Moncrieff, Anthony, producer 104, 316
Monet, Claude, french impressionist painter 132
Mondrian, painter 30
Monkees, The, pop group 225

Montgomery, Field-Marshall 319
Montgomery, Patrick, Anti-Slavery Society 236, 237
Monterchi, Italian painter 27
Moore, Ray, broadcaster 229, 232
Moran, Lord, the Queen's physician 123, 124n
Morris, Desmond, Curator of Mammals, London Zoo 313, 314
Morris, Professor J. N., medical authority 182, 288, 289
Morris, Johnny, zoo man and broadcaster 79
Morris, Pauline, author 100
Morrock, Michael, broadcaster 72
Morrow, Ed, popular American TV presenter 247
Moses, Old Testament prophet 91
Mossman, James, political commentator 254, 326
Mottram, Eric, linguistician and grammarian 285
Muffin, Pamela, hotelier 160-161
Muggeridge, Malcolm, broadcaster ... 53, 56, 145, 146, 163, 248, 278, 326
Muncaster, Claude, painter 277
Munro, Matt, popular vocalist 225
Murdoch, Iris, novelist 326
Murphy, Nigel, interviewer 292
Murray, Gilbert, scholar, poet and translator of Greek classics 188
Murray, Pete, disc jockey 225
Murray, Stephen, actor, broadcaster 202

Napoleon (See Bonaparte)
Nash, Ogden, American humorist 110, 146, 270, 331
Nasser, Gamel Abdel, President of Egypt 260, 261, 262, 301, 322
Nelson, Horatio, admiral 262
Neruda, Pablo, South American poet 215
Nesbitt, Robert, broadcaster 123
Newbolt, Sir Henry, poet 200
Newbould, Dr. Palmer, FRS 288
Newman, Cardinal Henry 78n, 324
Ni Chen 211
Nicholls, Beverley, novelist 132
Nicholson, Sir Nigel, of Sissinghurst 118, 119

Nijinsky, Madame Tomola, wife of Nijinsky 118, 119
Nijinsky, Vaclav, ballet-dancer 118-120, 353
Nixon, Richard, American President 336
Noel-Baker, Francis 257-258
Norbury, James, expert on knitting 245
Norwich, Dame Julian of, medieval anchoress 167
Novakov, Olga, godchild of the Tsar Nicholas 267

O'Brien, Conor Cruise, Professor of Humanities, New York University . 326
O'Faoláin, Seán, Irish writer 34
O'Higgins, Professor Paul 272
Olivier, Laurence, actor 330
Osborne, John, playwright and 'Angry Young Man' 330
O'Shea, Kitty, mistress of Parnell 266, 267
O'Shea, Tessie, music-hall coedienne 127
Orr, Peter, author of *The Poet Speaks* 218-219
Orwell, George, novelist 53, 59, 71, 92, 93, 141
Osborne, Sir Cyril, M.P. 276
Owen, Anne, writer and broadcaster 182

Paddick, Hugh, comic actor 123
Pain, Nesta, producer 148, 153
Palmer, Barbara, Lady Castlemaine, mistress of Charles II 154
Palmer, D. J., reader 34
Pannikar, Dr. Raymond, political commentator 304
Papadopoulos, Colonel, head of Greek military junta 258, 335
Parker, Derek, broadcaster 52, 112, 279
Parma, Prince of, Admiral of the Spanish Armada 149
Parnell, Charles Stewart, Irish politician 266, 267
Parra, Nicanor, poet 21, 213, 214, 215
Parry, conspirator 111
Pascal, Blaise, French philosopher 169
Pasmore, Victor, painter 29, 31n, 330
Paul, King of Greece 258
Patterson, 'Banjo', Australian poet 199
Patti, Madame Adelina, prima donna 117

Paulet, Sir Amyas, custodian of Mary Queen of Scots 150-152
Paxinou, Katina, Greek actress 186, 187, 188
Pedrick, Gale, producer, presenter of 'Pick of the Week' 78, 286
Penn, Patricia, writer and broadcaster 180, 310
Perowne, Lesley, broadcaster 66, 112
Pertwee, Bill, actor 123
Phelps, tom, Thames waterman 165
Philips, Lohter, German economist 270
Philby, Kim, spy 332
Phillips, Arthur 134
Pierce, Dr. Tim, Esso Petroleum 270
Pindling, Lyndon, Prime Minister, Bahamas 294
Pinter, Harold, actor, playwright 333
Plath, Sylvia, poet 334
Plowden, Alison, producer 150-153
Pocock, Robert, presenter 53, 54, 112
Podro, Michael, writer 31, 32
Pompidou, President of France 336
Pope, Alexander, poet 36, 219
Pope, His Holiness the 86, 333
Portsmouth, Duchess of, French mistress of Charles II 154
Potter, Gillie, humourist and entertainer 46
Potter. Professor Simeon, authority on the English language 107
Pound, Ezra, American poet 204
Powell, Enoch, MP 326
Power, Gary, American pilot 330
Priestley, J. B., author 56, 65, 247
Presley, Elvis, pop idol 230
Prévert, Jacques, French poet 183-184
Pritchett, V. S. writer 54, 56
Profumo, John, Secretary of State for War 332
Pullen, John, actor 152, 153
Pyke, Dr. Magnus, nutritionist 39, 41
Pythagoras, Greek philosopher and mathematician 196

Queen Elizabeth II 124, 148, 149-151

Queensberry, Marquis of, inventor of boxing rules 266
Quietus, Chinese philosopher-poet 211

Rabelais, French Renaissance satirist 285
Ransome, Arthur, journalist and author of *Swallows and Amazons* 68
Raphael, Florentine artist 27
Rasputin, Gregor, Russian priest and mystic 21, 252, 253
Rathbone, Eleanor, campaigner for women's suffrage 247
Rattigan, Terence, playwright 330
Ray, Dr. Isaac, physician (see George III) 156
Ray, Clive, ... 46
Raymonde-Hawkins, Miss M., animal welfare 39,40
Rees, Geronwy, politician (see Rhys) 112, 246
Reith, Lord, BBC 323
Rembrandt, Harmensz van Rijn, Dutch painter 32
Rhodes, Cecil, founder and Governor of Rhodesia 302
Rhodes, Mick, producer 182
Richard, Cliff, popular singer 226, 231
Richards, Frank, novelist 21, 59
Richardson, Sir Ralph, actor 54
Rimbaud, Arthur, French symbolist poet 70n, 285
Ritchie Calder, Lord, Committee for Overseas Volunteers 54, 305, 306
Ritsos, Yannis, Greek poet 196
Robb, Brian, Senior Tutor, Royal College of Art 35
Robbins, Professor R.H., linguistician 40, 45, 332
Robey, George, music-hall comedian 127
Robinson, Bishop of Woolwich 332
Rodgers and Hammerstein, creators of musicals 228
Rodin, Auguste, French sculptor 46
Rogers, Eddie, presenter 226
Roosevelt, Eleanor, American First Lady 247
Rossetti, Christina, poet 76
Rossetti, Dante Gabriel, painter and poet 33
Rossini, Gioachino Antonio, Italian composer 201
Rousseau, Jean-Jacques, French philosopher 142, 236
Rowse, A. L., critic and authority on Shakespeare 332

Royal Family, The, ... 110
Rubner, Professor R. H., authority on lotteries 276, 277
Rudé, Professor George, historian 141
Ruskin, John, art historian 27, 28, 34, 36
Russell, Sir Bertrand, philosopher 21, 212, 317
Russell, Paul, student of law 160-161
Ryder-Smith, Janet, producer 236
Rylands, George, Fellow of Kings College Cambridge 220
Ryle, Professor, philosopher 162

Sackville-West, Vita, writer on gardens 132
de Sade, Marquis 211
Salmon, Tom, interviewer 38
Salisbury, Lord, Prime Minister 267
Sampson, Anthony, journalist and writer 332
Sandford, Jeremy, author of *Cathy Come Home* *39,249*
Sargant, William, psychologist, St. Thomas's Hospital, London 184
Saud, King of Saudi-Arabia 333
Schiller, Johann Christoph Friedrich, German dramatist, poet ... 31, 32, 32n
Schönberg, Arnold, avant-garde composer 219
Schooling, Anthony, broadcaster 249
Schopenhauer, Arthur, philosopher of pessimism 32, 32n
Schubert, Franz, Austrian composer 201
Schumann, Robert, German composer 216
Scofield, Paul, actor 118, 119, 120
Scott, George Walton, writer 35
Scott, Sir Peter, ornithologist, writer and artist 46-48
Scott-Kilvert, Ian, translator of Greek poetry 196
Searle, Humphrey, jazz musician and broadcaster 209
Secombe, Harry, singer, star of *The Goon Show* 224
Sellers, peter, film actor 333
Seymour, Mrs Frances, Victorian traveller. 296, 297n
Shadwell,, Arthur 270
Shakespeare, William, dramatist 60, 170, 198, 230, 330
Shaw, George Bernard, playwright, 21, 46, 56-57, 62, 116-118, 179, 183, 219
Shaw, George Bernard 229,232

Shaw, Sandie, pop star 229, 232, 278
Shelley, Percy Bysshe, poet 199, 208
Shepherd, Alan, American astronaut 331
Sidney, Sir Philip, poet and courtier 221
Simmonds, John, producer 124
Simmons, Winifred, friend of H.G. Wells 53
'The Singing Farmer' 323
Sitwell, Dame Edith, poet 21, 205, 217
Smalley, Roger, composer 195
Smee, Michael, writer and broadcaster 176
Smith, Dan, authority on economic planning 249
Smith, Douglas, broadcaster 123
Smith, Leslie, presenter 276, 277
Smith, Paul Duval, interviewer 24, 58
Smollett, Tobias, novelist 24, 58
Smyth, Brigadier Sir John ,VC 112
Snagge, John, broadcaster 96, 96n
Snell, Gordon, interviewer 39
Snow, C. P., novelist 333
Soulie, Marguerite, wife of Arnold Bennett 62
Southey, Robert, poet 200
Spark, Muriel, novelist 331
Sparks, John, producer 47
Spencer, Anthony, contributor 86
Spenser, Edmund, Elizabethan poet 288
Spice, Michael, actor 124
Sproxton, Vernon, religious broadcaster 165, 166
Stalin, Josef, Head of Government, USSR 256, 262
Stead, W.T. journalist 265
Steele, Tommy, pop idol 226
Steiner, George, linguistician 234
Stephenson, Paul, BBC producer 109
Sterne, Sir Frederick, owner of Highdown, Worthing 132
Stessinger, Professor. Authority on Chinese politics 256
St. John Stevas, Norman, MP 277, 317
Stevens, Cat, pop singer 231

Stockhausen, Karlheinz, *avant-garde* composer 194
Stocks, Baroness MP, popular broadcaster 81, 317
Strauss, Levi, French politician 192
Strong, Patience, poet 134
Stubbs, John Heath, poet 220
Studdert-Kennedy, Rev. ('Woodbine Willie') war poet 112
Supremes, The, pop group 230
Swann, Donald, composer and entertainer 232, 270
Symonds, David, disc jockey 225, 231
Swinburne, Algernon Charles 211. 212
Swingler, Stephen MP, Parliamentary Secretary, Ministry of Transport . 243
Swinnerton, Frank, contributor 55, 62
Swinson, Arthur, writer 266, 268

Tao Chu, Chinese Head of Propaganda 256
Taylor, A. J. P., Fellow of Magdalen College, Oxford, historian 326
Taylor, Cyril (See Percy Dearmer)
Taine, Hippolyte, French philosopher 106, 109
Tanner, Dr. James, medical practitioner 176, 177
Tarne, Nathaniel, poet 214
Taylor, Cyril, writer and presenter 84
Taylor, Rev. Robert 156, 157
Taylor, Ruby, presenter 160
Tchelitchew, Pavel, painter 205
Tennyson, Alfred Lord, poet 21, 33, 34, 71, 92, 200, 206, 217, 315
Tereshkova, Valentina, USSR astronaut 333
Thackeray, William Makepeace, novelist, author of *Vanity Fair* 50
Theodorakis, Mikis, Greek composer 196
Todd, John, writer and broadcaster 86
Thomas, Dylan, poet 21, 207-210
Thomas, Paul, industrial training instructor 160
Thomas, Tony, broadcaster 308
Thompson, Lord, newspaper magnate 334
Thomson, David, writer and compiler 43
Thornton, Frank, actor 124
Thorpe, Jeremy, Leader of the Liberal Party 335

Thorpe, Professor, Cambridge pathologist 290
Throckmorton, conspirator 150, 152n, 330
Tolstoy, Russian novelist 169, 171
Took, Barry, script-writer 124
Toscanini, Arturo, orchestral conductor 112
Towers, Bernard, lecturer in Anatomy, Cambridge University 166
Trollope, Anthony, novelist 66n, 70
Trotsky, Lev Davidovitch, Russian revolutionary 252
Tsar Nicholas II of Russia 252, 267
Tse Tung, Mao, President of Chinese Republic (see Mao) 163. 227, 255, 320
Turgenev, Ivan, playwright 21, 264, 265
Turner, Ken, artist 30
Tusa, John, presenter and newscaster 254, 257
Twisk, Russell, editor of *The Listener* 327

Uccello, Paolo, Florentine painter 35
Ustinov, Peter, playwright and *raconteur* 21, 104, 302-304, 323
Usupov, Prince, assassinated Rasputin 253

Valentino, Rudolph, film actor 230
Valéry, Paul, French poet 219
Van Den Bergh, Tony, presenter 97, 180
Vassall, William, spy 331
Verlaine, Paul, French symbolist poet 212
Verne, Jules, French science fiction writer 56, 61
Viardot, Louis, translator of Cervantes 264
Viardot-Garcia, Pauline, opera-singer 21, 264-265
Victoria, Queen 157, 267, 268
Villon, François,15th century French poet 213
Vinci, Leonardo, Florentine artist (see da Vinci) 30, 211, 285
Voltaire, French political philosopher 169
Voysey, Michael, writer 117

Waddell, Helen, poet and translator 203
Waddington, C. H. FRS, of Edinburgh 288
Wain, John, novelist 62, 68

Wall, Rachel, historian 140
Wakefield, authority on English. *See Hornby* 107
Waldegrave, Lord 135, 145, 146, 248, 278
Waley, Arthur, translator of Chinese lyrics 202-294, 205
Walker, Bob Danvers, broadcaster (see Danvers-Walker) 134, 138
Walsingham, Sir Francis 150, 152, 153
Walton, Sir William, composer 215, 217
Ward, David, broadcaster 292
Warden, May, actress (see Freddy Frinton) 128
Warner, Rex, actor 186, 187, 188
Warwick, David, Eskimo descendent 292
Watkins, Vernon, poet 208
Watkinson, Ian, writer 134
Watson, Gary, reader and broadcaster 264
Waugh, Evelyn, novelist 228, 280
Weekes, Dr. Claire, contributor, 'Woman's Hour' 104, 241
Weil, Simone, French left wing philosopher 21, 86-89, 168
Wesker, Arnold, playwright 332
Wells, Frank, son of H. G. 53, 54, 55
Wells, Professor G. P., son of H. G. 53, 54
Wells, H. G., novelist, science-fiction writer 21, 52-56, 57, 70n, 71
Welsh, John, actor 46
Westbury, Marjorie, actress and reader 135
Wheldon, Huw, broadcaster...................................98, 209
Whicker, Alan, television broadcaster, contributor *The Listener* *327*
Whistler, James Abbott McNeill, American painter 33
Whitelock, Trafford, producer 96
Whitfield, June, actress 125
Whitman, Walt, American poet 201
Wilde, Oscar, playwright, poet and essayist 211, 212, 266
Wilder, Thorton. American playwright 169
Wilcocks, Dr. David, King's College, Cambridge 76
Williams, Emlyn, actor-playwright 216
Williams, Kenneth, actor and comedian 123
Williams, Vaughan, composer 47, 85, 112
Williamson, Stanley, producer 266, 268

Wilson, Colin, author 70, 70n
Wilson, Harold, Labour Prime-Minister 82, 332, 333, 334
Wilton, Robb, entertainer 271
Wimbush, Mary, actress and broadcaster 152, 153
Wölfflin, art historian 27, 28n
Wood, Wee Georgie, music hall artist 56
Wordsworth, William, poet 42, 77, 198
Worswick, David, Director Nat. Inst. Economic & Public Affairs . . 143-146
Wright, Basil 187
Wright, Captain Peter, prosecution witness in Gladstone case 266-269
Wyatt, Honor, broadcaster 227
Wyman, Laurie, scriptwriter 124

Yates, Ivan, correspondent, *The Observer* 317
Yeats, William Butler, Irish poet . . 21, 93, 169, 182, 202, 211, 217, 239, 323
Yee, Chiang, author of *The Importance of Living* 104, 106, 109
Young, Mrs. Elizabeth, writer 312

Zola, Émile, French novelist 64, 87
Zombies, The 230
Zoroaster (Zarathustra) founder of primitive religion 221